1001
Surprising Things You Should Know about Christianity

Jerry MacGregor and Marie Prys

Baker Books

A Division of Baker Book House Co
Grand Rapids, Michigan 49516

Published by Baker Books
a division of Baker Book House Company
P.O. Box 6287, Grand Rapids, MI 49516-6287

Printed in the United States of America

Library of Congress Cataloging-in-Publication Data

MacGregor, Jerry.
    1001 surprising things you should know about Christianity /
Jerry MacGregor and Marie Prys.
    p.   cm.
    Includes bibliographical references and index.
    ISBN 0-8010-6394-9 (pbk.)
    1. Church history–Miscellanea. I. Title: One thousand and one surprising things you should know about Christianity. II. Prys, Marie. III. Title.
BR153 .M23 2002
270—dc21

270
Macg

2001052841

Scripture quotations are taken from the HOLY BIBLE, NEW INTERNATIONAL VERSION®. NIV®. Copyright © 1973, 1978, 1984 by International Bible Society. Used by permission of Zondervan Publishing House. All rights reserved.

For current information about all releases from Baker Book House, visit our web site:

http://www.bakerbooks.com

For Brad and Julie
with thanks for your friendship
—Jerry

For Jeremy
—Marie

Contents

Introduction

Somewhere around the year 336, Eusebius, bishop of Caesarea, wrote the first history of the Christian church. This treasured volume tells the story of the early church's triumph in the face of persecution and begins with these words:

> At the outset I must crave for my work the indulgence of the wise, for I confess that it is beyond my power to produce a perfect and complete history, and since I am the first to enter upon the subject, I am attempting to traverse as it were a lonely and untrodden path. I pray that I may have God as my guide and the power of the Lord as my aid, since I am unable to find even the bare footsteps of those who have traveled the way before me, except in brief fragments, in which some in one way, others in another, have transmitted to us particular accounts of the times in which they lived.

With less than four centuries to chronicle, this church father faced the difficulty of summarizing an immense period of time into one book. With the addition of seventeen centuries, the number of interesting facts to be found has grown considerably.

1001 Surprising Things You Should Know about Christianity covers more than two thousand years of stories and topics, from the tragic to the outrageous. This collection is not made up of the 1001 "most important" facts, the 1001 "best" facts, or even what we might consider the 1001 "most-necessary-to-a-complete-education" facts. Rather, we have picked what is unique, unfamiliar, and that which might not be included in a scholarly examination of the church, yet what is indeed still a part of our Christian heritage. All 1001 were checked and considered, but this isn't what you might consider a "researched" volume. Instead, it's fun. And true.

So while we admit this is not a perfect and complete history, Eusebius's prayer continues with us: May God be our guide and the power of the Lord our aid!

Jerry MacGregor and Marie Prys

1

Persecutors and Persecutions

1. The Pharisees were a group of Jewish clerics who felt that their strict obedience to Jewish traditions set them apart from the rest of the culture. Their name means "the separated ones." They were intolerant of anyone considered ritually unclean, and they persecuted many people. Their reliance on rules made them appear pious to the masses. However, Jesus criticized them for having an outward show of piety while inwardly they were proud, pompous sinners.

2. The Sadducees were the Jewish aristocracy who rather enjoyed the artistic and political advantages that came from being allied with the Roman Empire. During Christ's life they controlled the high Jewish council, called the *Sanhedrin*, but they were haughty and generally disliked by the common people.

3. The Zealots were a Jewish resistance force at the time of Christ, basically a guerrilla army fighting the Roman Empire. They were inspired by the Maccabees of two hundred years earlier, who had fought and overthrown their Greek rulers. Headquartered in Galilee, they generally took action by destroying symbols of Roman rule.

4. On July 19, A.D. 64, a fire swept through Rome. It raged for seven days, consuming block after block of the working-class section of the city. Of the fourteen sections (or wards) of Rome, ten burned to the ground. While there is significant evidence to suggest that Emperor Nero set the fire to rebuild the city to his liking, and indeed some contemporaries accused him of that very thing, Nero blamed the Christians. There is no evidence that Christians set the fire, nor would there have been any benefit in their doing so. Nevertheless, Nero vowed to hunt them down and kill them, ushering in a wave of persecution that was to last four years. While that was happening, Nero seized a substantial section of land, heavily taxed the citizens, and built what he called the "Golden Palace."

5. The persecution of Christians was not an endless battle between Christianity and Rome. Rather it was a series of sporadic incidents that occurred over two and a half centuries, occasionally flaring up because of public incidents or a local official's prejudice. Nero began the official persecution of Christians by having them rolled in oil and set afire, their burning bodies lighting the Roman roads at night. He also began the practice of using Christians in public spectacles—battling dogs or lions while dressed in animal skins or re-enacting famous battles of the past. Amazingly, each time persecution erupted, the church experienced growth. That led Tertullian, a second-century writer, to opine, "The blood of the martyrs is the seed of the church."

6. King Herod, the man Rome attempted to install as "King of the Jews," was neither a king nor Jewish. His father was owed a favor by the emperor and was given Judea as a payback. Herod built many grand public buildings, including "Herod's Temple," but he was never popular with the people. His son, Archelaus, was such a disaster that Rome recalled him and sent a "governor" or "procurator" in his place—Pontius Pilate. He didn't last long either and was replaced after a few short years by a succession of other governors, including Felix and Festus, the latter before whom the apostle Paul appeared for trial.

7. The destruction of Jerusalem in A.D. 70 came after a five-year uprising against Roman rule. Governor Florus (who had replaced Festus), in need of money to pay for a rather extravagant lifestyle, sent his troops to seize the silver from the Jewish temple. That sparked a guerrilla war, which included the temple guard attacking a Roman garrison. Titus, the son of the new emperor, Vespasian, lay siege to Jerusalem and starved the city. He created new tactics, including the first known use of catapults, to breach the walls of Jerusalem. The Roman armies then burned the temple, knocked down the walls, dispersed the bricks, and poured salt on the ground. They were determined that the Jewish state would end. Vespasian then instituted the diaspora—the dispersion of the Jews throughout the Roman world. That marked the end of Israel as a nation until 1948.

8. The Love Feast was used by early church critics to suggest that Christians were having secret sexual orgies. Similarly, the Lord's Supper was misunderstood, and charges of cannibalism were directed at first-century believers. Pliny, a governor in Palestine, wrote to the emperor to ask if just being a Christian were enough to punish a person or if that person must have actually committed a crime. Pliny's approach was to order Roman citizens who admitted they were Christians to Rome. Those who were not citizens, he sentenced to death because their obstinacy deserved to be punished.

9. The charge of atheism was often made against Christians in the Roman Empire because the Romans could not understand a religion without images. Thinking Christianity insulted the Roman gods, they persecuted Christians. In *Apology*, which was written in the second century, Tertullian noted, "If the Tiber floods the city, if the Nile refuses to rise, if the sky withholds its rain, if there is an earthquake, famine, or pestilence, at once the cry is raised, 'Christians to the lions!'"

10. Emperor Nero is the most famous persecutor of Christians. He had believers arrested, tortured, and crucified. More than once he had women tied to mad bulls and dragged to death. At times he had them sewn into the skins of wild beasts, then he had hunting dogs loosed on them so that the Christians were torn to pieces. Nero also had Christians act out battles in public spectacles, so that they were killed by soldiers or beasts. Early church history tells us that both Peter and Paul were martyred in Rome by orders from Nero.

11. Many of the apostles were martyred for their faith. Matthew the tax collector was pinned to the ground and beheaded in Ethiopia. James, the brother of Jesus, was cast down from the temple tower and had his head smashed by a club. Andrew was crucified on an X-shaped cross in Edessa. Bartholomew was beaten to death by pagan idolaters. Thomas was tortured, run through with spears, and thrown into flames. And Peter was crucified upside down, saying he did not consider himself worthy to be crucified in the same manner as the Lord.

12. Emperors Domitian, Trajan, and Adrian persecuted Christians in the late first century and early second century. Adrian is known to have had more than ten thousand believers killed, many of them with crowns of thorns and nails through their hands as a mockery of Christ's death. When one of his generals, Eustachius, refused to join in the slaughter, Adrian had him and his entire family killed.

13. Clement of Rome served as the fourth bishop of Rome in the first century; some speculate he was mentioned in the Bible, in Philippians 4:3. He was exiled by Domitian for his Christianity and sent to the labor mines. He refused to remain silent about what Jesus Christ had done in his life and continued to win converts among others suffering imprisonment. Domitian had him thrown into the sea with an anchor around his neck. The anchor remains a symbol of hope for Christians everywhere in memory of Clement's efforts in the midst of bitter trial.

14. February 23 is Polycarp's birthday, a day celebrated for centuries as the first "Saint's Day." An eyewitness at Polycarp's martyrdom at the stake claimed that the fire did not consume his body, but that instead Polycarp appeared "as gold and silver refined in a furnace." That account went on to claim that when an executioner stabbed Polycarp's body, the blood poured out and quenched the flames. This account, which spread widely through Christian churches, led many to venerate his birthday. One follower even claimed that he had retained Polycarp's burned bones. Thus began the tradition of commemorating the lives of the martyrs.

15. Emperor Marcus Aurelius (better known as "Marc Antony") turned the persecution of Christians into a science of torture. He had their feet crushed, then forced them to walk over thorns. Others were burned with hot metal plates. Blandina, a middle-aged Christian woman, was placed into a bag and tossed by wild bulls. When that didn't kill her, she was placed in a red-hot metal chair. Refusing to recant her faith, she was eventually killed with a sword.

16. Further persecutions took place under Emperors Septimus Severus, Valerian, and Aurelian. Marcus Claudius Maximus developed mass graves for his victims. Emperor Decius brought the worst persecution to the church. Taking the throne in 249, Decius had been a military leader and would not tolerate disobedience. When he commanded all citizens to sacrifice to the traditional Roman gods, many Christians refused. Angry and wanting to discredit Christianity, Decius ordered those who would not sacrifice to be tortured until they said, "Caesar is Lord." Those who were killed were called "martyrs," which means "witnesses."

17. Anterus was elected pope in 235. He was martyred by the Romans after only a few weeks of service for ordering "the acts of the martyrs" to be written down and kept in the church library. Other Christians of that era and far beyond drew strength from the testimonies of those fallen in the name of Christ, and Anterus knew keeping such a record was imperative.

18. The martyr Apolloinia died on February 9, 249. She was an older Christian and refused to make blasphemous statements. Roman officials broke all her teeth and then made a large bonfire in front of her and the rest of the people of the city. She was told to recite the statements or be burned to death. She countered by asking for a moment and without flinching jumped of her own will into the fire and burned to death.

19. The record of martyrs was kept carefully by the early church, and the day each died was considered cause for celebration, because it recounted the day the individual left this life to join the Lord in heaven. By the year 250, some churches were having celebrations at the tombs of the martyrs on the anniversary of their death. The concept of "saints" first began with these morbid celebrations.

20. Bishop Sixtus II was martyred while preaching at a secret Christian service in a cemetery in 258. He was beheaded by order of the Roman Emperor Valerian, who believed Christians had caused many of the problems that plagued his reign, such as earthquakes and plagues.

21. Cyprian of Carthage had a similar fate after being banished from Rome. He was an ardent Christian and brought many followers into the bishopric of Carthage, but because of his views on several doctrinal issues, including the laying on of hands, the papacy threatened to excommunicate him. Cyprian was eventually martyred in Carthage.

22. Vincent of Saragossa is one of the most famous martyrs of the church. In 304, he was starved and then forced to suffer the rack. He refused to sacrifice to pagan gods. The torturers roasted him on a gridiron and then threw him into prison. Finally, they set him in the stocks. Still he refused to sacrifice. Augustine claimed Vincent of Saragossa's fame was known throughout the Roman Empire.

23. Forty Christian soldiers were left naked on a frozen pond in Sebaste, Armenia, in 320. Baths of hot water were placed around them as a temptation so that they would renounce Christianity. One soldier did succumb, but when the pagan guard saw the faith of the other Christians, he converted and joined the thirty-nine. They were all martyred for their beliefs, but their deaths inspired many more followers of the faith.

24. Losing riches and property was a common threat to the early Christians who would not renounce their beliefs. Those in authority knew this and went after the Christians with land first, assuming that if they renounced their beliefs, other Christians would follow. Though more Christians with land did renounce their Christian beliefs than those Christians who had less to lose, this fact did little to stem the tide of Christians who died faithfully proclaiming their love and loyalty to Christ.

25. Emperor Diocletian remains an enigma. A pagan and an effective leader, for eighteen years he ignored the Christians under his rule. He had Christian advisors, allowed Christian churches to be built—even his wife and daughter were reportedly believers. But in 303, Diocletian ordered the Christian community destroyed, all believers imprisoned or killed, and their Scriptures burned.

26. Euplius was one of Diocletian's victims. He died a martyr's death in 304. His faith is a good example of the practice of many Christians who not only expected to be martyred but even wanted to die in that manner. Euplius always carried the Scriptures with him, and he went out of his way to identify himself as a follower of the teachings of Christ.

27. Emperor Galerius, who took the throne after Diocletian gave it up, was clear in stating that he meant to "exterminate" Christianity. Believers were tortured, maimed, imprisoned, and killed by the hundreds. Bibles were burned, churches razed, and services prohibited. In 305, Galerius began the extermination of Christ's followers in the Roman Empire. Men were beheaded, women raped, and babies taken away to be raised by pagans.

The killings became so frequent that eventually even pagans refused to participate.

28. The Great Persecution that took place in the last few years of the third century and the first few years of the fourth century under Caesar Galerius occurred while he was trying to modernize the empire. There was a uniform currency, a uniform army, and a uniform political system, so Galerius logically decided there should be a uniform religion. In 298, he rooted out the Christians in the army and civil services, and in 303 cracked down on the church. The holocaust continued until April 30, 311, when Galerius, on his deathbed, issued an edict of toleration legalizing Christianity. Galerius persecuted Christians because he had once lost a battle after watching a Christian soldier cross himself.

29. Saying prayers for martyrs was a regular practice of the early church. By the fourth century, it was common practice for martyrs' remains to be placed beneath the altar in the Christian church (copying the vision the apostle John saw in Revelation 6:9–10). Those worshiping in the churches would pray for the martyrs who had faithfully departed. It was a commonly held belief that the martyrs heard such prayers and in turn prayed for those still living.

30. The Confessors were those Christians who had been tortured so that they would renounce their faith but had refused to do so. In the fourth century, the belief arose that Confessors were given special powers by God to heal others, prophesy, and, in particular, absolve others of their sins.

31. Pelagius was a British monk of the fifth century. He denied the doctrine of original sin and claimed that people could become righteous solely by the exercise of their free will. He was executed as a heretic in 417. It was in opposition to Pelagius's teachings that Augustine promoted his doctrine of grace—that sinners are saved by faith, which is a gift of God not the result of "good works."

32. Methodius was persecuted in an unparalleled manner for his work to protect icons in the ninth century. This Eastern Church leader was forced by Emperor Theophilus to spend seven years living with a decaying corpse. Methodius survived the persecution and outlived his sentence. Ironically, the emperor's wife, Theodora, took up Methodius's cause of protecting icons after her husband died.

33. As one bishop of Carthage found out c. 860, many people were unsympathetic to the cause of Christians living under Muslim rule. The bishop was tortured for not accepting the Muslim religious policy handed down from the authorities. He was later admonished by the pope for not quietly accepting the ruling and instead attempting to convert his persecutors through such tactics. Even worse, he eventually suffered persecution from Christian leaders for his actions.

34. In 1100, Rufus, acting king of England and a persecutor of Christians, was killed by a stray arrow while hunting. The murderer was never found, but no one seemed to mind. There was no mourning for the unloved king, and it was assumed he was eternally damned.

35. "False Martyrs" was the title given to many Christians who were killed by Muslims. Because Muslims and Christians share several key beliefs, it was assumed (wrongly) that Muslims would not persecute fellow believers. Therefore it was assumed any suffering caused by them was not the result of trying to stop the spread of the gospel or teachings about Christ, so the fallen Christians were referred to as victims instead of martyrs.

36. When Muslims took over Constantinople in 1204, Christianity suffered a strong blow. Though not openly persecuted, Christians were put under stringent rules and could expect a much better life if they abandoned their Christian beliefs. Believers were forced to wear a distinctive style of clothing and pay heavy taxes. Their children could be seized to serve in the Muslim army, and they were not allowed to hold meetings or have any religious processions. Furthermore, they were threatened under penalty of death not to try to convert Muslims.

37. William Sawtrey was an English priest who followed the teachings of John Wycliffe. He was burned for heresy in 1401, the first martyr in England.

38. Balthasar Hübmaier was called by his enemies "head and most important of the Anabaptists." He was burned at the stake in Vienna after being deemed a heretic by a Roman Catholic court. He penned one of the earliest arguments for religious toleration.

39. Anabaptist Jakob Hutter was tortured, whipped, and immersed in freezing water (to mock baptismal practices) at the order of King Ferdinand in 1536 that all Anabaptists be persecuted. Hutter was then doused with brandy and burned. The king had ordered the persecution in reaction to revolutionary Anabaptists in Münster, Germany.

40. The Massacre of Vassy occurred in 1562. Many French Protestants were killed by Roman Catholics; the action set off a series of eight religious wars that lasted thirty-six years.

41. Japanese Christians in the sixteenth and seventeenth centuries suffered greatly for their faith. In 1597, in one day alone, twenty-six Christians were crucified by the government for refusing to deny Christ. By 1640, thousands more had been martyred.

42. Cyril Loukaris lived in Constantinople in 1629 and was strongly influenced by the Reformation in the West. After having issued a written confession of his faith, he was strangled by Turkish authorities. An anti-Protestant reaction followed on the part of the Eastern Church.

43. On January 31, 1686, King Louis XIV of France ordered all Waldensian churches to be burned. He had previously revoked the Protestant-tolerating Edict of Nantes. This pre-Reformation tradition was soon devastated. Over two thousand members were killed, some two thousand evidently converted to Catholicism, and another eight thousand were imprisoned.

44. The castle of Hara, on the Japanese island of Amakusa, was held by thirty thousand Christian troops under the leadership of Masada Shiro. The island was captured in 1638, the defenders set fire to the castle, and all the Christians perished in the flames or by the sword. From then until 1873 (235 years later), Christianity was banned in Japan under penalty of death.

2

Monks and Nuns

45. The Monastic Movement stretched from the middle of the third century until the time of the Protestant Reformation. Those seeking a deeper walk with God fled from the influence of the world and sought solitude. Nearly all were ascetics, renouncing the comforts of the world for the reward of self-discipline. While most Roman Catholics see value in the monastic life, most Protestants, following the lead of Martin Luther, worry that it denies active love for one's neighbor and encourages self-righteousness.

46. The first monks were "hermits"—a name coming from the Greek word for "desert." The movement began in Egypt, where a short trip either east or west of the narrow strip of the Nile Valley put the monk into a scorched plain. The first hermit was Anthony, who gave up a wealthy existence for a life of solitude in a tomb.

47. Anthony was a well-to-do young man who heard Christ's command to the rich young ruler, "Go and sell all you have." Anthony did just that, selling everything and giving the money to the poor. After learning about self-denial from an elderly Christian brother, he decided to withdraw from the world and lived in a tomb for twelve years. From there he moved to an abandoned fort, had his food thrown over a wall, and did not see another human face for twenty years. During the persecution of 311, Anthony left the fort to minister to Christians forced to work in the imperial mines. Many people, including the emperor, sought his advice. Worried that a cult might form, he withdrew again and insisted on being buried secretly. He died at the age of 105, and a wildly popular account of his life, *St. Anthony of Egypt,* claimed that he did battle with demons and worked all sorts of miracles.

48. Pachomius was a young follower of Anthony's. Originally a hermit, Pachomius called other followers of Anthony to live together in a community in Tabennisi in c. 320. That group became the first Christian monastery and fostered the notion that a genuinely devout person withdraws from the world, marriage, pleasure, and family and friends. That idea would hold sway for a thousand years. Pachomius established a common life in which the monks worked, ate, and worshiped together. He arranged a fixed schedule, insisted on uniform dress, and laid down some strict rules of behavior. From Pachomius's base in Egypt, the monastic movement spread to Syria, Asia Minor, and Europe.

49. Simeon Stylites is famous for making his home on top of a pillar during the "hermit" stage of monasticism. After spending approximately thirty years on top of a pillar so he could better pray, fast, and occasionally preach, this holy man died in 459. While he was alive, his disciples sent food up in a basket. Incidentally, his first pillar was just nine feet tall, his last over fifty feet. He inspired many followers.

50. When it comes to ascetics, Origen is the most well-known. The third-century Christian writer slept on a bare floor, the better to "keep prayer" continually in his life. Following the literal words of Jesus to the disciples, Origen owned only one coat and no shoes, and c. 210 he followed Christ's words in Matthew 19:12, castrating himself in order to defend against fleshly temptations.

51. Monastic prayers were an essential ingredient in Christian society, and monasteries were expected to be in prayer for the good of the people, king, and country. As one writer said, "The people depend on their [monks'] prayers as if on God himself. . . . Through them the world is kept into being."

52. Monasteries and nunneries served as both schools and libraries, as well as training centers for missionaries. These havens were also in charge of caring for large holdings of land and organizing their cultivation by laypeople. The organizations oversaw the economic wealth of their holdings. Most importantly they brought religious conscience to society.

53. Athanasius introduced monasticism to the West in 335 when he was banished to Trier in Germany. A writer and staunch opponent of heresies that denied either the humanity or the divinity of Christ (including those of his friends Arius and Apollinarius), he is remembered for having authored *St. Anthony of Egypt,* which glorified the life of the hermit.

54. The Parabolani or "reckless ones" were a group of fierce lay monks that was instituted by Cyril, bishop of Alexandria in 412. Their purpose was to rid the early church of anti-Christian influences. They terrorized pagans, Jews, and nonorthodox Christians. The band grew to around five hundred to six hundred members.

55. Benedict of Nursia established the monastery as a self-contained, self-supporting community, with its own fields, barns, and workshops. Benedict wanted to establish a "spiritual fortress," so he set up the monastery at Monte Cassino, tearing down a pagan temple and establishing a Christian site that remains to this day. He insisted monks grow their own food, make their own furniture, even weave their own cloth. Recognizing that not everyone could survive that sort of life, Benedict also created the notion of a one-year novitiate, in which the young monk could decide if the lifestyle suited him. After the one-year period, each monk would make three vows: a vow of poverty, a vow of chastity, and a vow of obedience to the leaders. Benedict died in 543. By the ninth century his rule of monasticism was the standard one and had formed the basis for many new orders.

56. Life in a monastery might seem boring, but Benedict, who began the first self-contained monastery, declared that "idleness is the enemy of the soul." Every monk took part in cooking, cleaning, farm work, and crafts. They attended seven services each day, including a vigil service at two every morning. While modern Christians accuse monastic communities of "hiding out from the world" (and indeed, it was thought that outside the walls lay danger), those inside prayed diligently for the outside world, focused on a simple life of service, and found peace and order in a rather brutal world. Within the monastery, members made their own cloth, grew their own food, and worked in the shop or field to sustain the community. Most monasteries had a library, and Christendom owes a debt of gratitude particularly to the Benedictine monks who copied and preserved many of the earliest Christian writings.

57. The Rule is the monastic term for the set of regulations that members of a monastery live by. If it were too strict, it would scare away potential members; too lenient and it would create a haven for the lazy and the fearful.

58. The monks were taught that the body and its desires were evil and that the greatest spiritual gift that could be rendered was the suppression of passion. That made the monastic movement largely unnatural, requiring members to abandon families, give up relationships, shun marriage and children, and forgo normal interaction with those outside the inner circle.

59. The vows of poverty, chastity, and obedience allowed the monks to revive the faith in the fourth and fifth centuries. Rather than living as apostolic heroes, they substituted ascetic spirituality, transforming the notion of martyrdom from "dying for the faith" to "dying to self." In denying themselves pleasure and comfort, the monks sought to rid themselves of ego and any obstruction to godliness.

60. For nearly two hundred years, almost every significant Christian leader was a monk. During the fifth and sixth centuries, the monastic "cells" became the places of scholarship in the church and the center ring for leaders.

61. Many who became monks and nuns were introduced to their lifework at an early age. The story of Edburga, a tenth-century nun, was a common one. By the time Edburga was the age of three, her parents were convinced that she should be sent to a convent. Supposedly, she supported this decision. She was said to have chosen religious objects over secular ones as a toddler when given the chance. Her parents took this as a sign and brought her to the convent to be placed under the care of an abbess.

62. Hildegard of Bingen lived between 1098 and 1179. She was a well-known visionary and was the head of the Benedictine convent of Disebodenberg, Germany. Hildegard was in close contact with many important church officials as well as two emperors. She believed she had the power of divine light, and yet she did not fall into trances like other women. She was well respected and highly regarded for her spiritual knowledge and was a strong proponent for reform within the church. Above all, she spoke out on the authority of Scripture and of the saving work of Christ as the authority people needed to look to, not the priests or pope.

63. Bernard of Clairvaux founded a monastery in 1115 with thirty followers. His message was that individuals should have their lives transformed by the Spirit of God, which would require personal Bible study and prayer. That idea went against the grain of the hierarchical church, but Bernard's message reformed the monastic movement by putting the responsibility for a strong spiritual life back on the individual. Bernard's message also put him into a position of power, and he used that power to personally select a pope, introduce the worship of Mary, and trumpet a second crusade.

64. Dead saints were considered as important and powerful as live ones, particularly to monks. Some monks made the most of this commonly held belief, as in the tenth and eleventh centuries when French monks would carry a statue of St. Faith around the countryside to bring bad dreams to noblemen who desired to take a monastery's land away.

65. Peter Waldo, a wealthy young man influenced by the story of the rich young ruler from the Bible, taught voluntary poverty to his followers, sending them out two by two to teach their way of life to others. Calling themselves "the Poor in Spirit," Waldo and his followers got in trouble because they preached without the authority of the church. After Waldo and his friends were excommunicated in 1184, they set up a separate church, meeting together for worship in simple services. Many historians consider the Waldensians some of the first "Protestants."

66. Spaniard Dominic Guzman founded the Dominican Order. He had few followers until late in his work. Five years prior to his death in 1221, he had only six followers. At his death, there were thousands. Dominic's creed was "Have charity among you, hold to humility, possess voluntary poverty." He had noticed that missionary priests were depending on pomp and show to win pagans to Christ and decided monks should rely on poverty and simplicity instead. Gathering followers around him, Dominic called them "friars" (which means "brothers") to distinguish them from the more wealthy monks of his day.

67. Mendicant means "beggar" and was first used to describe the followers of Dominic Guzman in the early 1200s. Choosing to live among the people rather than separated from them as the monks were, they lived simple lives and were known for their desire to meet the spiritual needs of the commoners. Eventually, they became known as "Dominicans."

68. Johannes Tauler lived out his commitment to Christ through a lifetime of service to the suffering masses in the fourteenth century. It was a time of bitter suffering for many and was marked by periods of civil war and natural disasters. He nursed the sick during the Black Plague in 1347, a fortunate survivor when nearly half of all the total populations of Europe died. As a Dominican he suffered the fate of being run out of Germany at the pope's order shortly after the plague. He accepted this bitter course but never stopped looking for God's leading in his life.

69. The Lollards were a group of English priests in the late 1300s who took a vow of poverty and, in defiance of Roman church hierarchy, took the Bible to the common people of England. Originally they were simply called "the poor priests," for they wore no shoes and relied on the goodwill of others for their daily food. But their enemies began referring to them as "lollards"—a derogatory name for someone who mumbles—because they would quietly quote Scripture to people.

70. Girolamo Savonarola was a pious Dominican monk who lived in the corrupt, worldly city of Florence in the late fifteenth century. His preaching caught the attention of the masses and turned the city upside down—many came to Christ, gambling and prostitution were significantly reduced, and a new spirit came over Florence. But Savonarola attacked the church, particularly the wealth it had accumulated and the leadership given it by immoral Pope Alexander VI. In 1497, the pope excommunicated Savonarola and demanded he come to Rome. Savonarola refused, so the pope sent two papal ambassadors, who burned him at the stake in Florence's main piazza.

71. António des Montesinos served as a Dominican in the 1500s. His work among the Indians of South America and on their behalf helped many escape from the slavery code enforced by Spain. Thanks to his preaching on Christmas Day in 1511 in Santo Domingo and later appeals made directly to Spain, a colonial code was established that proclaimed the Indians free men.

72. The Society of Jesus, better known as the Jesuits, was founded in 1534 by a wounded Spanish soldier named Ignatius of Loyola and was approved by the pope in 1540. His book, *Spiritual Exercises,* is a paean to papal obedience, and the young men he gathered around him were to be at the command of the pope in order to "expand and preserve" the Roman Catholic Church.

Pope Paul III, recognizing the potential for having his own military-like devotees, used them to stem the Protestant tide by winning kings and princes to the Roman religion, to send them as missionaries to new parts of the globe, and to carry out his personal wishes.

73. Juan de Zumárraga, a Franciscan, served as the first bishop of Mexico c. 1530. He believed the Catholic Church was in need of reform and believed that through education the church would improve. He had a printing press brought to Mexico and printed many books to instruct the Indian people, as well as the other monks, on a variety of topics. It was the first printing press in the Western Hemisphere. Zumárraga founded the University of Mexico.

74. Katherine von Bora was sixteen years younger than Martin Luther, her famous husband. She was a nun of the Cistercian Convent of Nimbschem prior to becoming his wife. Her future husband saved her from punishment when he sneaked her and eleven other nuns out of their convent in empty herring barrels after the nuns became convicted of the tenets of the Reformation and wanted to leave the entrapments of monastic life. Punishment, had they been caught, would have been corporal and possibly fatal.

3

Councils

75. The Council of Carthage, called in 251 by Cyprian, gave incredible power to church leaders. Cyprian, who was clearly more pastor than theologian, wanted to unite a divided church. He testified at the council that "outside the church there is no salvation" and "he cannot have God for his Father who has not the church for his mother." Unfortunately, that meant important historical elements of the faith, such as pastors, the sacraments, and even the Bible, had no significance apart from church. Bishops were given the authority to determine church membership—in effect giving them the power to declare who is and is not saved. And rather than relying on the Spirit to move individuals, Cyprian claimed that the Spirit worked through the bishops in the church, thus forging a split between clergy and laity. Needless to say, the bishops of the day thought Cyprian's ideas were grand, and they endorsed a strong hierarchical structure for the church. In trying to bring about unification, Cyprian created the biggest rift in history.

76. The Council of Nicaea in 325 was the first great ecumenical council. It was set up to quell the disagreements that arose over the teachings of Arius, who claimed that Jesus was divine but not God. Arius, influenced by Greek mythology, saw Jesus as a created being, with great powers *like* God, but not *truly* God. Emperor Constantine called together the bishops, who denounced Arius's view and decided to create a statement of faith that declared Jesus as "very God of very God, begotten, not made, being of one substance with the Father." While the council settled the theological debate, it also created two precedents: that the bishops would decide disputes for all believers, and that the bishops would act together with the political leader in making decisions.

77. The Council of Constantinople was held in 381 in response to the teaching of Apollinarius, who claimed that Jesus was God but that he was not fully a man. That was followed fifty years later by the Council of Ephesus, called in response to the teaching that Jesus was something else entirely. So in three councils, over the course of a hundred years, the church declared Jesus Christ to be fully divine, fully human, and fully unified as both God and man.

78. The Council of Constantinople took place when Emperor Theodosius called together the bishops to confirm the Nicene Creed. But he only called the *eastern* bishops, neglecting Rome, and he asked that the bishop of Constantinople take precedence "because his city is the New Rome." Damascus, the bishop of Rome, disagreed and called for a synod the next year, attended by only *western* bishops—a move that called for the Roman Church to take precedence. This was the first time the argument was made that Christ's words to Peter, "Upon this rock I will build my church," applied to the church in Rome.

79. The Council of Hippo, which met in the year 393, was the first group to fix the canon of the New Testament to its current twenty-seven books. In 367, Athanasius, bishop of Alexandria, wrote an Easter letter naming the twenty-seven books and excluding such works as *The Shepherd of Hermas, The Revelation of Peter,* and *The Wisdom of Solomon.* Athanasius stated that some works, such as *The Didache* and *The Letter of Barnabas,* may be useful for private devotions but were not part of the "canon" or standard. Relying on the suggestion of Athanasius, the members accepted the books we now call "The New Testament," and rejected *The Shepherd of Hermas, The Letter of Barnabas, The Revelation of Peter, The Acts of Peter,* and *The Didache.*

80. The Council of Carthage in 397 confirmed the twenty-seven New Testament books. Several lists had been created prior to that time, but each excluded some books or included others. While most Christians acknowledged the four Gospels and the letters of Paul as inspired, there was great debate over Hebrews, James, 2 Peter, 2 and 3 John, and Revelation. The council confirmed the decision of Hippo, using the two criteria of apostolic origin and wide church use.

81. The Council of Ephesus was called by Emperor Theodosius II in 431 to look into the teachings of Nestorius. Cyril, the patriarch of Alexandria, slandered Nestorius because of his teaching that there were basically two Christs—the natural and the supernatural. Cyril got Nestorius thrown out before his supporters could arrive from Syria, then the Syrians complained about the political manipulations of the council, and eventually the emperor's representatives arrived and settled the argument in favor of Cyril.

82. The Robber Synod took place at Ephesus in 449. At that time there were two "sides" to the church—Alexandria and Rome formed one side; Antioch and Constantinople formed the other. They were always trying to outdo one another, making charges against personalities in each other's camps and fighting over doctrine. Eutyches, the head of a monastery, declared that Christ's human nature was lost in the divine nature, "like a drop of honey, falling into the sea, is dissolved." Antioch and Constantinople condemned Eutyches as a heretic, while Dioscurus, the leader of Alexandria, called for a council, invited only those sympathetic to his positions, and voted to uphold Eutyches. Pope

Leo labeled the gathering a "robber synod," refused to recognize it, and excommunicated Dioscurus at the next gathering of bishops.

83. The Council of Chalcedon in 451 was another attempt to explain Christ's nature and resolve some of the arguments over his divinity and his humanity. A number of proposed solutions had been developed, many of them heretical. The bishops created a statement that read, in part, Christ has "two natures, without confusion, without change, without division, without separation . . . coming together to form one person." It was the first council in which the bishop of Rome appeared as "pope," and it significantly increased tensions between Rome and Constantinople. It was stated that Chalcedon was more "in Christendom" than Rome, which made many Christians very angry. The statement was eventually reverted, but East and West would never meet in an official session again.

84. The Synod of Whitby was called in 664 by King Oswy of Northumbria to settle the question of the date to celebrate Easter. The king was a Celtic, from the Irish tradition of independent churches and monasteries. But his queen was a Roman, and her church had strong ties to the worldwide church structure based in Rome. Unfortunately, the two traditions used different dates for Easter, which kept Oswy from celebrating with his bride. Church leaders from both traditions met and discussed their reasons, but King Oswy sided with Rome, explaining that the Roman leaders had quoted Saint Peter, and he held the keys to the gates of heaven. While the decision reached at Whitby was minor, the results were not. The two traditions began working closely with each other throughout Britain. The Celtic Church remained strong but benefited from Roman organization.

85. The Seventh General Council was held in Nicaea in 787. More than 350 bishops assembled to condemn the iconoclasts. They were led by John of Damascus, who argued that an icon is an imitation of something holy, so to deny the power of an icon is to deny the possibility of the incarnation. That led to the acceptance of icons for Mary, angels, the apostles, and the like, and it led eventually to the Feast of Orthodoxy, a celebration in the Orthodox Church each spring that commemorates the worship of icons.

86. The Council of Clermont occurred in 1095. Urban II, a French pope, proclaimed a great expedition should be made to take back Jerusalem from the Muslim invaders. Jerusalem was successfully taken in 1099.

87. The Fourth Lateran Council, held in 1215 as an exercise in power-grabbing by a dedicated autocrat, might have been the all-time low point for theological debate. At the behest of Pope Innocent III, the council issued the following decrees: Every person must make an annual confession to a priest; the bread and cup during communion transformed into the actual body and blood of Jesus; the Roman Church was the only means of salvation; the pope was all powerful; anyone disagreeing with the pope was a heretic and could be punished by having all his or her property confiscated; excommunication prohibited one's salvation; Jews were to wear special identity badges; and Christians were to avoid all interactions with Jewish people.

88. The First Council of Lyons came about in 1245. This council was important in part because of how different it was from previous councils. Its focus was largely outside of the church, dealing with the Mongolian threat as well as the emperor himself, but it made no decisions about the church itself or even pastoral improvements.

89. The Second Council of Lyons and the Council of Florence were held in 1274 and 1483–1489. The purpose behind these two councils was largely to reunite the Christian East (Greek) and West (Latin) after the Crusades. The reunion was little more than an agreement on paper because many of the East clergy and laity openly rejected the decisions made at the councils.

90. The Council of Constance was held from 1414 to 1418. This council succeeded in forcing three rival popes to abdicate while at the same time accepting a fourth, Martin V. Jan Hus was condemned and executed at this council as well. Furthermore, it was decided in Constance that the church would have councils on a regular basis.

91. The Council of Ferrara-Florence met on January 8, 1438, in an effort to create an alliance between the Orthodox and Roman Catholic Churches to save Constantinople from the Turks. Though a temporary union was made, Constantinople fell to the Turks anyway in 1453, effectively ending the Byzantine Empire.

92. The Diet of Worms was a council gathering in 1521 in which the Roman Church ordered Martin Luther to retract his views on the Church. Led by Germany's young emperor Charles V, who called Luther a "devil in the habit of a monk," it was a kangaroo court, a mock court. Luther, standing before an angry emperor who was about to declare a death sentence, stated, "Here I stand. I can do no other. God help me. Amen." Within a week he was covertly squired away by the prince of Saxony to Wartburg Castle, where Luther lived under the assumed name of "Junker George" and translated the Bible into German.

93. The Diet of Speyer in 1529 proclaimed Anabaptism a heresy and asked courts to condemn its followers to death. The Anabaptists supported the right to make Christianity a personal decision and to rebaptize adult believers. The Zurich authorities refused to agree with the Anabaptists and adopt these doctrines. As a result, more than four thousand Anabaptists were executed—generally by drowning, which was a cruel action taken against those who believed in baptism by immersion.

94. The Council of Trent, which met from 1545 to 1563, was one of the most important church gatherings in history. The church had become wealthy, the clergy worldly, and the monastic orders scandalously immoral. People were leaving to join Protestant denominations, so Pope Paul III called a gathering of leaders to reform the church. Rather than reform it, the council reaffirmed the Roman doctrines of transubstantiation, works contributing to salvation, the seven sacraments (rather than the Protestant two) and their necessity for salvation, and the importance of the formal Latin mass. They also refused to use the vernacular translation of Scripture and insisted that the church hierarchy alone could understand and interpret the Bible. A meeting that could have brought the two sides together ended up splitting Catholics and Protestants permanently.

95. The Great Council of London, called by Archbishop Thomas Cranmer on March 20, 1552, never came about. Having watched the Roman Catholic Church convene the Council of Trent, Cranmer thought the Protestants should get together and clarify issues concerning the church, communion, and the role of pastors. He invited John Calvin, Heinrich Bullinger (successor to Zwingli), and Martin Luther's right-hand man, Philipp Melanchthon, to a "godly synod" for "the refutation of error, and for restoring and propagating the truth." However, Mary became queen soon after, and London was no longer safe for Protestants, so the great synod never occurred.

96. The Westminster Confession of Faith was created in 1646 by a short-lived assembly of English and Scottish parliamentarians. King Charles I called Parliament together in hopes of strengthening the government's rule over the church, but when they didn't agree with him, he tried to have the members arrested. That sparked a civil war. Parliament abolished the episcopal system, set up a Presbyterian church in its place, beheaded the king, and gathered 151 pastors and scholars together to define the "new church." They created the strongly Calvinistic *Westminster Confession*, which included the divine inspiration of Scripture, predestination, and the importance of Sabbath rest and worship. Though often considered severe and humorless, the assembly began their shortened version of the *Confession* with a joyous understanding of the relationship of man to God: "The chief end of man is to glorify God and enjoy Him forever."

97. The First Vatican Council was called in 1869 to stem the tide of nationalism in Europe. People sharing a language and geography were calling for the establishment of countries, so Pius IX fought that notion by declaring himself head of the church, political leader over all Catholics, and infallible when he spoke in his capacity as pope. Such awesome power didn't last long. Two months later, Victor Immanuel captured Rome, and the people voted to form the nation of Italy.

98. Vatican Council II was called by Pope John XXIII in 1962, in an attempt to bring the church up to date. More than two thousand cardinals, bishops, and abbots attended, making it the largest Catholic council ever. At the council they changed the mass from Latin to each area's native language, pronounced the supremacy of Scripture over tradition, decreed that laypeople could share ministerial functions, renounced political activism by the church, and decided that an individual could be a Christian without being a Catholic. The council's actions significantly changed the entire Roman Catholic world overnight.

4

Ideas

99. The Trinity, as a theological concept, was first clearly defined by the Carthaginian writer Tertullian in the year 195. Relying on legal terms from the Roman court system, he explained that three *personae* (the Father, Son, and Holy Spirit) could share one *substantia* (literally "property rights"). In other words, God is one substance, consisting of three persons. Tertullian wrote his treatise in Latin, and thus popularized that language for all the Christian writers who would follow him for the next fifteen centuries.

100. The Rule of Faith said that all Christian churches would share the same doctrine. Hegesippus, a well-traveled historian of the second century, noted that orthodox teaching was everywhere: "In every city what the law and prophets and the Lord preached is faithfully followed," he wrote. To support his argument, Hegesippus drew up a successive list of the pastors of all the major churches, going back to the apostles.

101. Baptism in the early church was believed to cancel all sins committed *up to that time.* Sins occurring after baptism required special treatment. In particular, murder, sexual immorality, and denying the faith would cause an individual to be excluded from the fellowship of the church. Before the fifth century the commonly-held view was that sins (especially mortal ones) committed after baptism was administered were unforgivable or nearly impossible to do penance for.

102. While the Lord's Supper and baptism were the only sacraments of the early church, a third was developed in a remarkable way during the third century. Novatian, a respected leader in Rome, argued that those who had renounced their faith during persecution should never be allowed back into the church. Cornelius, the bishop of Rome, believed that God would forgive everyone, even those who had renounced him. In setting up a system by which a lapsed believer could re-enter the church, Cornelius helped create the sacrament of penance.

103. The idea that a worship service is a sacrifice of Christ's body and blood was first suggested by Cyprian, the bishop of Carthage, in 251. Cyprian, who was trying to unite a divided church, decided to elevate the role of the priest to better bind the body of believers together under one authority. He claimed that during a mass the body of Jesus was to be sacrificed anew, and the priest, functioning on behalf of the Lord, was the only one prepared to perform the sacrifice. That more or less put the priest on a par with the high priest of the Jewish faith and significantly changed his role during the worship service. Instead of being a fellow worshiper, the priest became the specially anointed leader.

104. "Catholic" was a term coined in the fourth century. The goal of the church was to establish Christianity as the universal religion of the empire. The term "Catholic" comes from the Greek words *Kata* and *holos,* meaning "universal." By the end of the fifth century, the term "Catholicism" became synonymous with Western Christianity.

105. Humanism, the belief that every person has dignity and worth, has its roots in Christianity. The poet Petrarch discovered some ancient Latin manuscripts that elevated the role of man, and popularized the study of them in Europe. Slowly the focus of philosophy turned from the church to humankind, ushering in the Renaissance.

106. Patriarchates, the administration of a local church's affairs by a bishop from a major city nearby, became the policy of the church at the Council of Nicaea in 325. The members recognized the bishops of Alexandria, Antioch, and Rome as "preeminent" in their geographic areas.

107. Ecumenical councils were "universal" or all-encompassing meetings which allowed those involved to see God's continuing presence in his church. Seven such councils were recognized between 325 and 787. The councils were an important tool of keeping the two factions of the church, East and West, together as one.

108. At the General Council at Constantinople in 381, church representatives agreed that Jesus grew hungry, weary, suffered physical pain, and died—aspects that point out his humanity. If Christ did not become fully a man, they reasoned, he could not fully appreciate man's condition.

109. The sacrifice of the mass came about largely due to a mystical experience of Gregory the Great. Believing the bread and cup actually become the body and blood of Christ during communion, Gregory once asked friends to partake of communion for thirty days straight in hopes of releasing a deceased friend from purgatory. On the thirtieth day, he had a vision that the man had been released. When Gregory shared his vision with local priests, they theorized that there is "power" in the Eucharist when it is specifically offered for the sins of someone, whether alive or dead. That doctrine caught on and helped define the mystical tone of Christianity in the Middle Ages.

110. The measurement A.D. didn't come about until five hundred years after the death of Christ. The A.D. system was introduced in 550 by Dionysius Exigus, a monk in Rome. A.D. stands for *Anno Domini,* "in the year of our Lord," and is used to distinguish between the time before Christ and the time after Christ.

111. The treasury of merit was a Roman Catholic doctrine that claimed the good deeds of the highly spiritual were kept in something akin to a giant box and could be credited to another person's account—generally for a fee. It led to the sale of indulgences, in which a wealthy person could buy the spiritual acts of a saint to escape time in purgatory.

112. Anselm is most famous for being named archbishop of Canterbury by William the Conqueror in 1093 and refusing the post on the basis that a king should not appoint a church leader. He did eventually accept the post, however. His best contribution to the church was his treatise *Why Did God Become Man?* In it, Anselm put forth the notion that God's honor was offended by man's sin. Though God wishes to forgive our sin, he cannot simply "overlook" it; satisfaction must be made. Therefore God became man in Jesus Christ, and the one offering satisfaction is both God and man. Anselm's idea became known as the "Satisfaction Theory," and it remains the most widely held explanation for Christ's death on the cross.

113. Celibacy among high clergy members of the church came to be expected and ultimately required in the third and following centuries. However, it was common for village priests to have families through the medieval era in some parts of Europe (the bishop collected an annual fee or tax to allow the arrangement). Whether priests might marry depended somewhat on where they lived. The parish priests of the Greek (Orthodox) East were generally married men living with their families. In the Latin (Catholic) West parish priests were required to be celibate, especially after the eleventh century.

114. The inner call of God is a phrase that comes from the writing of Catherine of Sienna. In a male-dominated, strongly hierarchical church, Catherine became famous for calling people to remember the fact that God speaks to us as individuals. In the mid–fourteenth century, while Catherine was living in a convent and shut off from the world, the Black Death swept across Europe. Her response was to re-enter the world and minister to the sick and dying. She also began evangelizing condemned prisoners, something the church had stopped doing years earlier. Through her letters and writings, Catherine eventually became a counselor to popes as well as prisoners.

115. The practice of excommunication was used as a tool to coerce political leaders in the thirteenth century to submit to papal power and authority. It was practiced so often that Pope Innocent III created a new ceremony for it, in which the "anathema" (curse or judgment) was announced, the name was revealed, saving grace was set aside, a bell rang as if for a funeral, a book was dramatically closed with a loud thump, then a candle was extinguished—all to symbolize the "cutting off" of the guilty party. If an excommunicate entered a worship service, the mass would be halted until the person could be escorted out.

116. Baptism was one of the earliest acts of defiance in the Protestant Reformation. Those who practiced it were doing so without the approval of Rome and were severely punished. Withdrawing to the countryside, they began forming the first "free churches"—that is, independent churches that were free of state control and state ties.

117. The German liturgy marked a seminal change in the Christian church. Luther translated the Latin liturgy into the language of the people, changed the focus from "sacrifice" to teaching the Word of God, and invited believers to partake of the bread *and* the cup, rather than having the priest partake of the cup on behalf of his congregation. Those remain the hallmarks of all Protestant worship services today. Luther also reintroduced the singing of hymns, even writing Christian lyrics to the popular drinking songs of his day.

118. Jansenism is the term applied to followers of Cornelius Jansen (1585–1638) in his battle against the accommodating theology of the Jesuits, who were moving among the wealthy and powerful of Europe. A faithful follower of the writings of Augustine, Jansen argued that their emphasis on good works and confession had cheapened the redeeming work of Christ. Humankind is lost, Jansen noted, so good works can never earn salvation, which is available only through God's grace as expressed in Christ's death, and repeated confessions are no compensation for a dissolute lifestyle. The Jesuits, worried about losing influence, had Jansen excommunicated.

119. **"Wholesome Laws"** is the phrase used by Puritans to describe the agreement they lived under. Aiming to knit together a community of faith under God's design, they believed that the government must base all its laws on a shared moral covenant. That became the basic premise behind American government.

120. **The Deists** claimed theirs was the "original religion," and that Christianity was simply a concoction of priests who desired to enhance their own power. Voltaire, their most active spokesman, predicted that within twenty years of his death the Christian church would cease to exist. A few years after his death in 1778, his home was purchased by a ministry that used it as their Bible printshop.

121. **The Watchmaker God** was the term applied to the Almighty by the Deists. Accepting the notion of a supreme being, but rejecting the idea that he is involved in the world, they followed the writings of Voltaire (1694–1778), who saw God as a giant watchmaker—he set things into place, then simply backed away and let the world run its course.

122. **"The second work of grace"** was a phrase used by holiness churches, most notably the Church of the Nazarene, to denote a more complete Christian life. Sometimes called "entire sanctification" or a "second blessing," the late nineteenth-century notion grew out of the John Wesley tradition that there is an "average" Christian life and a "deeper" Christian life, and that by yielding to the Holy Spirit, believers can find such a walk with God.

123. **Children born on Sunday** brought embarrassment and sometimes scandal to their parents in eighteenth-century Puritan America. It was believed that babies were conceived on the same day of the week they were born. The Puritans looked down

on such acts being committed on Sunday; it was considered sinful and scandalous. Some ministers refused to baptize such children as they were thought to be "born in sin." Incidentally, Jonathan Edwards, one of the greatest preachers of his era, was the father of eleven children, six of whom were born on Sunday.

124. Postmillennialism is the belief that the Christian faith is expanding, thus continually improving the world. Throughout the eighteenth and nineteenth centuries, theologians posited that the "church era" would eventually bring all things under the headship of Christ, ushering in an era of peace that would last one thousand years.

125. Premillennialism isn't a new invention. Manuel de Lacunza, a Chilean monk in the mid–1700s, was the first modern scholar to suggest a premillennial return of Christ. Lacunza said the world would head toward destruction, but Christ would appear and remove his faithful from the worst of it (the tribulation) before returning to establish his one-thousand-year reign. Written during a time of almost universal postmillennialism, Lacunza's words were ignored for almost two centuries.

126. March 21, 1844, was William Miller's proposed date of Christ's return. But nothing happened. He then changed the date to October 22, 1844. That date too passed without incident. His followers were embarrassed and disillusioned, and many dropped out. The doctrine of premillennialism experienced a setback as a result.

127. Amillennialism has been around longer than either of its counterparts. The Book of Revelation is read by amillennialists as symbolic rather than literal, and the coming of the kingdom of God is a two-part event. The first part began when Christ came to earth and continues even now; for the amillennialist, the final things are essentially accomplished already, though not by sight but by faith. The second part will begin at his second coming. Christ is ruling on high in the present age, which is seen as being symbolized by the thousand-year reign discussed in Revelation. Evil is fully present (note Christ's parable of the wheat and the tares growing next to each other), but Christ is dominant. The kingdom of God is present through the church, but this is not a presence that is moving toward fulfillment because fulfillment will come with the glory of heaven, not with the earthly church.

128. "Neo-orthodoxy" was the term used to describe the theology of theologian Karl Barth. While recognizing the reality of God, sin, and the salvation that comes through Jesus Christ, Barth also rejected much of the historicity of the Old Testament, leaving many conservatives ambivalent about the value of his work.

129. "Minister" is descended from Middle English. The term meant "lowly person" and was originally adopted as a term of humility for men of the cloth.

5

History

130. The Great Divide began in 286, when Diocletian split the old Roman Empire into Eastern and Western empires (a division that became permanent in 395). Rome was capital in the West, Constantinople in the East. After the conversion of Constantine, the churches in those two cities vied for religious and political control of the faith. Though each city would eventually be sacked by nomadic armies, the churches would continue their battle throughout history. Eventually Constantinople, capital of the Byzantine Empire, was defeated by Muslim armies and lost its place of leadership. The name of the city was changed to Istanbul in 1453 after being conquered by the Turks.

131. Constantine was the second most powerful man in Rome when the emperor died, leaving an internal struggle for power that meant Constantine would have to go to war. In October of 312, as he was marching to the battle of Milvian Bridge, the general looked into the sky and saw a cross with an inscription on it: "In this conquer." He immediately ordered his soldiers to paint crosses on their shields, and Constantine won the battle (and the empire). With that one step, Christianity became the official religion of Caesar, and the fortunes of all Christians changed. Though it's hard to know if Constantine really believed, he presided over the first ecumenical council at Nicaea and on his deathbed asked to be baptized a Christian.

132. The conversion of Constantine offered the Christian church official "protection," but in another way it precipitated danger. Prior to Constantine's conversion, the church consisted of dedicated believers. After his conversion, the churches were filled with the ambitious, the shallow, and those who merely wanted protection and who would bring pagan activities into the church.

133. The Edict of Milan was given by Galerius in 313 and was the result of Christianity triumphing over paganism. Religious toleration was granted to all Christians as well as adherents to other faiths throughout the Roman Empire.

134. Byzantium, a city on the Bosporus Strait, became the "new Rome" in 330 when Constantine moved his imperial residence there and renamed it "Constantinople."

135. The Emperor Theodosius moved the Christian church from a passive role in society to an aggressive one. In 380 he declared, "It is our will that all the peoples we rule shall practice" Christianity. Then he went on to add, "The rest, however, whom we adjudge demented and insane, shall sustain the infamy of heretical dogmas . . . they shall be smitten first by divine vengeance and secondly by the retribution of our own initiative, which we shall assume is in accordance with divine judgment." Rewards for believing had given way to punishment for not believing. Theodosius also forbade religious arguments because of fears of heretics affecting both the civil and religious order of Rome.

136. The first Christian riot occurred when Theophilus, a militant bishop, encouraged Christians and soldiers to fight pagan-

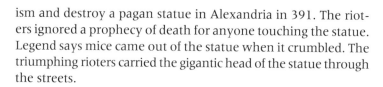

ism and destroy a pagan statue in Alexandria in 391. The rioters ignored a prophecy of death for anyone touching the statue.
Legend says mice came out of the statue when it crumbled. The
triumphing rioters carried the gigantic head of the statue through
the streets.

137. The Massacre of Thessalonica took place in 390, when a
charioteer was accused of being a homosexual. The governor had
him arrested, but the arrest occurred just before the racing season began. The people cried out for his release, and when the
governor refused, they rose up, killed the governor, and freed
the charioteer. Emperor Theodosius, incensed at their behavior,
sent soldiers to the next race. Posting them at all the gates, they
entered the structure and killed seven thousand Thessalonians.

138. The response of Ambrose, bishop of Milan and the conscience of the empire, was to call for Theodosius to repent.
Ambrose refused to offer him communion, and Theodosius was
forced to take off his imperial robes in front of a crowded church,
kneel, and ask pardon for his sins. With that done, the church
discovered a weapon they could use to keep political leaders in
line: the threat of excommunication.

139. The Edict of Valentinian III was given in 445. This edict
established the authority of the pope over the church. It was
given to maintain order among the bishops so that they would
not act against the customs or traditions set down by the pope.

140. The Banquet of Constantine was a celebration that followed the Council of Nicaea. The ruler of the empire sat together
with the bishops of the largest cities, and later, in the words of
Eusebius, "Some of them sat on the same couch as the emperor,
while others rested on cushions on either side of him. One could
easily imagine this to be the kingdom of Christ; a dream rather
than a reality." One man, Paphnutius of Egypt, who had lost an
eye during the persecution of Diocletian, was kissed on his eye-
less cheek by Constantine.

141. The Age of Imperial Power created problems for the
church. The emperor had the power to hire and fire bishops,

and many were called and banished several times, depending on which group was advising the leader. Athanasius, bishop of Alexandria, was banished from his church five times and brought back five times—each reinstatement occurred because of a change either in emperors or advisers.

142. Charlemagne became king of the Franks in 771 and spent the next thirty years conquering neighboring lands and expanding his borders. On Christmas Day, 800, Pope Leo III crowned Charlemagne emperor, finally stabilizing western Europe. It was significant for several reasons: First, because the world had largely been in chaos since the fall of the Roman Empire in 406; second, because it was the pope who took the authority to crown the emperor; and third, because Charlemagne was the first to unite the political and the spiritual leadership in one person. The idea that Europe needed a "Christian king" would influence politics and the church for centuries.

143. The donation of Pepin, father of Charlemagne, was the gift of land (including the bulk of Italy) given by the king of the Franks to the pope in 756. The land was donated so that the pope could start a Holy Roman Empire, and it was retained until the late 1800s.

144. The "Dark Ages" is a term that refers to a period of time in which culture and learning were largely lost. Scholars normally begin a discussion of the Dark Ages with the year 410—the year in which Rome fell to the Visigoths—and end with the year 962 when the German King Otto the Great revived the Roman Empire. Libraries in the West were burned, the acquired knowledge of Greek and Roman civilization could be found only in a few monasteries, and few individuals received any schooling. The result was that many of the artistic and technical skills developed over the centuries were lost, and the political vagaries of the time made for a brutal and dangerous world for most Europeans. However, it should be noted that during the Dark Ages in the West, the Byzantine Empire in the East was healthy, and the Islamic culture was at its zenith.

145. Feudalism arose out of the collapse of Charlemagne's empire. In feudalism, political power is held by a private individual rather than the state, and on his land (or "fief") live vassals who are under his leadership and must pay homage to him. The church became part of this system in medieval times, and a vestige of it still exists in England, where a vicar serves at the appointment of a lord, who owns both the church building and the land it rests upon.

146. Investiture took place when a vassal would kneel before his lord, swear on a Bible to be faithful to him, and then be handed an object by the lord that signified the lord's jurisdiction over him. A soldier was handed a lance or sword, a servant was handed a glove or pillow, and a farmer was handed a hoe or a bit of straw.

147. At its height, the papacy helped to defeat the kings of France, England, and the Holy Roman Empire, settled doctrinal debates via the Fourth Lateran Council, and took control over the lives of common people by seizing control of the church bureaucracy. However, the church began a long decline in authority during the fourteenth and fifteenth centuries due to a series of events, such as the following.

148. The rise of monarchs and the subsequent decline of feudalism led to a developing sense of "nationality" and the accompanying loyalty of people to their king and country. People began to see themselves as Englishmen and Frenchmen rather than as members of the Roman Church. With the rise of strong national leaders such as Philip IV of France and Edward I of England, the influence of church politics began to wane.

149. The alienation of commoners due to the confiscatory taxation practices of the church and the excesses of the Spanish Inquisition led to a marked decline in the church's influence throughout Europe. Showing increasing opposition to oppressive practices, common people were getting fed up with an arrogant, out-of-control church hierarchy.

150. The decreasing morality of the clergy, most notable in the 1400s, eroded the church's voice on moral issues of the day. The plague had brought death to tens of thousands. The Hundred Years' War had brought unceasing sorrow. And marauding bands of warriors (following the warlike path of the crusaders) had cheapened life and hardened spirits. With more than one-third of Europe wiped out because of war and sickness, the average person began to doubt the goodness of God. Watching the clergy become morally lax caused many more to follow their example.

151. The Renaissance (fourteenth to sixteenth centuries) brought about an emphasis on relativism, in contrast to the rigid standards preached (but not followed) by the church. With the Renaissance's emphasis on humanism and individualism, people began to abandon the corporate demands of Roman Catholicism.

152. The rise of the middle class began an extension of wealth to more individuals, ushering in an era in which those who were formerly poor began to concentrate on improving their lives on earth, rather than expending all their efforts on preparing for the hereafter. This led to a further secularization among church attendants.

153. The crazy-quilt politics of Europe helped usher in the Reformation. Hundreds of principalities switched allegiances with the various super-powers of England, France, Spain, and Portugal. The Holy Roman Empire was largely a German entity, at war with the Ottoman Empire and afraid of the growing Muslim nations to the southeast. In addition, the New World had been discovered, and nations were establishing outposts in South America, India, Africa, and the Far East. In the midst of political turmoil, it was impossible for the Roman Catholic Church to establish unified control.

6

Crusades

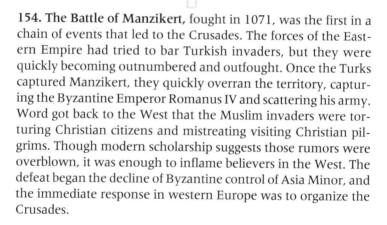

154. The Battle of Manzikert, fought in 1071, was the first in a chain of events that led to the Crusades. The forces of the Eastern Empire had tried to bar Turkish invaders, but they were quickly becoming outnumbered and outfought. Once the Turks captured Manzikert, they quickly overran the territory, capturing the Byzantine Emperor Romanus IV and scattering his army. Word got back to the West that the Muslim invaders were torturing Christian citizens and mistreating visiting Christian pilgrims. Though modern scholarship suggests those rumors were overblown, it was enough to inflame believers in the West. The defeat began the decline of Byzantine control of Asia Minor, and the immediate response in western Europe was to organize the Crusades.

155. There were eight Crusades during the years 1095 to 1291, and they represent everything from religious fervor to adventurous spirits to personal profit. They came after two centuries of peaceful Christians traveling to Palestine to see the birthplace of Christ and the sites in Scripture. But the rise of Islam and the loss of territory to Turkish Muslims, along with the rising incidents of mistreatment of Christians, led to the call for believers to retake the Holy Land.

156. The word "crusade" comes from the Latin term to "take the cross." Each crusader wore a cross over his breast on his way to the Holy Land and on his back during the trip home. They were promised forgiveness for all past sins if they went.

157. At the Council of Clermont, Pope Urban II preached a stirring sermon in which he cried out, "An accursed race utterly alienated from God has invaded the lands of Christians . . . by sword, plunder, and fire." He then called on believers to "tear that land from the wicked race." In response, his audience stood and shouted, "God wills it!" Urban then declared that the warriors who fought and died would immediately enter heaven, stealing an idea the Muslims had propagated for three centuries.

158. Urban II launched the First Crusade in 1095 allegedly at the behest of Emperor Alexis of Constantinople, who needed help fighting the Turks. In reality, Pope Urban II was looking for a way to unite squabbling European Christians and gain leverage over the Eastern Church. Sending representatives throughout Europe to recruit knights who would gain back the holy sites of Palestine, the church found men ready for war and adventure. Unfortunately, when those soldiers arrived in Constantinople, Emperor Alexis thought they were a threat to his throne, and he immediately made a treaty with the Muslims. Undeterred, the crusaders left the city, traveled to Antioch and Jerusalem, and captured those cities after a terrible bloodbath.

159. Promises made to the crusaders by the church for participation in the holy battles were often tied to heavenly rewards. The gift of eternal life was "assured" to all who died in battle. Warriors were offered forgiveness and relieved from doing penance, and land was also promised to those who conquered it. The promise of land was a powerful incentive for those who were poor and without property in their native land.

160. The First Crusade came in response to Alexis I, emperor of the East, who was being besieged by Turkish invaders. Pope Urban II called for volunteers to "enter upon the road to the Holy Sepulchre and wrest the land from that wicked race." Five thousand knights from France, Germany, and Italy drove the Turks from Constantinople and then captured the city of Jerusalem. By 1153 the knights regained the entire Syrian coastline.

161. Evangelism was never the main priority of the crusaders' quest. They did not emphasize sharing the gospel with Muslims as a main priority, despite the fact that missionaries traveled to nearly every other part of Europe with evangelism as a mission during the same time period.

162. The Latin Kingdom of Jerusalem was the name the first crusaders chose for their new home after having attacked and taken the city. They elected Godfrey of Bouillon as their ruler and decided to build castles for their leaders. However, the battle to capture the city had been so bloody and offensive to the locals (one poet wrote that the soldiers "rode in blood to their bridle reins") that they immediately had to go on the defensive and would battle a guerrilla war for the next one hundred years.

163. The Knights Templars were Christian soldiers who formed a fellowship in Jerusalem c. 1119 during the First Crusade. Originally called "The Poor Fellow Soldiers of Christ and the Temple of Solomon" because they had taken a vow of poverty and their lodgings were on the old temple grounds, they existed to protect pilgrims on the way to and from the Holy Land. Though originally poor, once the pope took a shine to them, the knights became wealthy and powerful. They entered the banking business, created "temples" or lodges in cities throughout Europe, and emerged as a formidable military group. Eventually King Philip IV of France had to wage a campaign to suppress their work. Members were imprisoned, tortured, and made to confess to dishonesty and unnatural practices.

164. The Knights of Saint John, also called *The Knights Hospitallers* or *The Knights of Malta,* was a religious order founded in the late eleventh century by a Jerusalem monk named Gerard. At first their work was aimed at assisting spiritual pilgrims in the Holy Land, but then they fought in the Crusades and gained tremendous influence. When the Knights Templars were abolished, the Knights of Saint John took over their money and property. They moved to Cyprus, then to Rhodes, and finally to Malta, where they were known for preparing for battle by carrying an eight-pointed cross (now called a "Maltese Cross"). Some people believe they still exist but are a secret society.

165. The Second Crusade was led by Bernard of Clairvaux, a mystic who claimed he had been instructed by God to free the city of Jerusalem. Joined this time by European royalty, he and other crusaders set out in 1147 and caused much slaughter (one chronicler speaks of their sawing bodies in half in search of gold, another of their roasting and eating the flesh of infidels). After two years, they accomplished nothing, and the various knights began drifting back to Europe.

166. Bernard urged the crusaders to take up the sign of the cross in the battles to come. Whether the crusaders believed the symbol would protect them is unclear, but so many people put on cross patches that Bernard ran out of them and had to make more from his own robe.

167. The first Islamic "jihad," or "holy war," was declared by Saladin, sultan of Egypt, during the Second Crusade. Calling for all Muslims to fight and die for the glory of Allah, Saladin created a massive army of pilgrims, who never fought because their leader negotiated a peace before war broke out. No one used the term again for centuries.

168. The Third Crusade was launched in 1189 by three famous kings: Richard the Lion-Hearted of England, Frederick Barbarossa of Germany, and Philip Augustus of France. They sailed to fight Saladin, sultan of Egypt, but Frederick fell overboard in his armor and was drowned. Philip got tired of arguing strategy with Richard and returned home, and, upon arriving, Richard was offered Saladin's sister in marriage as a means of arriving at peace. Instead, the two antagonists agreed to a three-year truce, making meaningless one of the most expensive armed conflicts in history.

169. The Fourth Crusade was called by Pope Innocent III in 1198 as a way to increase papal lands. The crusaders were supposed to attack Palestine, but once they got underway, they decided to attack the town of Zara to find gold. With that taste of success, they proceeded to sack the city of Constantinople, thus enraging Innocent, who railed against them, calling them robbers and rapists. Angered, the crusaders decided to end their journey, never coming near Jerusalem.

170. The Children's Crusade, one of the strangest footnotes in Christian history, was called by mystics who believed God would deliver Jerusalem to the poor and weak. Thousands of boys and girls from France and Germany, aged ten to eighteen, marched to the shore of the Mediterranean in 1212. Many starved or froze to death during a brutal winter storm. Having been told God would part the Mediterranean Sea so that they could cross in safety, the children were disappointed to be herded onto boats. Some children drowned in high seas, some returned home in shame, but many were sold as slaves to Muslims. None reached the Holy Land.

171. The Fifth Crusade was called in 1217 by Pope Honorius III in what was largely an attempt to rid Europe of undesirable characters. The ragtag army captured Damietta in Egypt, and then they were starved into submission during a siege. They called for a truce and returned home, taking out their anger on European towns and villages by burning and pillaging.

172. The Sixth Crusade was launched and led by Emperor Frederick II in 1228. But instead of fighting, he marched to the gates of Jerusalem and negotiated a peace treaty with the Muslim sultan. A battle was never fought, which enraged the pope, who was hoping to declare a victory under his reign.

173. The Seventh Crusade was led by King Louis IX of France—the man referred to as "Saint Louis." His plan was to attack Egyptian cities in order to negotiate the capitulation of Jerusalem, but he was such a weak military leader that his army was defeated and Louis himself was captured in 1254. He spent four years in captivity before being freed for a huge ransom.

174. The Eighth Crusade was also led by King Louis IX, this time in 1270. He landed his army at Tunis, immediately became sick with a fever, and died. His men, wanting to treat their king's body with respect, kept it too long. A plague broke out as a result, devastating the troops. The survivors sailed back, never having fought a battle.

175. Pope Pius II was searching for support for a new crusade against the Turks in 1460. He delivered a three-hour sermon to an audience of princes who were quite interested and eager by the end of the long talk. Unfortunately, then Cardinal Bessarion gave an additional three-hour sermon. The princes lost interest and the hoped-for crusade was never mounted.

176. Unfair decrees made living under "Christian" rule difficult for many Muslims. Christian leaders steadily restricted Muslims within Christian lands socially and financially as well as persecuting them physically. Clement V (1305–1314) decreed that the presence of Muslims on Christian land was "an insult to the Creator."

177. The persecution of Muslims cannot be disputed. By 1500, no Muslim community that had been overtaken during the Crusades by the Christians was surviving, largely due to intense persecution by Christian society. In contrast, the Muslim conquests of Christian and Jewish settlements were much more successful and ultimately peaceful.

178. "Be a man, Father. Arise!" These are the words of Catherine of Sienna to Pope Gregory XI in 1375, trying to get him to begin yet another crusade to the Holy Land. Catherine, a mystic who wrote voluminously about her visions and trances and who promoted crusades continually, urged the pope to "do God's will and mine! . . . I demand that you set forth to fight the infidels." The Great Schism prevented any such undertaking.

179. The word "Christian" was first used by those who were involved in the First Crusade (1095). This term came from the Latin word *Christianitas,* which means "Christianity" and "Christendom." Its use helped unite the churches within Europe under a common identity and basic, universal term.

180. The Crusades were a failure for regaining lost Christian territory, but they introduced the notion of foreign travel to a wide audience and certainly enriched the economy—particularly in the cities of Venice, Genoa, and Pisa, which prospered by carrying the crusaders to the Middle East and selling them supplies. With the end of the Crusades, Europeans began looking across the seas to a New World where they could spread Christianity.

7

Battles

181. The Battle of Adrianople helped bring about the demise of the Roman Empire. The armies of the Visigoths, under the leadership of Fritigern, crushed the legion of Emperor Valens at Adrianople (present-day Edirne, Turkey). This defeat led the Roman armies to begin allowing in new racial and ethnic groups—further weakening their own sense of unity.

182. The Roman legions were a fighting formation, a rectangular arrangement of men in lines that were trained to move in sequence. The first three lines were spearmen or pikers who had shields and whose job it was to stop attacks and charges by the enemy. Behind them were foot soldiers with swords and spears, called a "cohort" and expected to fight in tandem with those around them. At the back were the archers, firing arrows into the enemy lines.

183. The defeat of Rome took place in 410 when Alaric, leader of the Visigoths, besieged and stormed the city. It was the first time in 620 years that an enemy had defeated Rome. After the Visigoths charged through the streets and plundered the city, Alaric insisted on inspecting the booty. Separating out what he considered "church" treasures from personal effects, he ordered his soldiers, out of respect, to carry all the religious and sacred objects to the churches named for Peter and Paul, and leave them there for the priests to use.

184. The Battle of Chalons, in northeast France, was fought in 451 as the Roman Empire was beginning to fade. Attila the Hun and his armies had overrun most of central and eastern Europe, but the discipline of the Roman legions under Aetius, supported by Visigoth cavalry, saved western Europe from invasion and certain destruction.

185. Muhammad claimed to have received a new religious system from God in 622. It claimed one God, a strict code of conduct, and the merging of political and religious authority in a way that would unite the diverse nomadic tribes of Arabia. By 636 the Muslims controlled Palestine, and by 700 their armies had captured the entire Middle East and northern Africa (areas still under Muslim control). By 711 they had crossed into Spain and expanded eastward to India. Seeking to control the known world, they attacked France. Charles Martel, king of the Franks, fought them back in a series of battles in 732 that kept the Muslims out of Europe and preserved Christianity in the West.

186. The Battle of Tours is generally considered the most important fight in the history of Christendom. The battle was fought in 732 by Charles Martel, king of the Franks, and the Christian armies of modern-day France and Germany defeated the Muslim armies that had swept across northern Africa and southern Europe. The territory the Muslims won in the early eighth century is still under Islamic control and violently resistant to Christianity fourteen centuries later, so it is safe to say that Martel and his army retained Europe for the Christian faith.

187. In conquering the Bavarians and Saxons of Germany, Charlemagne tried to force the tribes into Christianity. When that proved a difficult task, he proclaimed some rather harsh laws: Eating meat during Lent was punishable by death by hanging. The old pagan practice of cremating the dead was punishable by death by burning. Pretending to be baptized was punishable by death by drowning.

188. The Battle of Hastings changed the course of history. Harold Godwin became king of England in 1066, but William of Normandy claimed that he had been promised the crown. When a third claimant, the king of Norway, invaded the north, Harold took his armies northward and defeated them. That allowed William to invade the south unimpeded, then attack Harold's fatigued soldiers at Hastings. Harold's men held the high ground and might have won, but William had his army pretend to retreat in disorder, causing the English to race down the hill after them. The Normans then turned, splitting the English into several small groups, and won the day.

189. The Battle of Crecy in 1346 saw the English army under the leadership of Edward III defeat the larger, more experienced French army of Philip VI by employing the tactics of the Roman legions and using "longbows" to rain artillery fire onto the enemy. Weighted down by armor and crowded onto narrow paths, the French were destroyed. Under Edward's strategic leadership, England became a world power for the first time.

190. The Ottoman Turks in the 1300s were the first to hire and train a professional army since the demise of the Roman legions. Called "Janissaries," they served during peacetime as a national police force. In 1445, King Charles VII of France hired companies of mercenaries on a permanent basis, setting up the first regular army in Europe.

191. The Hundred Years' War (1347–1453) separated England not only from France but from the pope. Due to an inability of either side to forge a comprehensive victory or find a reasonable conclusion, the war dragged on through innumerable treaties and interruptions. With the unending warfare came a marked disregard for church leadership.

192. The Italian Rebellion broke out when the papal states became a battleground in the late fourteenth century. The popes and the majority of cardinals were French, and the Italian people grew to hate the pope, his mercenaries, and his French legates, or representatives. When the pope embargoed grain to Florence during the famine of 1374, Italians took up arms against the Catholic Church.

193. The War of the Eight Saints took place in 1377. The entire city of Florence had been excommunicated by the French pope in response to their uprising against his leadership. Pope Gregory then invited outlaws to prey on Florentine caravans. The Committee of Eight organized a strategy to seize ecclesiastical property, keep churches open, and protect its businesses against papal mercenaries. Those eight men became heroes to the cities of northern Italy.

194. The Bohemian Rebellion came about in 1415 when a group of followers under the leadership of Jan Hus requested they be able to partake of both the bread and the cup during communion. They called themselves "The Unity of the Brotherhood," and, though the Roman Church did everything they could to try to wipe them out, the group remained until able to join forces with the Protestants behind Martin Luther one hundred years later.

195. The Battle of Orleans took place in 1429 when the French army, led by Catholic mystic Joan of Arc, forced the English armies to abandon their siege of Orleans in France. French military leaders initially had no interest in the rantings of the nineteen-year-old Joan, but they quickly realized all went well when they followed her instructions (and, conversely, everything went to pieces when they did not). After only ten days, the English fled the field. Next, Joan led the French armies to several victories over the occupying English armies. Captured in an attempt to retake Paris, she was convicted of heresy and burned at the stake.

196. The Peasants' Revolt of 1524 is one of the sadder moments in the story of Protestantism. German peasants, encouraged by the reformers' concept that every man is free, revolted against their lords. Issuing a decree that in effect outlawed serfdom and slavery, they turned violent when the princes and lords rejected their ultimatums. Martin Luther wrote a pamphlet entitled *Against the Thievish and Murderous Hordes of Peasants,* calling on the royals to "strangle and stab" the "insurgents." An estimated one hundred thousand peasants died, and many rejected Luther as a false prophet.

197. The Battle of Kappel was fought on October 11, 1531. It was a battle between Catholics and Protestants of Switzerland, and it took the life of the influential Reformation leader Ulrich Zwingli. As a result of the Protestant victory, the city of Geneva became the center of Reformed Christianity in the world.

198. The Munster Rebellion began in 1533 when some followers of Jan Matthijs, a self-styled savior, began hearing him preach about the coming apocalypse and how it would bring Christ's thousand-year reign to the city of Munster. Their sometimes violent actions led to the archbishop sending papal troops to take control of the city, but the people closed the gates, leading to a siege. One of the extremists, Jan of Leyden, seized power in the city and began issuing directives he claimed came from God (including introducing polygamy and taking the title "King David" for himself). The citizens of Munster kept this up for a year before they were starved out.

199. The Schmalkald League was a band of Lutheran royals who fought a civil war against Emperor Charles V between 1521 and 1555. Wanting to free themselves of Roman Catholicism, but still desiring to control lands and churches, the participants all believed that the Christian faith held society together. Yet, each prince wanted to be the one to make the decision. The war finally ended with the Battle of Lepanto.

200. The Battle of Lepanto in 1571 saw a fleet of three hundred ships from the papal states defeat the 273-ship Turkish navy of Ali Pasha off the coast of Greece. The last of the great naval battles fought by oar-driven ships, it marked a turning point in the Muslim expansion into Europe.

201. The St. Bartholomew's Day Massacre is difficult for historians to describe. France was experiencing religious skirmishes, with the minority French Protestants (called "Huguenots") forming their own armies to protect them from French Catholics. A royal wedding was planned in an attempt to unite the two sides, but Catherine de Medici, the mother of the bride and a Catholic, used the festivities to try to arrange the murder of the Huguenot leader. It is believed by some historians that when the attempt failed, Catherine, in an attempt to cover up her crime, ordered the French army to massacre all the Huguenots gathered for the wedding. On August 24, 1572, the killing started. Soon bands of hoodlums were chasing down random Protestants for sport. The atrocities were appalling—one printer was roasted, along with his seven children, in a fire fueled by his own books. The death toll ran higher than forty thousand, and the civil war spread from Paris to the countryside.

202. The Spanish Armada, considered invincible in the sixteenth century, was defeated in a battle that took place in the English Channel in 1588. Lord Howard's 197-ship navy defeated Spain's 130-ship armada, dealing a severe blow to Spanish pride and putting a stop to their plans to force Catholicism on other countries. The battle made Britain a sea power—a title it would maintain for centuries.

203. The Thirty Years' War was the last great religious war in Europe. Starting as a civil war between Protestants and Catholics in Germany, it burst into flame in 1618 when Protestants in Prague stormed the royal palace and threw the governors out the window (they landed on a pile of manure and survived). Shocked, Holy Roman Emperor Ferdinand II sent troops into Prague to force all Protestants into exile, leading the Protestant king of Denmark, Christian IV, to attack Ferdinand in Saxony. The battle then raged through France, Germany, and Sweden, with nations and religious groups fighting a long series of battles over both territory and theology.

204. The Peace of Westphalia in 1648 put an end to the Thirty Years' War, though by that time Germany was in ruins and had lost one-third of its territory. However, the document is important in that it recognizes three forms of Christianity—Catholicism, Lutheranism, and Calvinism—and allows all three to exist in the same region. America's founding fathers insisted on "freedom of religion" after seeing the devastation brought about by religion in the Thirty Years' War.

205. The Battle of Blenheim, fought on August 13, 1704, was a turning point in European history. The allied Roman Catholic armies of France and Bavaria threatened to defeat Protestant Vienna, but the Duke of Marlborough brought English troops to the city, joined with the Austrians, and soundly defeated them. That effectively cleared French troops from Germany, allowing the Germans to see themselves as a nation and solidifying the national boundaries of Protestant and Catholic countries.

206. The Battle of Poltava followed in 1709. The Orthodox soldiers of Peter the Great of Russia crushed the Protestant Swedish armies of Sweden's Charles XII. The victory made Russia the dominant power in eastern Europe and led to the growth of the Eastern Orthodox Church throughout central and eastern Europe.

207. The Battle of Plassey, though one of the most brutal battles in history, is perhaps the most forgotten. The British armies, under the leadership of Robert Clive, defeated the Indian armies of Suraj-ud-Daulah in 1757, thereby gaining control of Bengal and leading to two centuries of British domination over India. Though largely a fight over the riches of India, it was presented to the English people as a fight between Christianity and the pagan doctrines of Buddhism.

208. The Battle of Yorktown, while not having clear religious overtones, nevertheless was seen by colonial Americans as a sign of God's blessing. The American and French armies, under the leadership of General George Washington, defeated the larger, better equipped, and much more prestigious British army of Lord Charles Cornwallis. With Cornwallis's surrender, the Revolutionary War effectively came to an end.

209. The Battle of Austerlitz was a major victory for Napoleon. In the battle, fought in 1805 in present-day Slovenia, French forces defeated a combined Austrian and Russian army. The result was that provinces of Austria were made part of Italy, the Holy Roman Empire was dissolved, and Napoleon became the ruler of all central Europe.

210. The Battle of Waterloo marked the ultimate defeat of Emperor Napoleon and the creation of modern Europe along nationalist lines. The small town of Waterloo, near Brussels, saw the larger, better-equipped French army attack the strong defensive positions of Britain, Belgium, and the Netherlands. Had he attacked in the morning, Napoleon would probably have won the battle and changed the course of history. Instead he waited until afternoon, so that the previous night's rainfall could dry, and allowed the Prussian army to reinforce the allied lines. The French were stopped, then defeated in a fierce bayonet counterattack. Napoleon then abdicated the throne and was exiled to the barren island of St. Helena.

211. The Battle of Normandy took place on June 6, 1944, when Allied troops landed on the French coast and drove the Germans out of France. While the religious aspects of World War II are often overlooked, Nazi Germany under Adolf Hitler was bent on driving Christ out of the lives of its people, and the extermination of the Jewish race was official Nazi policy. With the defeat of the heavily fortified Nazi positions, the German armies were in a race back to their homeland, and the end of the war was in sight.

8

Popes

212. The title "pope" comes from the word "papa," and refers to the fatherly leadership of some of the early bishops in the church. It wasn't reserved for the bishop of Rome until the sixth century.

213. Announcing Peter as the first bishop of Rome is a long-time Catholic claim, but it wasn't made official until 1870. Rome was certainly the premier city in the western world—the imperial capital, the eternal city, and the home of the largest and wealthiest church. Though some Christian historians (including Irenaeus in the second century) referred to Peter and Paul as the "founders" of the church in Rome, it should be noted that Irenaeus and others disagreed with the Roman Church when its bishop made some theological errors. In fact, up to the time of Constantine, there is no evidence to suggest that the bishop of Rome held recognized authority outside of his own city.

67

214. The desire to name Peter as pope grew out of a desire to refute the gnostics, who claimed to have "secret traditions" of the Christian faith passed down to them by first-century believers. In the second and third centuries, many Christians felt that a list of leaders, traced back to Paul and Peter, was a way of safeguarding the true gospel.

215. Fabian was elected pope in 236. He served fourteen years before being martyred by Emperor Decius. After Fabian's death, the emperor was reported to have said, "I would far rather receive news of a rival to the throne than of another bishop of Rome."

216. Every pope wears a piece of jewelry known as "the fisherman's ring." A golden ring, it depicts Peter fishing, and is supposed to symbolize the pope's role as a "fisher of men."

217. Pope Leo I, a nobleman who had been sent by the emperor to arbitrate a dispute in 440, was in Rome when the bishop died. Asked to preach a funeral mass, Leo extolled, "the glory of the blessed apostle Peter . . . *in whose chair his power lives on and his authority shines forth.*" When it was seen that Leo believed the bishop of Rome was to lead the church, he was immediately acclaimed the new pope.

218. Leo made significant changes to the role of "bishop of Rome." Officially the Roman Catholic Church asserts that there were forty-eight popes prior to Leo, but historians cannot confirm many of them. There was apparently no pope at all during the years 304 to 308, and some of the earliest names ("Telesphorus" and "Hyginus") have almost no historical support.

219. "Leo's argument," that Christ anointed Peter as head of the church, flew in the face of Scripture and church history. Jesus himself was clear that his followers were not to pattern themselves after princes, lording authority over others. And the idea that Christ's words were for the office of church leader, rather than a reference to the truth of Peter's words ("You are the Christ"), is not evident in the text. There's also the problem of Peter's questionable character—he denied Christ, was often overcome by emotions, and was once called "Satan" by the Lord Jesus (Matt. 16:23). Paul tells of having to rebuke Peter for hypocrisy in the Book of Galatians. But in 445, Emperor Valentinian III proclaimed that the papal court in Rome was preeminent over all others, effectively turning Leo's claims into law.

220. The Vandal Plunder escalated the power of Pope Leo. When the Vandal hordes came to the city gates, Leo met their leader, Geiseric, and begged for mercy. Geiseric agreed, and though his armies sacked the city and took not only all the valuables but several hostages for ransom, they neither burned the city nor killed its inhabitants. The citizens of Rome, recognizing Leo's role in saving their city, gave him the ancient heathen title, *Pontifex Maximus*—the high priest of religion in the empire. Thus the pope came to rule over the eternal city.

221. Celibacy was a Roman Catholic doctrine that arose during the ascetic movement of the second and third centuries. But in 1522, Martin Luther noted that celibacy was not a biblical mandate (he also noticed that Peter, whom the Roman Church claimed was the first "bishop of Rome," must have been married, because both Mark and Luke refer to his "mother-in-law"). So in addition to abolishing the office of bishop, Luther announced that priests could marry. He then married a former nun, Katherine von Bora.

222. Gregory the Great is generally regarded as the first true pope. While others had begun recognizing the archbishop of Rome as first-among-equals, the brave and highly organized Gregory gave the role an entirely new profile. Originally the prefect of Rome (the highest civil office), Gregory resigned to enter a monastery. His administrative abilities attracted attention, and in 590 he was elected bishop despite his own objections. When the city was attacked and the Roman armies fled, Gregory mustered his own troops and negotiated a treaty. He established churches in Britain and elsewhere, making sure they were subservient to the Roman Church. He also wrote *Pastoral Rule*, an excellent handbook for local priests that became the most widely read book of his day. While he never accepted the title of "patriarch," he saw himself as the leader of the world-wide church.

223. When Pope Gregory was elected in March of 590, there had been no pope for six months. The previous "pope," Pelagius II, had died of the plague, along with half the city of Rome. Gregory, upon hearing the news, refused the office. When pressed, he fled the city and hid in a forest. Church officials had to send a search party to find him and drag him back to Rome. He wasn't officially installed until September 3, and at that point he was fifty, bald, and in poor health. To show his lack of desire, Gregory's first announcement was that there would be a public act of humiliation, and he led seven processions through the streets, singing dirges and reading aloud sad prayers. With that, the plague seemed to stop. The citizens of Rome, overjoyed, put up a statue of the archangel Michael on the banks of the Tiber—a statue that stands to this day. Gregory is now remembered as "Gregory the Great," and is considered one of the best church administrators of all time.

224. On March 26, 752, Stephen III assumed the papacy after Stephen II died. Many historians refer to the successor as Stephen II because the *real* Stephen II died only four days after his election.

225. The kidnapping of the pope occurred on April 25, 799, when some armed men, loyal to the previous pope, grabbed Pope Leo during a St. Mark's Day parade. Accusing him of perjury and adultery (they were probably correct), they whisked him off to a cell in Greece. But because there was only one guard to watch him, Leo's friends were able to release him and return him to Rome. That prompted Leo to appeal to Charles the Great, king of the Franks, for military assistance—and that marked the beginning of the "Restored Christian Roman Empire," putting the pope in league with the king of France.

226. A legend, supposedly started by the Dominicans, claims that there once was a female pope. Historians disregard the possibility that a woman could have risen to the position of popess and believe instead that it was an act of satire against Pope

John VIII, a weak and ineffective pope. The name Johanna supposedly took. The legend claims that Johanna (Johannes) filled in for more than two years between the reigns of Pope Leo IV and Benedict III (847 to 855), and that she was disguised as a man. Legend has it that she went by the name Pope John VIII.

227. Benedict IX was only eleven years old when, in the eleventh century, he was made pope of the entire Christian empire!

228. Pope Sergius III, who served between 904 and 911, maintained a mistress, Marozia, who, with the help of her mother and sister, managed to control and fill the papal chair with men of questionable morals, including her illegitimate son, between 904 and 963. This papal time period was known as the rule of harlots.

229. The pope was elected by the local congregation in Rome for centuries. In 1059, Pope Nicholas II declared that only cardinals could be papal electors. In 1179, it was determined that the election of a pope requires a two-thirds majority of all voting cardinals, and that they must all be in attendance in Rome. The declaration that a pope must be elected within twenty days of the death of the previous pope was made in 1274 by Gregory X.

230. The reform of the papacy took place under the leadership of Hildebrand, who served as Pope Gregory VII from 1073 to 1085. In an attempt to pull the church out of feudalism and the Dark Ages, he claimed unprecedented power, even announcing that papal authority took precedence over state authority. In 1075, Gregory announced that no Christian should be involved in the practice of investiture (taking an oath to a lord to serve as his vassal). He even excommunicated the emperor and absolved his subjects from their oaths of allegiance. This was in effect a declaration of war on Europe's wealthy leaders. Remarkably, Gregory won. The emperor came to him as a penitent and was welcomed back into the church.

231. Pope Innocent III, who served from 1198 to 1216, may have been the worst power monger the church has ever seen.

In an attempt to centralize church administration, he proclaimed himself Christ's representative on earth, "a mediator between God and man; below God but beyond man." He excommunicated all those who disagreed with him and declared that anyone excommunicated would be condemned to hell. Innocent also pushed through a number of ecclesiastical doctrines like demanding annual confession and insisting that the Roman Church was "the repository of spiritual truth." He created a list of all the popes that had served before him, though some of it was clearly imaginative, having no historical basis or support, and announced that Christians were to avoid all Jewish people, who he declared were to wear identifying badges. Some historians refer to him with terms like "hard-driving" and "ambitious," but in reality he was a racist megalomaniac.

232. Pope Gregory VII, who reigned from 1073 to 1085, was the father of the Gregorian Reform movement. A friend once described him as "holy Satan." He was responsible for excommunicating Emperor Henry IV for not abiding by church decisions.

233. Cardinal Robert of Geneva, the pope's representative in Italy, was an imposing, autocratic spokesman for the church. To put down the Italian rebellion, he hired mercenaries from the French coast who spread terror across Italy. He eventually became known to the common people as "the Butcher."

234. "There is no doubt that he [Innocent IV] is the true antichrist." Around 1254, Holy Roman Emperor Frederick II and his followers added up the value of the Roman letters of "Innocencius papa" (using the Greek value sixteen for the letter P) and came up with a total of 666. Armed with this knowledge, they made this statement. It should be noted here that Innocent IV believed Emperor Frederick II was the antichrist.

235. Pope John XXI carries with his name the distinction that he did not follow a Pope John XX. John's XXI title came after John XIX. It is unknown why the "twentieth" Pope John was skipped. Pope John XXI died in 1277 when the ceiling of his home fell down on him.

236. Cardinal Gaetani was so desperate to become pope that he pretended to be a voice from heaven and spoke on his own behalf to convince Pope Celestine V to resign. Celestine V had served in that role for just fifteen weeks, but Gaetani proved successful and became Pope Boniface VIII in 1294. He immediately imprisoned the tricked pope, and Celestine remained incarcerated until he died.

237. Pope Boniface VIII, who served from 1294 to 1303, went to great lengths to defend his authority when challenged. King Philip IV of France prohibited the export of money from France to Rome in order to defend his authority. Boniface responded by issuing the *Unam Sanctam* bull, which restated his claim of authority in all such matters. Philip responded by sending an agent to seize the pope and plunder the papal palace. Boniface was threatened and imprisoned for several days and died within a few weeks.

238. Bad feelings developed between the people and the pope during the late 1300s. There were a number of incidents that caused problems, including the pressure for donations and the immoral behavior of priests, but one incident in particular caused havoc: The nephew of the abbot of Montmayeur broke into a married woman's house, raped her, and then watched as she attempted to escape via a third-story window, lost her balance, and fell to her death. When outraged citizens demanded justice, the abbot simply replied carelessly, "What then? Do you suppose all Frenchmen are eunuchs?"

239. The Atrocity at Cesena occurred on February 3, 1377, after the citizens of that city took up arms against papal mercenaries who were stealing supplies. Cardinal Robert persuaded the people to surrender their arms, swearing "a solemn oath on his Cardinal hat" that they would not be punished. Then he ordered a massacre. Five thousand people were butchered, some by drowning when they tried to escape via the moat and were forced to stay in the water at swordpoint. Eight thousand refugees fled the sacked city. When an English soldier asked if he should continue killing unarmed innocents, Robert replied by shouting, "Blood and more blood!"

240. The Papal Schism of 1378 to 1417 brought about an almost complete secularization of the church. Some historians have referred to this period as the "paganized" stage of Christendom. When the resolution of first two, then three popes finally came to an end, the process was under the leadership of politicians and Renaissance artists rather than devout believers in Jesus. Leo X, the pope at the beginning of the Reformation, led an extravagant life of banquets and balls, art shows, and dramas. It was his actions, in an attempt to raise money to build St. Peter's Church in Rome, that led him into conflict with Martin Luther.

241. Pope Alexander VI wanted to keep peace as parts of the world were being discovered. Knowing Spain and Portugal were the main contenders in exploration, in 1493 he drew a line down a map of the Atlantic and awarded discoveries in the West to Spain and in the East to Portugal. Alexander intended the New World for the Spanish, leaving Africa and the Orient to the Portuguese. Unbeknownst to him, the line he drew dividing the two countries' possessions (45 degrees longitude) crossed Brazil. Thus, Brazil today is Portuguese in origin. This was known as the Treaty of Tordesillas.

242. "The wisdom of Solomon" was the joke offered by terrorist Sir John Hawkwood when, after watching two of his men fight over a nun during the Atrocity at Cesena, he took his sword and cut her in half. Hawkwood was so feared by the people that he lived the last twenty years of his life in riches, collecting extortion money from the cities of northern Italy by promising not to attack them.

243. Rodrigo Borgia, better known as Pope Alexander VI, was probably the most immoral man to ever serve in the role. While holding the office from 1492 to 1503, he busied himself with Italian politics and the local artistic community, paying bribes and hoarding wealth. Grossly immoral, he openly acknowledged that he had several children by different women. Some blame Alexander and those who came before and after him for the estrangement of the pope and the rise of the Protestant Reformation.

244. On February 25, 1570, Pope Pius V excommunicated Protestant Queen Elizabeth I of England. He declared her a usurper of the throne. This was the final instance of a pope using his power to "depose" a reigning monarch.

245. Clement XIV demonstrated very well the delicate power struggles that played within the high ranks of the Catholic Church. Because he felt threatened by the power and popularity of the Jesuit Order of monks, he had them disbanded in 1773. The Jesuits had become a truly admired group of people who were devoted to serving the poor, providing for orphans, and developing missions. His decision was revoked forty-one years later by Pope Pius VIII.

246. The Conciliar Movement in the first half of the fifteenth century sought to limit the power of the papacy. The council claimed to be superior to the pope, and called for regular meetings, but Martin V declared the meetings illegal and disbanded them. Discredited, the movement died out, allowing some of the worst popes in history to follow.

247. The infallibility of the pope was proclaimed in 1870 by Pope Pius IX, the same man who had declared that the Virgin Mary was immaculately conceived. In an attempt to stem the rise of doubt and rationalism, Pius simply declared there were certain things a Roman Catholic could not believe. His list included socialism, civil marriages, and salvation through any other church besides that of Rome.

248. The pope has to wear certain clothes each day: black trousers, a collarless white shirt, a clerical collar, a white skull-cap, short red shoes, and a long white garment called a "cassock," with a sash. For public appearances, he'll don a short red cap (a "mozzetta") and a circular collar of white wool (a "pallium") which rests on his shoulders. The pallium is embroidered with six black crosses.

249. The Pectoral Cross is the gold cross that hangs around the neck of the pope. It must be worn at all times when the pope can be seen by others.

250. The Second Vatican Council opened on October 11, 1962. It was directed by Pope John XXIII and proved to be the Catholic Church's most searching self-examination in its history.

251. Pope Paul VI celebrated mass in Italian instead of Latin on March 7, 1964, at a Roman parish church. This marked one of the most significant changes of the council that had been held in 1962: worshiping in the vernacular.

252. A private mass is held by the pope each morning. It is to be a private time of reflection, unlike the "general audience" that is held every Wednesday in St. Peter's Square. That service may attract up to forty thousand participants.

253. How many popes? Since Saint Peter, who is assumed to have been the very first pope, there have been 262 men who have served in this position.

254. Voting for a pope is an interesting procedure. Each cardinal is handed a blank ballot and asked to write one name on it, walk to an altar, place the ballot under a plate, then pledge allegiance to the name he voted for. After ballots are counted, they are burned. If a majority is not reached, they are burned in a way that produces black smoke. They continue this process until a majority is reached. Once someone is elected, the ballots are burned with a chemical to produce white smoke.

255. The pope lives in Vatican Palace, but during the summer he often moves to a papal villa in the small town of Castel Gandolfo in the Alban Hills southeast of Rome. Though unknown by most Catholics, it is referred to as "Vatican South" by those in the press.

256. The pope earns an annual salary of about eighteen thousand U.S. dollars per year. It is paid by the annual "Peter's Pence" contribution that is collected by Roman Catholic churches around the world each year.

257. Pope John Paul II, who led the Roman Catholic Church during the late twentieth and early twenty-first centuries and worked to expand the pope's role in international affairs, was born in Poland. This is significant because the last non-Italian to hold the office of pope was Martin V, who took office in 1417.

258. Pope John Paul II made history in 1992 when he upheld Galileo's view of the sun and the solar system. The pope formally withdrew the Roman Catholic Church's condemnation of Galileo Galilei nearly 360 years earlier (Galileo was forced to defend his view in 1633) for believing the sun was the center of the universe.

9

The Schism

259. The Great Schism began in 1378 when Pope Gregory XI died. France had dominated the papacy for decades, and the pope eventually moved to Avignon. When Gregory died, the new pope, Urban VI, proved unpopular. When he moved back to Rome, the cardinals elected another pope, Clement VII, who remained in Avignon. For thirty-nine years there were two popes, each claiming to be the "Vicar of Christ." There were also two colleges of cardinals, who both continued electing new popes when their pope died.

260. The Babylonian Captivity of the church occurred when the pope moved to Avignon because of political pressures from the king of France. Those outside French borders saw the pope as the tool of France, and even followers within France recoiled at the bureaucracy and extravagance of the papal estate.

261. Pope Gregory XI, knowing that the breakaway cities of northern Italy were about to invite Rome to join them in rebellion, decided it was time for the pope to return to Rome in 1377.

262. "Rome is wherever the pope happens to be."—the words of Emperor Charles V, who tried to keep Pope Gregory from returning to Rome. Though Gregory was born in France, and his aged father threw himself across Gregory's doorframe in an attempt to prevent his leaving, he sailed for Rome only to be embroiled in local politics, endangered by antipapists, and ceaselessly hounded by French cardinals to return to Avignon. He agreed to do so in the spring of 1378 but died before he could leave the city.

263. The Conclave of Rome took place in 1378, with sixteen cardinals charged with electing a new pope. One cardinal was Spanish, four Italian, and eleven French—but the French cardinals were from two parties fearful of electing someone who would support the other side. The citizens of Rome, seeing a chance to end the reign of French popes, sent a committee of leaders to plead for a Roman one. When the group could not agree on a candidate, it decided to compromise by electing an outsider it could control: Bartolomeo Prignano, a quiet unknown man who took the name Pope Urban VI.

264. The False Pope was the aged Cardinal Tebaldeschi of Rome, who on April 8, 1378, was forced to put on the papal mitre and wave to the crowds outside, pretending to have been elected pope. The cardinals were afraid of the crowds thronging St. Peter's Basilica, shouting, "We want a Roman!" and making threats against the French. The appearance calmed them, and the next day the cardinals announced the election of Urban before leaving town.

265. Pope Urban VI was one of the biggest mistakes in church history. Totally unprepared for such high office, he allowed power to go to his head. Berating those around him without tact or dignity, he yelled at one cardinal to "shut your mouth," screamed at another that he was a "half wit," and had to be restrained from slapping a third. Plunging into secular government affairs, he announced that the ruler of Naples, Queen Joanna, was incompetent to lead because she was a woman. He then threatened to put her in a nunnery. Those closest to him thought he was mad.

266. *Furiosus et melancholicus* was the charge brought by French cardinals against Urban when he refused to return to Avignon. In July 1378, they announced that he had been elected under the duress of mob violence (though his election came about *before* any threats were made) and was unfit for office due to mental illness. The cardinals called him "anti-Christ, devil, apostate, tyrant, deceiver, elected-by-force." There was no official means for repudiating a pope, so the French were hoping Urban would simply step down or, at worst, be forced out. Instead, Urban hired an army.

267. King Charles V of France, an otherwise wise ruler, called the French cardinals together, gave them his support, and watched them elect a new pope—Pope Clement VII, none other than Cardinal Robert of Geneva, the "Butcher of Cesena," a man despised throughout Italy. It was such an arrogant display of power and such a cynical and cold-hearted response to the situation that the historian Michelet would later describe it by saying, "No epoch was more naturally mad."

268. The Condottieri, or Italian "contract workers," were mercenaries hired by Pope Urban to maintain his position by force. They drove out the forces supporting Clement, then helped elect a new College of Cardinals, so that there were now two popes, two church hierarchies, and two armies supporting them. England, in natural opposition to France, supported Urban. Scotland, in opposition to England, supported Clement. Spain supported Urban, Portugal went for Clement. All of Europe was divided.

269. The madness of Urban grew as some priests close to him deserted in favor of Clement. Once, while besieged by an army, Urban mounted the battlements four times per day, at precise intervals, to "excommunicate" the soldiers. When a group of cardinals planned to create a regency council to govern while holding Urban in a cell, he learned of the plot, had them arrested and tortured, and walked back and forth beneath the windows, reading out loud from the Psalms while listening to the screams of the victims. Eventually, he became as hated as Clement.

270. "Who can be sure of salvation?" This was a question asked by a writer after each pope had excommunicated the followers of the other. Every Christian was under penalty of damnation by someone. In some cities there were two competing priests, each condemning the services of the other. Though the schism had not started for religious reasons, it was the single greatest impediment to the faith of people.

271. The church faced bankruptcy due to revenues being cut in half. To stave off a catastrophe, priests performed simony, sold benefices and promotions, and charged for the smallest service. The sale of indulgences became important, undermining the faith of the common people.

272. "Like a prostitute found at the scene of a debauch," wrote the Monk of St. Denis about the fourteenth-century church, "she has become a subject for satire and object of laughter for all peoples of the world. . . . They make up songs about her every day."

273. The Duke D'Anjou, brother of King Charles, supported Clement. When asked by the pope for military support, D'Anjou required as payment "the kingdom of Adria"—that is, all the land alongside the Adriatic. Clement eagerly agreed, because he knew there was no such kingdom, and the opposing cities in that region would doubtless never agree to be united. When the faculty at the University of Paris called for a church council to settle the schism, D'Anjou had their leaders arrested, causing the rest to flee to Rome and side with Urban.

274. An Ecumenical Council was the clear solution to the problem of the schism, but both popes adamantly rejected it, for fear of losing control. Though the schism would go on for forty years, damaging both the church and society, one pope held out in Rome, the other in Avignon. Their supporters continued electing successors, having created two different Colleges of Cardinals.

275. The Council of Pisa met in 1409 to determine the true pope. The participants decided to sack both Clement and Urban, and called a new man, Alexander V, as pope. Unfortunately, Clement and Urban had supporters, so there were now three popes. However, Alexander's reign was short-lived.

276. John XXIII, Alexander's successor, is thought to have poisoned Alexander. It is believed that this notorious pope began his career as a pirate. He was deposed by a council that locked the doors of the council chamber and sent all outsiders away before they would even read aloud the charges, so horrendous and long was the list of misdeeds he committed. Among other charges, it was this pope's idea to sell indulgences to make money (presumably to line his own pockets).

277. The Council of Constance met in 1414, which was possibly the world's first version of the United Nations. Bishops came from every country, grouped by nationality, and included laypeople. Each nation was given one vote. To solve the problem, they fired two popes, convinced another to step down, and settled on one man: Martin V, who immediately repudiated the council, claiming they didn't have authority over a pope.

278. The Great Schism brought John Wycliffe to a turning point. Originally wanting to reform the church, he watched the abuses on both sides and concluded that the entire church hierarchy should be swept away. "Each that shall be damned shall be damned by his own guilt, and each man that is saved shall be saved by his own merit," wrote Wycliffe. In transferring salvation from the agency of the church to the individual, Wycliffe introduced Protestantism and ushered in the modern world.

10

The Reformation

279. The term "Reformation" was not used in reference to the birth of Protestantism until the seventeenth century. Prior to that, the word "reform" was used mainly to refer to the need for change within the Catholic Church.

280. One of the earliest voices against the growing wealth of the Roman Church was Arnold of Brescia, who argued that the practice of clerical vice was an attempt by the pope to control the world. In a famous series of sermons, he urged the church to surrender all its property, sell all its goods, and give the money to the poor. Banished from Italy for this kind of talk, he eventually returned and led an overthrow of the pope, but he was arrested and executed by Emperor Frederick Barbarossa in 1155.

281. In the century prior to the Reformation, there was increasing religious interest throughout northern Europe. Monasteries gained members, increasing numbers of people made pilgrimages, and many more factions and heretical groups emerged. All of these instances were signs of discontent with the current state of the church. People were searching beyond Sunday mass and confessions for spiritual hope, and many were frustrated with the lax discipline of the clergy, the never-ending political squabbles, and the endless rituals and requirements.

282. The Council of Basle, 1431–1449, was one instance of the need for reform within the church. Convened in 1431 by Pope Martin V, the council had an agenda that included a variety of issues, including reform of church finances and the ongoing difficulties with the Hussites, whose leader had been condemned and executed in 1415 at an earlier council. Also discussed was the possibility of reunifying with the Eastern faction of the church. In 1433, Pope Eugene IV came under fire for his "disobedience," as both the emperor of Rome and the council ruled that the pope was under the authority of councils and had been disobedient. The pope responded by denouncing the council in 1437 as heretical. Such political squabbles dragged on for years. Later the council transferred to Ferrara to discuss unity with the Eastern Church, and a new pope was elected (considered an antipope by some).

283. The sale of indulgences has a long history in the Catholic Church, but the man who brought it to the forefront was Johann Tetzel, a Dominican monk and the "commissioner of indulgences." Seeking to find a fund-raising gimmick to help build a new basilica in Rome, Tetzel began selling forgiveness. He preached sermons declaring that the audience's dead relatives were in purgatory, awaiting redemption gained by the giving of a monetary gift to the church. "As the coin in the coffer rings, a soul from purgatory springs," he said. The money raised was then sent to Rome.

284. The Unity of the Brethren was the name the church in Bohemia gave itself after throwing off the Roman Catholic Church and the German Empire. Relying on the writings of John Wycliffe and Jan Hus, they were repelled by the extravagant lifestyle of the pope and the idiosyncratic doctrines being announced in Rome. In particular, they demanded each person in a worship service be allowed to partake of both the bread and the cup, rather than having the priest take it on their behalf. Pope Alexander V tried desperately to put down the rebellion, but it remained and was one of the seeds of the Reformation.

285. Martin Luther, a scholar and priest, tried to find forgiveness through a life of penance. He once climbed Pilate's stairs in Jerusalem on his knees, praying and kissing each step in an attempt to find God. His efforts left him filled with doubts, to the point that he once cried out to his confessor, "I hate God!" But a quiet study of Paul's letter to the Romans caused him to stop and consider these words: "The just shall live by faith." The implication was that monks, masses, saints, the intercession of priests, and the mediation of the church in Rome were superfluous. That idea changed the world.

286. When Martin Luther died on February 18, 1546, two interesting items were found in his pockets. One was the beginning of a projected manuscript aimed against Roman Catholics. The second was a slip of paper with a saying reminding him, "We are beggars, that's the truth."

287. The Ninety-five Theses were the list of grievances Martin Luther posted on the door of the Wittenberg church in Germany in 1517. The list included the selling of indulgences, the worship of relics, and other questionable practices. It was a rather restrained list, considering the debates about the role of the church going on across Europe. The door to the church served as a sort of community bulletin board, so one could argue that Luther was doing nothing more than calling for a discussion.

288. The Protestant Reformation cannot simply be defined by the actions of Martin Luther. While his nailing of the Ninety-five Theses is largely recognized as the first significant break with Rome, the connection between the Roman Church and the lives of Europeans had been slowly eroding. The actions of Peter Waldo, John Wycliffe, Jan Hus, Girolamo Savonarola, and Jan Van Ruysbroeck's Brethren of Common Life all preceded Martin Luther, and in many ways mirrored his beliefs and actions. What we consider "the Reformation" can really be broken down into several mini-Reformations.

289. The Lutheran Reformation took place largely in Germany and Scandinavia. Instigated by the selling of indulgences and enlarged by the excommunication of Luther, it was marked by three distinctives: *sola fide* (justification by faith alone), *sola gratia* (salvation by grace alone), and *sola scriptura* (the authority for doctrine and practice is found in the Bible alone).

290. The Swiss Reformation was led by Ulrich Zwingli and John Calvin and spread throughout Germany, Switzerland, Holland, England, Scotland, Hungary, and parts of France, eventually moving to New England and the New World. It was marked by an emphasis on election, the sovereignty of God, and the Lord's Supper as a symbol of Christ's sacrifice rather than a spiritual presence that somehow affects the lives of believers. Those who followed Calvin's writings generally tried to impose their theology onto the workings of local government.

291. The French Reformation was largely due to the decay of the Roman Catholic Church in France. Inspired by the writings of John Calvin, many educated people left the Roman Church to follow Protestantism, therefore inviting persecution. Though many young noblemen defended the "Huguenots," the unstable political atmosphere in France led to religious civil war—sometimes fomented by England and Spain, which were intent on keeping France unstable.

292. The English Reformation was begun by Henry VIII as the result of his desire to divorce his wife, developed by Edward VI in an effort to reshape English worship, advanced by Mary I when she persecuted Protestants, and finally established by Elizabeth I when she ended both the persecutions and the alliance with Spain. Though opposed by both Puritans and Separatists, Elizabeth's "Middle Way" created the modern Anglican Church.

293. The Scottish Reformation was given impetus by the fact that the Catholic clergymen in Scotland were perhaps the most depraved of all Europe. Under the leadership of Patrick Hamilton, George Wishart, and John Knox, and influenced by the teachings of Wycliffe and the ideas of the Celtic Church, the Scottish people flocked to Protestantism even though there were no Protestant preachers or an organized Protestant Church. The fact that Bibles, books, plays, and songs were being distributed in both the English language and the Scottish dialect no doubt propelled the movement.

294. The Netherlands Reformation was really begun when both Catholics and Protestants banded together to expel the Spanish armies from modern-day Holland and Belgium. When that task was done, they began to battle each other, which turned into an eighty-year civil war. Though the Spanish would come back in on the side of the Catholic south, England would send reinforcements to the north, helping them hold the line of battle at the Rhein River for twelve years. With the defeat of the Spanish Armada in 1588, the northern Dutch territories declared independence and began settling Dutch Reformed communities all over the New World.

295. Philipp Melanchthon was both a colleague and close friend of Luther. Melanchthon taught Greek at the University of Wittenberg and was a gifted writer and editor. It appears he was something of a cheerleader for Luther's work. He used his talents to help give structure to Luther's writings, but in his own right, Melanchthon was responsible for much of the formulating of the Augsburg Confession of 1530 and the defense that went along with it. He is considered a founding member of early Lutheranism.

296. The Leipzig Debate was a public theological debate that ran for eighteen days in the spring of 1519. The representative of the Vatican, John Eck, challenged Martin Luther, who had declared that a papal decree was not enough to prove heresy—the pope must rely on the Bible to prove Luther's theology incorrect. "Neither the church nor the pope can establish articles of faith," said Luther. While that may be so, at the close of the debate Eck immediately moved to have Rome declare Luther a heretic.

297. The early reformers called themselves "evangelicals"; their individual congregations were all part of one universal church, the catholic church (as the Apostles' Creed states) on earth. It wasn't until the seventeenth century that the various denominations of Reformed and Lutherans considered themselves separate church bodies.

298. "Protestant," the term commonly applied to the reformers following the Reformation, came about at the Diet of Speyer in 1529. The "evangelical" nobility as well as whole cities objected to the decree that Catholic masses were to continue and be tolerated in every principality. This refusal by the church to make amends and to take the Reformation seriously prompted protests on the part of the evangelicals. The term "protestant" became synonymous with those who objected to the church.

299. John Calvin was French and the father of Calvinism. Persecuted by Catholics, the young man was forced to leave France one night in 1533 by way of his window, being lowered out with a rope made of bed sheets. He disguised himself as a farmer and spent three years as a fugitive from the Catholic authorities before going to Geneva and reforming it into what became a model city for Protestantism. His contributions, which included *The Institutes of the Christian Religion,* proved invaluable in spreading Reformed doctrine throughout the world. "To omit Calvin from the forces of Western evolution is to read history with one eye shut."—John Morley, British statesman.

300. William Farel played an important role in the changes that occurred in Geneva, Switzerland, during the Reformation. Farel, who had played an important part in earlier ridding Geneva of popery, urged Calvin not to retreat into his studies when he was so desperately needed as a figure of leadership in the daily affairs of the Reformation. Later the two wrote the *Confession of Faith* that summarized the main doctrines of Calvinism.

301. Ulrich Zwingli was a pastor in Zurich who in 1519 announced that he and his church would no longer follow the prescribed Catholic lectionary, but instead he would preach through the Book of Matthew. He followed that by allowing priests and nuns to marry, removing the relics and Catholic images in the sanctuary, and replacing the formal mass with a simple worship service focused on preaching the Bible. Swiss churchmen rallied to his side, establishing the Reformation in Switzerland. Zwingli, who opposed war, was killed while fighting as a soldier at the Battle of Kappel—a fight between Catholics and Protestants.

302. Zwingli had a similar experience to Luther and his Ninety-five Theses in that he wrote a list of articles (there were sixty-seven) discussing his own beliefs of doctrine as well as the grievances he held against the established church. These included his disagreement with the pope, the mass, monastic vows and celibacy, indulgences, and teachings on purgatory as well as other subjects. On January 29, 1523, he appeared before six hundred men with his Latin, Hebrew, and Greek Bibles open and ready to be used. His audience was pleased and grew enthusiastic, so it was ordered that the priests should promote the theses.

303. Zwingli was married twice. He and nine other priests appealed to their bishop for his blessing on their decisions to get married. However, the bishop refused them all in 1522. Zwingli married in secret, outside of the church, and resigned from the priesthood later that same year. He was married again to his wife in a formal church ceremony in 1524.

304. "We have become the spectacle of the world."—Martin Luther's comment was justified; the Reformation remains an unparalleled event in the history of the church.

305. Heinrich Bullinger succeeded Zwingli as the minister of the Zurich Great Church. Bullinger sought to unite the various reform movements that spread throughout Europe by establishing alliances to help the reformers broaden their movement.

306. The revolt against Rome occurred in 1521 and 1522, as German princes and dukes defied the pope's condemnation of Martin Luther. Claiming that the church needed "pastors and not dignitaries," Luther returned to Wittenberg, abolished the office of bishop, and announced that priests and nuns could now marry.

307. Michael Sattler became converted and led the movement of the Anabaptists, who were inspired to their beliefs by the preaching of Zwingli, much to his dismay. Sattler presided at the Schleitheim Conference but was arrested in Austria that same year. He was tried and found guilty and was burned to death as a heretic.

308. The Schleitheim Conference of 1527 resulted in the oldest creed of the Anabaptists. The conference produced a document that called for more than mere acceptance of correct doctrine; the Anabaptists desired a daily walk with God. The participants agreed to live communally, to reject all forms of warfare, and to rely on congregational church authority. Wanting to separate church and state, they preached religious liberty, insisted on the Bible as their final authority, and considered each believer both a priest and a missionary.

309. One cold winter day in 1535, twelve Anabaptists ran naked through the streets of Amsterdam. Protestants and Catholics were equally angry at the spectacle and demanded that the Anabaptists do something to control their more zealous members. The leader of the Anabaptists complied and eventually the group as a whole became more disciplined.

310. *Cujus regio, ejus religio.* "The religion of the prince determines the religious allegiance of the state." This principle was adopted at Augsburg in 1555. If the king was Catholic, his countrymen were also required to be Catholic.

311. The Belgic Confession of Faith was written in 1561 by Guy de Bres and several other reformers. The document was revised by Francis Junius of Bourges. Though it was originally written in French, it was quickly translated into Dutch and Latin. The confession covered many of the same theological topics as had been covered in other Reformed confessions written up to that time.

312. The Heidelberg Catechism was commissioned by Elector Frederick III, ruler of Palatinate, the most important German province, from 1559 to 1576. The purpose of the catechism was to guide ministers and teachers as well as the common people in the Christian faith. The name "Heidelberg" was adopted after the new form was approved by a synod in Heidelberg, Germany, late in 1562. It is believed Zacharias Ursinus and Caspar Olevianus authored the document, but this cannot be proved without doubt. Other editions have followed, and the Heidelberg Catechism is still used today by many Reformed churches throughout the world.

313. The Latin version of the Heidelberg Catechism was divided into fifty-two separate sections called "Lord's Days." The purpose of these divisions was to encourage ministers to cover the catechism in the space of one year. The catechism was to be used regularly and thoroughly, and the divisions were an easy way to encourage ministers to be thorough. These groupings of questions and answers within the catechism remain today.

314. "Religion is not changed as easily as a shirt."—King Henry IV of France, who was raised in the Protestant tradition, became a Roman Catholic in 1593. He and many others knew all too well the truth of the statement.

315. The Synod of Dort met in Dordrecht, the Netherlands, from 1618 to 1619. The purpose of the gathering was to respond to the Arminian heresy present within the Reformed Church. Followers of Arminius presented their views on five specific points in the Remonstrance of 1610. The document that came out of this meeting became known popularly as the Canons of Dort and was essentially an argument against the Remonstrance of 1610. Five main doctrines were covered in the canons' documents (total depravity, unconditional election, limited atonement, irresistible grace, and perseverance of the saints). Interestingly, though the gathering was essentially national, involving churches of the Netherlands, there were twenty-six delegates from foreign countries as well.

316. Despite their theological differences, Protestants and Catholics shared common ground in regard to their dislike for drama and plays, grisly sports, festivals, dancing, disorderly funerals, breaking the Sabbath, gambling, blasphemy, drinking of toasts, and wrongful use of church property.

317. "Protestantism . . . is the Lutheran rebellion, whose evil virus goes wandering about in almost all nations."—Pope Leo XIII, in *Militantis Ecclesiae,* 1897

11

The Church
Harms Its Own

318. In 1492, the year Columbus sailed to the New World, Spain officially expelled all Jews from the land. The church and state were very connected in Spain, as they were in all other European countries at this time. The Catholic Church was intolerant of other beliefs and began hunting out those who held "questionable" beliefs. What followed was the Spanish Inquisition.

319. Jan Hus was known to be a man who lacked tact and was outspoken when it came to the sins of the church. He was a diligent scholar and believed the common people desperately needed their own translation of the Bible. He translated the Bible, which was a great achievement, but his contribution was not welcomed. Hus was condemned and his Bible rejected as

heretical by the Catholic Church. Promised a safe hearing at the Council in Constance by the Holy Roman emperor in order to discuss the matter, Hus came out of hiding and traveled to Constance. He was seized and promptly and unfairly tried. He was then burned alive.

320. Felix Manz was the first Protestant martyred by other Protestants. Manz was a Swiss Anabaptist reformer and traveled far and wide to preach. He was drowned in 1527 as punishment for preaching the doctrine of adult baptism.

321. In an attempt to purge Paris of overzealous Protestants and their placards denouncing the Catholic Church, many of the royal family, church officials, and other political figures held a torch-lit procession from the Louvre to Notre Dame on January 29, 1535. Before the day was over, six Protestants were hung and then burned. This was largely in response to the actions of a Protestant by the name of Feret. He had sneaked into the palace and nailed a highly inflammatory statement to the king's bedroom door several months before.

322. In 1546, George Wishart, a Reformed pastor, was executed in England by Roman Catholics. Angered by the act and determined to retaliate, Scottish Protestants seized and murdered Cardinal David Beaton in St. Andrews, Scotland.

323. Michael Servetus was burned at the stake in 1553 in Geneva, Switzerland, a Calvinist stronghold, for his beliefs (considered heretical) regarding the Trinity. Geneva was at that time a model city of Protestant belief and was firmly controlled by John Calvin. Servetus was asked to keep quiet about his differing views and even to leave the area, upon the threat of death if he refused. He continued to openly disagree and was burned at the stake.

324. "Bloody Mary" restored Roman Catholicism to England in 1554. Mary Tudor, daughter of Henry VIII (who was a Protestant), was determined to return England to the Catholic Church. Three hundred Protestants were burned at the stake, and four hundred more died by imprisonment and starvation.

325. The St. Bartholomew's Day Massacre occurred on August 23, 1572. Between five thousand and ten thousand Huguenots (Protestants of France) were massacred by Catholics in Paris during the reign of King Charles IX (who was very young at the time) and his mother, Regent Catherine de Medici. The Protestants had come to the city for a royal wedding, and though there is no historical evidence to prove whether the orders were given by the queen or not, the massacre was carried out by arch-Catholics (ultra Catholics) who feared a Protestant takeover.

326. The Netherlands was touched by the Reformation in 1582. King Philip II of Spain, staunchly Catholic and very much against the spread of Protestantism, sent ten thousand troops to "control" the rebellion. A total of eighteen thousand people were killed as a result.

327. "You have struck me with roses." Obadiah Holmes uttered these words in 1651 after suffering thirty lashes for preaching Baptist doctrine in Protestant England. Holmes's experience did not deter others from joining the Baptist tradition; in fact, it served to encourage more followers.

328. America was not born a land of tolerance. There was plenty of disagreement but little room for it among the groups who came to the New World. Thankfully the land was plenteous, and people were able to spread out. However, there were still Catholics persecuting Huguenots, Dutch Reformed Christians jailing Lutherans, and Puritans actively persecuting Quakers, Anglicans, Presbyterians, and Lutherans.

329. Quakers were persecuted in the New World just as they had been in the Old. In 1656 eight Quakers came to Puritan Massachusetts from England, but they were not welcomed. Instead they were imprisoned (with no trial) and then sent back to England according to the wishes of the Massachusetts Bay Company.

330. The Salem Witch Trials are a well-known event in the early history of the United States. Those accused suffered unfair trials, imprisonment, and, for some, death at the hands of Christian Puritans. The number of women accused of witchcraft was no less than 150 in Salem, Massachusetts, in the year 1691. Nineteen of those accused were eventually sentenced to death and hanged.

331. Massachusetts citizens held a day of fasting to repent of the Salem witch trials (held five years earlier) on January 15, 1697. According to record, the special day was instituted so that "all of God's people may offer up fervent supplications unto him, that all iniquity may be put away, which hath stirred God's holy jealousy against this land; that he would show us what we know not, and help us, wherein we have done amiss, to do so no more."

332. Christianity was banned in France by revolutionaries in 1794. The "reign of terror" followed, in which fourteen hundred people died. Napoleon ended the ban in 1804 and imprisoned Pope Pius VII.

333. Bethel African Methodist Episcopal Church was started in 1794 in Philadelphia under the pastoral leadership of former slave Richard Allen. He and other liberated African American Christians were discriminated against and even asked to leave when they attended the predominantly white St. George's Methodist Episcopal Church. However, St. George's fought them at every turn when they tried to begin their own church, even threatening to dismiss all African American Methodists from the rolls of the church who had committed themselves to the new project. St. George's even went so far as to trick Bethel into signing over control, including their property. The last straw occurred in 1805 when an elder of St. George's made it his right alone to preach, to administer sacraments, and to forbid people the right to assemble. He also demanded payment for these rights. Richard Allen then consulted a lawyer and a supplement to the original charter was adopted. After several battles in court, Bethel was granted its independence. Eventually, other African American Methodist churches would join Bethel as a new denomination was born.

12

The Bible

334. The Bible is the world's best-selling book as well as the world's most shoplifted book!

335. Jerome, who was born in A.D. 340, began his ascetic lifestyle as a hermit but found he needed something to occupy his mind. He took up Hebrew and eventually began teaching classes in biblical interpretation. Eventually, he translated the Old and New Testaments from their original languages into Latin—what we call the "Vulgate," which the Roman Catholic Church used as its "authorized" version.

336. The tests of canonicity (the selection of which books were to be included in the Holy Bible) included: (1) the book had to have a history of being used in Christian worship; (2) the book had to be written by an apostle, or affirmed by an apostle; and (3) the book had to have evidenced power in the lives of believers. Justin Martyr, Theophilus, Victorinus, and Tatian are some of the early believers who became Christians simply by reading the New Testament books.

337. The Muratorian Canon is named for its discoverer, L. A. Muratori, who first published it in 1740. A fascinating look into the early church, it reveals that by the year 190, Christians had developed a New Testament and put it alongside the Jewish Scriptures—the former the fulfillment of the latter. It contains in order: Matthew, Mark, Luke, John, Acts, 1 and 2 Corinthians, Ephesians, Philippians, Colossians, Galatians, 1 and 2 Thessalonians, Romans, Philemon, Titus, 1 and 2 Timothy, the Apocalypse of John (Revelation), the Apocalypse of Peter, and the Wisdom of Solomon.

338. Some books of Scripture faced challenges. Christians in the West didn't like Hebrews, while those in the East opposed Revelation. Church historian Eusebius, writing in the fourth century, noted that James, 2 Peter, 2 and 3 John, Jude, and Revelation were the only books "spoken against." Martin Luther would challenge the Book of James in the sixteenth century, calling it "an epistle of straw."

339. The Apocrypha, a collection of books associated with the ancient church, was accepted as part of the Bible by Augustine in the late fourth century. Because much of Roman Catholic theology is based on the writings of Augustine, Catholics still accept the Apocrypha as part of the Word of God. However, neither the Jews nor Christians in Palestine ever accepted it as Scripture. Protestants during the Reformation rejected it as part of the canon, and it no longer appears in Protestant Bibles.

340. The allegorical method of interpretation went to extreme lengths to try to make the Old Testament into a Christian book. Origen, one of the first Christian theologians, believed that "the Scriptures were composed through the Spirit of God, and have both a meaning which is obvious and another which is hidden." He then proceeded to create all sorts of allegorical meanings to the Word of God. This infuriated his critics, who felt that Origen was crafting theological implications out of thin air.

341. Stephen Langton, who was archbishop of Canterbury in the thirteenth century, was the first to create chapter divisions for the Bible.

342. The Synod of Toulouse in 1229 forbade everyone except priests from possessing a copy of the Scriptures. At that gathering, Pope Gregory IX asked Dominican friars to question suspects and prosecute heretics, making the friars a powerful force and keeping the Bible out of the hands of laypeople.

343. The invention of movable type by Johann Gutenberg was recently hailed as the most important technical advancement of the last millennium. Gutenberg, a printer in Mainz, found a way to make many copies of a page by using letters made of lead. In 1456, he and his fellow printers created two hundred copies of Jerome's Vulgate Bible. Prior to that time, all books were hand printed on papyrus sheets or animal skin, making them expensive, time-intensive, and rare. Consequently, few people could read, and even fewer owned any books. Within twenty years of Gutenberg's first printed Bible, the printers of Mainz had created more Bibles than had been produced by hand in the previous fourteen hundred years.

344. The printing press did not only allow for the dissemination of the Scriptures but also for the spread of critical, sometimes satiric examinations of the church's excesses. These writings fit the growing mood in Europe that the Roman Church was out of touch with common people's lives.

345. Archbishop of Armagh, Ireland, James Ussher became famous for his chronology of the Bible (which placed the creation of the world in 4004 B.C.). He wrote a history of the Latin church as well as the articles of faith for the church in Ireland. Ussher was given a state funeral and buried in Westminster Abbey, a high honor.

346. The Great Bible (1539) was the first widely popular English translation of the Scriptures to be owned and read by the common people. Produced by William Tyndale, Miles Coverdale, and John Rogers, it was based on translations from the Latin

Vulgate, with additional notes from the writings of Martin Luther and Ulrich Zwingli. It was also a significant improvement over the earlier *Coverdale* and *Matthew* Bibles because of its readability and understanding of poetry.

347. The Geneva Bible (1560) was a product of the Calvinist movement in northern Europe. Rather than simply relying on Roman Catholic translations, the English exiles in Geneva created prologues to each book of Scripture, added marginal notes to aid understanding, and spent considerable time recrafting the poetic elements of the various books. One outstanding feature that the translators developed was the numbering of chapters and verses—something that not only made it a popular Bible but has also been copied by translators ever since.

348. The King James Bible, which was originally named *The Authorized Version,* was first suggested by the Puritans in 1604. King James, who disagreed with the Calvinist leanings of *The Geneva Bible,* wanted a version that supported the divine right of kings. He appointed fifty-four scholars divided into eight teams and demanded they examine all earlier English versions to aid in translation. Produced in 1611, the translation is marked by beautiful language, an accurate translation, and modesty when faced with embarrassing language and situations.

349. The first copy of the Gutenberg Bible took three years of constant printing to complete, and it was finished in 1455. It was done in two volumes, with 1,284 pages total. Two hundred original Gutenberg Bibles were printed, and forty-seven still exist.

350. The Wycliffe Bible was translated from the Vulgate Bible into English by John Wycliffe in 1384. The Catholic Church denounced Wycliffe as heretical for doing this, because it was forbidden to translate the Bible into English at that time.

351. The Tyndale Bible was published in 1526 by William Tyndale, an English Protestant reformer, from the ancient Hebrew and Greek texts. This version was also condemned by the church. An approved English translation was finally published in 1582: the Rheims-Douay Bible.

352. The Geneva Bible was the first to depict Adam and Eve wearing "breeches." The editors thought the passage where Adam and Eve are sewing fig leaves together for clothing (aprons) was too racy. The Bible was nicknamed the "Breeches Bible."

353. Hugh of St. Cher was a French cardinal and reportedly compiled the first Bible concordance; he is thought to be the first person to divide the Old and New Testaments into chapters.

354. The Aiken Bible was the first Bible printed in the United States. Congress authorized its publishing in 1781.

355. Biblical criticism was the attempt to examine the Word of God through the lens of science and historical theory in the late 1800s in order to find its exact meaning. "Lower" criticism meant seeking the earliest and most reliable text of Scripture. "Higher" criticism intended to find the hidden meanings of the words. Rejecting the miraculous and traditional understanding, the critics invented all sorts of new interpretations and imposed them on to the plain meaning of the text.

356. Adam Clarke, a Methodist circuit preacher of the nineteenth century, believed that only through regular Bible reading would Christians grow wise in their salvation. He said, "Read the whole Bible, and read it in order; two chapters in the Old Testament and one in the New, daily if you can possibly spare the time; and you will have more time than you are aware of; if you retrench all needless visits, and save the hours spent in useless or unimportant conversation."

13

Documents, Edicts, Bills, and Meetings

357. The Apostles' Creed wasn't written by the apostles, but it first appeared as a baptismal confession in Rome during the second century. An attempt to clarify the faith while battling gnosticism, it emphasizes that God created matter, that Jesus was born of a virgin, that Christ died, and that we will all be resurrected. Most importantly, it states that salvation and redemption don't come from secret knowledge but from faith in Jesus Christ.

358. The Nicene Creed was created in its first draft by Eusebius, bishop of Caesarea and writer of the first great book on church history. While sitting with other bishops at the Council of Nicaea, Eusebius recognized that the church needed a concise statement of belief, and so he created one. But because the council was meeting to clarify the nature of Jesus Christ, it inserted some words from Hosius of Cordova to help define the Lord Jesus Christ: "true God of true God; begotten, not made; of one substance with the Father." Though the participants wanted to refine the statement, an impatient Emperor Constantine insisted they ratify the statement as it stood, and it remains the standard in the Roman, Anglican, and Eastern Churches.

359. The Donation of Constantine was a forged document that claimed Constantine had "donated" half of his empire to the bishop of Rome. The idea behind the letter was to give land to the pope and therefore create a "Holy" Empire. In 756 the king of the Franks, Pepin, read a copy and decided he would also offer the pope a gift of lands. He donated the "papal states," a swath of land that stretched across Italy, so that the pope would have his own territory to govern. Vatican City, where St. Peter's Basilica now stands, is the only remaining portion of Pepin's donation.

360. British law required a three-year fast of those who offered sacrifices to fountains (holy wells). The early British Christians struggled with the loss of sacrificing (a pagan ritual). Evidently the need for legislation against it forced this law, which was imposed by seventh-century church leaders. Fountain worship was also denounced in the eleventh century by Archbishop Anselm.

361. The Truce of God Proposal established a "closed season" on fighting. The pope announced that there was to be no fighting in Christian nations from sundown Wednesday until sunrise Monday, nor was there to be any sacking or looting during Lent, Christmas, and Easter seasons. The proposal was largely ignored because it left only two and a half days of fighting per week.

362. The Peace of God Proposal banned anyone who had sacked a Christian city, pillaged a church or monastery, or killed noncombatants during war from taking communion. Inaugurated in the eleventh century, it was an attempt by church leaders to discourage knights and soldiers from running amuck in the towns and villages of Europe.

363. Canon Law was the name given to the body of rules and duties that applied to churchmen in the twelfth century. The pope, trying to gain support for a papal monarchy, had his legal experts draw up a systematic statement of theology, then added laws for the ecclesiastical courts, the rites and ceremonies associated with the church, and the rules for things like giving and fasting. It gave the church incredible power and was a crass attempt to control every aspect of people's lives.

364. The Interdict was one of Innocent III's ideas for increasing his control. While excommunication was aimed at individuals, an "interdiction" was a papal decree that an entire city or region was being excommunicated, generally because the pope didn't like their leader. In announcing an interdiction, Innocent would stop all church services, refuse to allow anyone to partake of communion, and at times even board up churches. In ten years, he pronounced an interdiction eighty-five times.

365. The Interdict of 1208 placed Britain under firm orders not to perform any Christian church services or burials. Churches were to remain closed, with harsh penalties for any who disobeyed. Pope Innocent III imposed the policy after Britain's king, John, disagreed with the choice Innocent had made for who would become the archbishop of Canterbury.

366. *Clericis Laicos* was the document issued in 1296 by Pope Boniface VIII, threatening excommunication to any ruler who tried to tax the clergy or the church. It came about because the feuding kings of France and England, Philip the Fair and Edward I, decided to tax wealthy clergymen to help offset the costs of the Hundred Years' War. Edward's response was to seize the church's property and strip unpaying clergymen of all legal protection. Philip's answer was to place an embargo on all gold, silver, and jewels entering Italy. Boniface backed down, so it was clear the pope no longer held sway over the monarchy.

367. The bull *Unum Sanctum* was issued in 1302. Within this document, Boniface VIII stated the absolute authority of the Roman Church over humankind in all regards, which meant the pope had more power than any king or emperor.

368. The Schleitheim Confession, produced at a conference on the Swiss-German border in 1527, emphasized four doctrines: *Discipleship* (that a believer's faith goes beyond accepting doctrine and transforms his manner of life); *Love* (that a Christian will take care of others and not fight in wars); *Congregationalism* (that decision-making in a church is done by the entire membership); and *Separation of church and state* (thereby giving freedom of worship to all citizens). The confession became a pattern for reformers and Protestants.

369. The Ninety-five Theses, 1517, were ninety-five arguments that Martin Luther nailed on the door of the church in Wittenberg, Germany. Posting arguments was a common practice, but this document stated the need for reform in the church as well as Luther's profession that faith in Christ is the only way to be saved. This action paved the way for the Reformation.

370. The Colloquy of Marburg occurred in 1529. This meeting was meant to unite the Lutherans of Germany (with Martin Luther leading them) and the Reformed believers of Switzerland (with Ulrich Zwingli leading them). Though they agreed on fourteen out of fifteen articles, they were divided over the single doctrine of the Eucharist. Luther believed the Eucharist somehow contained the grace of God; Zwingli saw the Lord's Supper as a symbolic act. As a result of the division, there was never a united front against the Roman Catholic Church by all Protestants.

371. The Augsburg Confession was the statement of faith produced in 1530 by Reformation leaders (Martin Luther was still considered an outlaw and was unable to attend). But Philipp Melanchthon, friend of Luther and the professor of Greek at Wittenberg, ably presented Luther's positions and drafted the Confession. Unfortunately, by that time Martin Luther had become an irascible old man. He endorsed the bigamous marriage of supporter Prince Philip, accused other reformers of being demonic, and sounded like a racist in denouncing the Jews.

372. John Calvin, the Geneva reformer, instigated a plan on January 20, 1541, to hold a "church court" each week in Geneva. The purpose of the weekly meetings was to keep tabs on the people, look for weaknesses in the system where discipline might be a problem, and judge those who had committed an offense.

373. In 1543 the British Parliament ordered that all commoners or, in its words, any "women or artificer's prentices, journeymen, servingmen of the degree of yeoman, or under, husbandmen or labourers" were forbidden to read any of the New Testament of the Bible that was printed in English.

374. The Six Articles of 1539 were a reaffirmation by the English church of Roman Catholic doctrine. The Six Articles included the need for clerical celibacy, the importance of confessing to a priest, the succession of bishops, and the perspective that a "mass" is a sacrifice of Christ. But one of the things it did away with was the monastic system. As a result, King Henry confiscated the land and sold it, replenishing his royal coffers.

375. The Forty-two Articles were the work of Thomas Cranmer in 1553 and defined the movement of the English church away from Roman Catholicism and toward Protestantism. Reversing the earlier Six Articles, it allowed priests to marry, did away with confession, and recognized only baptism and the Lord's Supper as sacraments.

376. Sebastian Castellio's pamphlet *Concerning Heretics Whether They Are to Be Persecuted and How They Are to Be Treated* was written in response to the 1553 martyrdom of Michael Servetus by the Calvinists in Geneva. Servetus was a heretic by the standards of most churchmen, and he narrowly escaped death by the Inquisition in Lyons before being recognized in Geneva on his way to Naples. He was burned at the stake; his death caused many to question the severity of punishment for theological disagreements. Through his death and the revulsion it caused, as well as Castellio's pamphlet, the idea of religious toleration and liberty began to grow.

377. The Peace of Augsburg Accord, crafted in 1555, adopted one simple territorial principle: The prince or ruler in each region would be able to decide the religion of his subjects. The idea grew from the ancient notion of a "Christian prince"—that one wise leader will decide for all. Unfortunately, it also spelled the death of Christendom. If one leader can announce that the truth is Roman Catholic, and another leader just a few miles away can announce the truth is Lutheran, then the concept that there is a "norm" for Christian truth is gone.

378. John Knox's Scottish Confession was written in 1560 in just four days. This statement of faith of the Church of Scotland remained a pillar of that institution until 1647 when the Westminster Confession superseded it.

379. The Thirty-nine Articles (1563) were Queen Elizabeth's attempt to find a middle way between Protestantism and Roman Catholicism. The articles retained the Catholic liturgy and the succession of bishops but rejected papal authority, proclaimed the Bible as the final authority for the church, and recognized baptism and the Lord's Supper as the only two sacraments. English churchmen praised Elizabeth's handling of the situation, which gave rise to the term *Via Media,* which means, "the Middle Way."

380. The Edict of Nantes in 1598 created a compromise solution to the French religious/civil war that had been going on for thirty years. Offering the Huguenots religious freedom while maintaining Roman Catholicism as the official religion, it came about largely because the nation was broke and both sides were completely fatigued by war.

381. The Millenary Petition was a document signed by a thousand churchmen of England and presented to King James I upon his succession to the throne in 1603. Heavily influenced by the Puritan and Separatist movements, the petition called for minor changes in the Church of England, including tolerance of independent churches. James made a pretense of hearing the petition, but when he called a conference of bishops at Hampton Court, he threatened to "harry out of the land" anyone who attempted to separate from the state church. However, there was one item in the petition that King James agreed to: the creation of a new Bible translation.

382. The Mayflower Compact is an agreement of principles signed by the forty-one male Separatists on board the ship *Mayflower* in 1620. The Separatists had contracted to have the ship take them to Virginia, where they would be under the authority of the king of England. But a bad storm blew them off course to the shores of Massachusetts, where they were under no state authority. Therefore the Separatists, who had begun calling themselves "Pilgrims," agreed to start a new colony for the advancement of Christianity. They committed themselves to be self-governing, to enact laws for the public good, and to uphold group solidarity. Though King James didn't like it, there was little he could do about it. Their sense of freedom, self-government, and public policy would shape the future of America.

383. Catholics and Jesuit priests were not allowed to enter Puritan areas of Massachusetts following a law that was passed in 1647. Second-time offenders of this law could face death if they were apprehended.

384. "No Christmas!" The British Parliament banned Christmas and other Christian holidays in 1647 because of the Puritan influence that deemed it necessary to abstain from such celebrations. The ban was later dropped.

385. The Rescissory Act was passed on March 28, 1661, by the Scottish Parliament. It repealed all church-state legislation created since 1633 (Charles I's reign). The purpose of the act was to restore the Anglican episcopacy to Scotland and break down the Presbyterian Church, which had become the national church in 1638. In 1690 Parliament again established the Presbyterian Church of Scotland.

386. The Act of Uniformity, written in 1662, made it a legal requirement that all English ministers publicly ascribe to the

Book of Common Prayer. The decision remains on England's statute book to this day, though it has been modified over the years.

387. The English Toleration Act of 1689 granted all "non-Anglican Protestants" the right to worship freely in England. The Act didn't protect the rights of people of other faiths, however, which included nonbelievers, Catholics, Jews, and others.

388. The Half-Way Covenant was a document that allowed occasional churchgoers in New England to baptize their children, attend social congregational activities, and vote, but it prohibited them from taking communion. The Half-Way Covenant was executed by the clergy and was in effect throughout New England.

389. The Schism Bill was meant to reinstate Catholicism in England in the eighteenth century. However, this bill died when Queen Anne (the bill's promoter) died in 1714. It was considered a "Protestant Passover" because the death of the bill meant deliverance for all dissenters who would have been affected by its regulation.

390. "Locking church doors is the law." In 1765 a law was passed in Massachusetts which stated that church doors should be locked during services in order to *prevent* people from leaving before the sermon was over.

391. The Concordat of 1801 restored Roman Catholicism as the state church of France. Though France was never going to be a culture held together by the church, Napoleon made sure, upon seizing power, to work out an agreement with the pope. The agreement assured him that the church would be on his side as he led France out of chaos and into the future.

392. The Disestablishment Bill was put into effect by the British. This bill dissolved the Church of Ireland. It passed in 1869.

393. The Eighteenth Amendment to the United States Constitution went into effect January 16, 1919. Thanks largely to Christian activists, it prohibited the sale of alcohol. Thirteen years later, Congress repealed the amendment.

14

Titles

394. The "Catholic" name was first applied to the Christian church in the late second century. The word "catholic" means "universal" and was intended to suggest that all Catholic believers shared the same orthodox theology about Jesus Christ. Irenaeus, a great historian from that time, explained that Catholic believers had their roots in the teachings of the apostles, while heretics were those who followed other teachings or claimed to have new, inspired teachings directly from God.

395. The Thirteenth Tomb was the place Emperor Constantine prepared for his own death. The city of Constantinople, which became the new capital of the empire, was presented as the center of the Christian world. The emperor built the Church of the Twelve Apostles, prepared twelve symbolic tombs for the twelve apostles, then in the center added a thirteenth tomb for himself. That caused the priests to refer to the emperor as "equal to the apostles."

396. "God's Consul" was the nickname given to Gregory the Great (540–604), whose great executive abilities and warm sympathy gave new life to the church after a series of wars, bad popes, and plagues had brought it to its knees. Gregory became mayor of Rome and planned not only construction projects but an economic plan and a welfare system for widows. He came up with the idea of enlisting monks as missionaries to take the gospel to the tribes of northern Europe, reformed the priesthood, and saved the church from pagan invaders. The prestige of the pope for the next thousand years came largely as a result of Gregory's reputation.

397. *Maleficiam* was the charge brought by the church against people doing evil. Because confessions in sorcery trials were routinely extracted by torture, they generally reflected the accusations of the prosecutors. Of course, then as now, some of the evildoers were cranks, so they readily admitted to consorting with demons.

398. The **"East Mark"** was the military province at the far eastern end of Charlemagne's empire. Set up in the valley of the Danube River, the area eventually became known by its Germanic name: Austria.

399. "The Governor of all things" was John Calvin's description of God. Reading Christ's words that not a sparrow falls to the ground without God knowing it, Calvin began preaching the absolute sovereignty of God. He focused on predestination—the idea that God has elected certain people for eternal life—and instructed his followers that they could use a simple yardstick to evaluate God's people: They will participate in baptism and the Lord's Supper, they will live an upright moral life, and they will make a public profession of faith.

400. *The Encomienda* was the name given to the official Spanish policy toward the Native Americans of the New World. Spaniards saw themselves as Christian princes who were there to offer leadership and salvation to ignorant pagans. Their policy called for Spanish rulers to use Native Americans for heavy and dangerous work (like mining and cutting new roads) while offering them "instruction in the holy faith." Because many of the Native American tribes had evil practices like idolatry and human sacrifice, the Spanish felt duty-bound to cease those religious practices.

401. *Libertas* was the slogan inscribed in gold on the red banners of the Anti-Papal League. The cities of Milan, Bologna, Perugia, Pisa, Lucca, and Genoa joined with the citizens of Florence (and the various potentates who had territorial ambitions) to throw off papal leadership.

402. The Holy Experiment was the name given to the Puritan idea of uniting church and state. In Massachusetts, the Puritans passed a law that all free people must be church members, and that only church members could vote. By the mid–1600s, they had to amend their experiment due to the worldliness of the citizens of Massachusetts.

403. Latitudinarians was the name given to a group of Anglican churchgoers who stressed the "proper behavior of Christians." Influenced by the Age of Reason, they rejected the emotionalism and "religious enthusiasm" they saw in the late seventeenth-century church. They called for quietness, respect, and a thoroughly colorless society.

404. "The Temples of Reason" was the name given to the Roman Church during the French Revolution. The People's Government imposed a loyalty oath on priests, removed all Christian dates from calendars, and replaced Christian parades with processions led by young people dressed as "Reason" or "Liberty." At one point, they even set up a "Goddess of Reason" in the cathedral of Notre Dame.

405. "Bobby Wild Goose and His Ragged Regiment" was the term given to Robert Raikes, founder of the first Sunday school, by Anglican churchmen who feared that having working-class children learn to read would hurt the economy by encouraging them to give up manual labor. As the Sunday school movement grew, so did the awareness of wealthy Christians that they had a responsibility to the poor. Not only did Sunday school revolutionize the church, it helped foster public education, sparked the printing of popular Christian books and tracts, and brought about the creation of special hymnals to be sung by children before their Sunday lessons.

406. "Sinners in the Hands of an Angry God" was a famous sermon by Jonathan Edwards. In 1741, Edwards assured listeners that only by strict adherence to the Puritan faith could they hope to avoid the eternal tortures of hell. "There is no want of power in God to cast wicked men into Hell at any moment," he warned. "O sinner! Consider the fearful danger you are in; it is a great furnace of wrath, a wide and bottomless pit." It was reported that one man, overcome by those words, clung to a support beam during the sermon out of fear that he was slipping into the fires of hell.

407. Risorgimento, or "rebirth," was the Italian movement of the mid–1800s that called for the creation of an Italian nation and the overthrow of all foreign authority in the Italian peninsula, including the papal states. Pope Pius IX remained in power only because the French Army protected him. On September 20, 1870, the city of Rome surrendered and the thousand-year rule of the pope came to an end.

408. "The prisoner of the Vatican" was the title given to Pope Pius IX in 1871. When newly crowned King Victor Emmanuel of Italy moved his residence to Rome, the pope protested and threatened to excommunicate him. But Victor ignored the threats and offered an annual subsidy if the pope would focus on spiritual matters. Pius rejected the offer and remained inside the Vatican until his death.

409. Tractarianism was the term given to a group of Oxford-educated pastors bent on rejoining the Church of England with the Roman Catholic Church. John Henry Newman, John Keble, and Richard Froude began anonymously writing and publishing four-page leaflets, called "tracts," that they bicycled around

and sold for a penny a piece. The tracts encouraged reconciliation between Anglicans and Roman Catholics and argued for
such things as transubstantiation, the worship of saints, and the
existence of purgatory. Eventually, the leadership of the Church
of England put a stop to it, and the authors departed their
denomination to become Catholics.

410. The Canvas Cathedral was the term given to the huge tent
set up at the corner of Washington Boulevard and Hill Street in
Los Angeles for the 1949 Billy Graham crusade. Looking for a
feel-good story, William Randolph Hearst ran a series of articles
highly praising the abilities of the North Carolina native, and the
publicity catapulted Graham to national prominence. Having
been heard by more than one hundred million people, Graham
has probably preached to more people than anyone in history.

411. "Amen" is a Hebrew word and means "true" or "certain."
It comes from another word, *aman,* which is Latin and means
"to strengthen." Christians use this word to close their prayers
and also to conclude the singing of a hymn. It is mainly an
expression of approval or agreement with the sentiments being
expressed.

15

Art and Music

ART

412. The original purpose of art within the church was as a teaching tool. Most people did not and could not read, and there were relatively few copies of the Scriptures available to those who could read. Paintings and sculptures were used early on to explain the stories of the Bible as well as the doctrines of the church. Symbols were a decoration, yet they stood for important concepts; they were engraved in stone, placed in stained glass windows, and painted on canvases.

413. Byzantine art used color to represent certain people. The idea was that the figures would then be immediately recognizable to those viewing the piece. Artists used yellow and light blue to represent St. Peter, deep red for St. Paul, blue for the

Virgin Mary. A deep red that was at times mixed with gold, or at times a deep blue, represented Jesus Christ.

414. "The vanities of life have taken from me the time to contemplate God" are the words of Michelangelo Buonarroti. Inspired by biblical subjects, his frescoes for the Sistine Chapel span from creation to the last judgment. He was also the architect for the Medici Memorial Chapel and redesigned St. Peter's Basilica in Rome. Though revisionist historians have tried to paint him as a libertine, late in life he wrote, "By the cross, by grace, and by diverse trials I am sure we will be in heaven."

415. The Sistine Chapel ceiling, painted by Michelangelo Buonarroti in 1512, contains not only nine scenes from the Book of Genesis and paintings of seven Hebrew prophets but it also includes five "sybils"—pagan prophetesses who supposedly foretold the coming of the Messiah. Begun at the urging of Pope Julius II, the paintings revealed an entirely new style of art by making the men and women of Scripture seem like real flesh-and-blood, rather than the ethereal, unrealistic beings of Middle Age art.

416. The Last Judgment, a painting by Michelangelo on the altar wall of the Sistine Chapel, depicts the bodies of the saved rising to heaven while the bodies of the damned descend into hell—all watched over by a strong and powerful Christ. Nothing like it had ever been seen before. When Pope Paul III first saw the painting in 1534, he gasped, "Lord, charge me not with my sins when you come on the Day of Judgment!"

417. The Artist of the Soul is the title given to Rembrandt van Rijn, a Dutch painter many consider the greatest artist of all time. Born into a pious Reformed family, Rembrandt moved away from the common practice of making Bible characters seem superhuman. Instead he used neighbors and normal people as models for his characters. Displaying an appreciation for God's creation and a talent for contrasting dark backgrounds with light faces, he created paintings that reveal the humanity of the Christian faith. In *Raising the Cross,* Rembrandt included a portrait of himself as one of the crowd helping to crucify Jesus Christ.

418. The Protestant Church did not appreciate art for much of its history because of the Reformation's reactionary thoughts against the idolatry of the Catholic Church and its use of icons and statues. As a result, art in general was thought to be sinful and distracting; it was preferred that buildings be neat, functional, and devoid of the relics and images of human saints. Protestants have only in the previous century begun to add art to their churches.

419. "Man just has and will have some religion," said William Blake (1757–1827), an artist and poet. "If he has not the religion of Jesus, he will have the religion of Satan." Blake's illustrations for the *Book of Job* were not popular in his lifetime, but his genius has been recognized by later generations. He is best remembered for his poem "Jerusalem," in which he likens the rebuilding of the ancient city to "England's green and pleasant land"—a phrase that has become the unofficial anthem of that country.

420. Themes that were important to the church are evident through the art of any given period. Early church art appears to call forth a greater awe than later periods. The Middle Ages were a time of reflection that was meant to bring people to conversion; subjects tended to be sorrowful and focused on darker topics that might lead one to seek salvation. Later eras focused on the grace that was brought out through revivals and awakenings—people were finding grace, peace, and forgiveness.

421. "You must see in nature the cylinder, the sphere, the cone, all put into perspective . . . the spectacle which the omnipotent eternal God and Father spreads before our eyes" was the advice of artist Paul Cézanne to writer Emile Zola.

422. "The works of God are appreciated best by other creators," said Leonardo da Vinci, inventor and painter of *The Last Supper* and *The Virgin on the Rocks*. A passionate student of the physical body, da Vinci once noted, "You think that the body is a wonderful work; in reality this is nothing compared to the soul that inhabits in that structure . . . the work of God."

423. "Have religion in your art," wrote Jean-Auguste-Dominique Ingres. "Do not believe that you can produce anything of worth without the elevation of the soul. To see anything beautiful you must see only the sublime. Do not look to the right, to the left, or below. Look only to heaven."

424. Pagan art was replaced by new art with Christian themes as Christianity expanded throughout the world. No land was "born" Christian. As a result, art, as an expression of the people who lived there, was not automatically Christian. Stories from the Bible as well as stories of the converted pagans became subject matter for new art that reflected the Christianization of these evangelized places.

425. "I believe I am nearer to God by being humble before the splendor (of nature);** by accepting the role I have been given to play in life; by honoring this majesty without self interest; and above all, without asking for anything, being confident that He who has created everything has forgotten nothing."—Pierre-Auguste Renoir, master of the impressionist painters

MUSIC

426. "May the Almighty grant me just enough strength before my end to enable me to express in music** the emotion which this undeserved act of spiritual grace has awakened in me." —the words of Franz Joseph Haydn after writing *The Creation*

427. Charlemagne, king of the Franks from 771 to 814, greatly enjoyed singing, but he would not perform solos, preferring to sing only with the rest of the congregation.

428. The first organ was most likely built for Louis the Pious in 826 by a Greek organ builder to accompany the singing of Psalms. A picture of it remains in the Utrecht Psalter, which dates to 830. The bellows were pumped by hand by several people standing around the organ as the organist played.

429. "Good King Wenceslas" was a ruler and patron saint of Czechoslovakia, but he was murdered by his brother in 929 after a very short reign. He is fondly remembered for working to unite nations, gain peace, and for taking a special interest in the poor of his country, and he is remembered with this hymn.

430. "Why should the devil have all the best tunes?"—the words of William Booth, founder of the Salvation Army, upon adding theological concepts and stories to Irish drinking songs. Martin Luther had done the same thing in the fifteenth century, adding Christian words to German drinking songs in an attempt to teach theological truth.

431. Old Version was a collection of the Psalms translated into English, given a meter, and set to a sort of tune. First published in 1562, it was an attempt to get churches singing—something the Anglican Church did not approve of. The attempt failed. In 1696, poet Nahum Tate came out with an up-to-date version, appropriately titled, *New Version.* Many groups rejected it because Tate occasionally used words not from the Book of Psalms. While Baptists and Separatists were trying to add some singing to their services, the church hierarchies in England and on the continent refused to do so.

432. Christmas carols were outlawed by the Puritans in the New World in 1647. The Puritans found them to be out of keeping with the true spirit of Christmas.

433. *St. Matthew's Passion* and *The Brandenburg Concerto* are two of the works written by Johann Sebastian Bach in the early 1700s. An extremely devout Lutheran, Bach wrote hundreds of concertos, oratorios, and cantatas, and each one had inscribed on it a verse of Scripture or a personal note to God such as "To God Be the Glory."

434. "God is a God of order," wrote Johann Sebastian Bach, a musician of such order that his children sometimes aroused his anger by playing only the first notes of a line of music, forcing Bach to hurry to the piano to finish playing the line. "God prescribes, calculates, and arranges everything, and thus explains

His will how He wants to be respected by us; therefore we should presume and do nothing without His revealed word."

435. Many thanks are due to German composer Felix Mendelssohn, who was a devout Lutheran, for his *Elijah* oratorio, which is considered second only to Handel's *Messiah*. He was also responsible for rediscovering Bach, whose music had been forgotten for eighty years.

436. The *Messiah*, often considered the finest oratorio ever written in English, was actually composed in 1741 by a German, George Frideric Handel, sung largely by an Italian opera company, and first performed in Dublin, Ireland. Handel, who came from a pietistic home, wrote the *Messiah* in just twenty-four days. He went on to write more than a dozen oratorios based on characters in Scripture, including David, Deborah, Moses, Samson, Saul, and Solomon.

437. "Joy to the World!" was a song made by two people: Lowell Mason and Isaac Watts. Mason took the music from a section of Handel's oratorio, the *Messiah*. Watts had written the words in 1719.

438. The First Presbyterian Church of Springfield, New Jersey, donated its church hymnals to the cause of the American Revolution in 1780. The pages were used as gun wadding by American troops to successfully stop the oncoming British from gaining more ground.

439. "Ye servants of the eternal King, His power and glory sing, and speak of all His righteous ways with wonder and with praise."—from a hymn by George Frideric Handel (1685–1759)

440. The first published book (1640) in the United States was Stephen Day's (Steeven Daye) *The Whole Booke of Psalmes, Faithfully Translated into English Metre whereunto is prefixed a discourse declaring not only the lawfullness, but also the necessity of the heavenly ordinance of singing scripture psalmes in the Churches of God.* The books sold for twenty pence each.

441. *Hymns and Spiritual Songs* was the first hymnal ever published in English. Though Martin Luther had drafted Christian words to German drinking songs, the Anglican and Lutheran Churches did not approve of singing in worship, claiming it was too emotional and did not aid in the understanding of theology. In stepped Isaac Watts, who used hymns to teach of Christ's birth, death, and resurrection. Two years later he produced *Psalms of David Imitated in the Language of the New Testament,* in which he included such winning tunes as "Joy to the World" and "O God Our Help in Ages Past." Christians began singing about the truths of God—though the Anglican Church still held out until the mid–1800s.

442. The first hymnbook with a musical score contained just thirteen tunes. This Massachusetts-printed hymnbook of 1798 was the ninth edition of *The Psalms, Hymns & Spiritual Songs of the Old and New Testament; Faithfully Translated into English Metre. For the Use, Edification, and Comfort of the Saints in publick and private especially in New England.*

443. Ira Sankey, the other half of Dwight Moody's evangelism team, was a gifted singer. Moody first heard him sing at an early morning Indianapolis prayer meeting. Moody asked Sankey to join him that very day in the Chicago evangelism project. The two traveled around the world and evangelized together for many years. Sankey popularized the religious hymns and melodies that went along with evangelism and helped to draw in large crowds.

444. "Almighty God touched me with His little finger and said, 'Write only for the theater' . . . and I have obeyed that supreme command"—Giacomo Puccini, creator of the timeless operas *La Bohème, Tosca, Turandot,* and *Madame Butterfly.*

445. Charles Wesley was a Methodist preacher best known for bringing great singing into Methodist churches. His hymns include "And Can It Be" and "Hark the Herald Angels Sing" and were a distinct break from the psalms used in his Anglican upbringing. Charles cofounded Methodism with his brother John in 1738. While lying sick, Charles heard a voice tell him to "rise and believe in the name of Jesus so that you will be healed." He believed and eventually was healed. Shortly afterward he wrote the famous hymn, "O For a Thousand Tongues" to remember that spiritual experience.

446. **"Art, to be truly art, needs the divine gift of creation,"** said Italian opera composer Pietro Mascagni. "Jesus was Divinity, and that indicates genius is a divine gift, because only Divinity can create that which does not exist."

447. John Newton was once a slave trader, but after reading Thomas à Kempis's book *Imitation of Christ* during one of his long voyages, he became converted. He became a prolific hymnwriter and eventually pastored a church in England. His most famous hymn, "Amazing Grace," written in 1779, was his testimony of the incredible work God's grace has brought to all.

448. **The most popular songwriter of the mid–1800s** was Philip Bliss, a Pennsylvania farm boy with no formal training, who penned the lyrics and tunes to such classics as "Let the Lower Lights Be Burning," "Almost Persuaded," "Jesus Loves Even Me," "Hallelujah, What a Savior," and "It Is Well with My Soul" (just the tune). Bliss and his wife were riding a train to join evangelist Dwight Moody when the Ashtabula Bridge in Ohio collapsed, sending the railroad cars 90 feet into a river. Ninety-two of 159 passengers died—the bodies of Bliss and his wife were never found.

449. **"O God! Thou art the true, eternal, blessed, unchangeable light of all time and space.** Thy wisdom apprehends thousands and thousands of laws, and yet Thou ever actest of Thy free will and to Thy honor. Thou wast before all that we worship. To Thee is due praise and adoration, for Thou alone are the true . . . the best . . . the image of all wisdom"—the words of Ludwig van Beethoven in 1814.

450. **"Everything is transitory except the Word of God, which is eternal,"** noted composer Franz Liszt, "and the Word of God reveals itself in the creation of genius." The most famous pianist of the nineteenth century, Liszt's genius is evidenced in his *Hungarian Rhapsodies.*

451. Horatio G. Spafford's four daughters drowned (their mother survived) in the North Atlantic in 1873 when their ship sank. As he traveled to England to join his wife after the tragedy, he crossed over their watery graves and was overcome with grief, yet he was comforted by Scripture. In response, he wrote the famed hymn "It Is Well with My Soul."

452. Joseph M. Scriven dedicated his life to the poor and suffered many difficulties, including the deaths of two fiancées prior to marriage. He is credited with writing "What a Friend We Have in Jesus."

453. Fanny Crosby is considered the best-known female hymnist. That she was blind from infancy was another matter. Her songs remain dear to the church, including "Blessed Assurance," "To God Be the Glory," and "Safe in the Arms of Jesus." Though she wrote more than nine thousand hymns, those that remain in use today were all written in the first ten years of her ministry.

454. "Nearer, My God, to Thee" is said to be the last song played by the band as the *Titanic* sank in 1912. Many of the remaining passengers were said to have joined in singing as they awaited the sinking of the ship.

455. "My artistic goal is to make an object," said violinist Igor Stravinsky. "I create the object because God makes me create it, just as He created me."

456. Inspiration for the hymn "This Is My Father's World" came to Pastor Maltbie Babcock as he was viewing Lake Ontario from the summit of a hill outside of Lockport, New York. The young man would tell his congregation he was going out to see his Father's world. He wrote the words to this special hymn one day while doing just that.

457. "Eternal Father, Strong to Save" is the U. S. Navy's official hymn. Calling for God's protection of his people on both dry land as well as the sea, it is a fitting anthem.

16

The Church in England

458. The Celtic people were an ancient people in western Europe who migrated to the British Isles. Their language, which evolved into Welsh and Gaelic, and culture were dominant in England for centuries, until the people were won to Christ by the preaching of Patrick in the fifth century.

459. When the Roman Empire was crumbling, its Christian leaders and the influence of Roman civilization as a whole left England. Thus for more than two centuries after the Romans left, newly evangelized areas were left on their own. Historians refer to this time as "the two lost centuries of English history" because little has been discovered that is reliable beyond assumptions made from archaeology.

460. The Celtic Church, a strong, worship-filled church, preached grace, respected creation, and was completely separate from Rome. Much of what is known of the "two lost centuries" comes from this church. It was the first to send missionaries to Europe after the Roman Empire pulled out of the continent. Celtic churches were built of wood or even mud and brush, and there are many remaining throughout England, Wales, and Scotland today. The places where these Christian communities thrived contained churches that were named after the saints who helped form the communities.

461. The construction of early churches in England and how they are situated on the land reflect the pagan influences that still affected new Christians and their beliefs even after conversion. The ground to the north side of a church building was called the "devil's side" and was meant, quite simply, to give the devil his due. Perhaps this belief was maintained in the hopes that the devil would stay on his side of the line!

462. Villagers avoided the north side, with some people even refusing to sit in the pews on that side of the church. Not surprisingly, no one wanted to be buried on the north side of the church property either. When British law made it a requirement for churches to make room for burials of those who were criminals, unbaptized infants, and those who had committed suicide, the churches would automatically place these reserved lots to the north of the church. The south end of the church lots are often crammed beyond capacity with ancient graves from a time when no one but a very few dared be laid to rest on the north end of the lot.

463. The Church of England, which is referred to as "Anglican" in Britain and "Episcopalian" in the United States, owes its history to an obscure verse of Scripture. Leviticus 20:21 says it is wrong for a man to marry his brother's wife, so King Henry VIII wanted his eighteen-year marriage to his deceased brother's wife, Catherine, annulled on the grounds that her inability to have a son must be a curse from God. When the pope demurred (largely for political reasons), Henry had an English court annul the marriage. He then married Anne Boleyn.

464. Saint Thomas à Becket, an English Roman Catholic, was appointed archbishop of Canterbury in 1162 and was at one time a close friend of King Henry II. When he sided against the crown in favor of the church in 1164, he was charged with misappropriating funds of the crown and was banished from England. Becket fled from England but returned in 1170 and became involved in the controversy surrounding the appointment of Henry II's son to the position of archbishop of York. Becket was murdered by four knights during a church service at Canterbury Cathedral by order of his former friend, Henry II.

465. Simon Fish was circulating his pamphlet, *Supplication of Beggars,* to the people of London as early as 1529 to arouse their feelings against the Church of England. Four years earlier, Fish had joined a religious group of young men who were unhappy with Henry VIII's cardinal, Thomas Wolsey. Eventually, Fish was found out and was exiled by Wolsey. However, when Anne Boleyn read a copy of his pamphlet and gave it to the king, Fish was embraced and given protection from the church. Fish died in 1531.

466. Thomas Starkey served as chaplain to Henry VIII and was a promoter of Thomas Cromwell's policies. In 1535 he wrote *[An] Exhortation to the People Instructing Them to Unity and Obedience.* This work promoted moderation, which was a common theme of Anglicanism. He drew on arguments of reason as well as Scripture, but also on the writings of Philipp Melanchthon, a more moderate Lutheran. Starkey urged the English to preserve unity as a church of believers despite the diversity separating papists from reformers.

467. The Act of Supremacy, passed by the English Parliament in 1534, declared King Henry VIII "supreme head of the Church of England." The Act came about because Henry, who wanted a son, was married to Catherine of Aragon, who had only borne him a daughter. Henry asked the pope for a divorce in order to marry Anne Boleyn, but the pope feared that would anger the Roman emperor Charles V, who was Catherine's nephew. When the pope stalled, Henry named Thomas Cranmer archbishop of Canterbury, and Cranmer quickly granted the divorce. Henry and Anne had a daughter, Elizabeth, the next year, and Parliament announced that the pope no longer had authority over the English church.

468. Poorly educated clergy were common in sixteenth-century England. The shortcoming was particularly noticeable in rural areas. In a test done early in that century, 168 out of 311 clergy were unable to repeat the Ten Commandments, and some could not recall who had composed the Lord's Prayer.

469. The *Book of Common Prayer* provided the sixteenth-century English church with a compromise. Because Henry VIII had named Thomas Cranmer archbishop of Canterbury, it was unclear if the churches of England were connected to or separated from the church in Rome. Cranmer put together a committee that created a liturgy pleasing to both Catholics and Protestants. It used the high language and ritual of Rome but removed the objectionable aspects of Catholic theology. In 1549, Parliament passed the Act of Uniformity, requiring the *Book of Common Prayer* be used in all English churches.

470. Thomas Cranmer became archbishop of Canterbury almost solely because he let it be known that he would grant King Henry VIII a divorce from his first wife. After Henry's death, Cranmer moved the English church away from Catholicism. Confessions were halted, priests were allowed to marry, relics were removed, and both bread and wine were reintroduced to communion.

471. Cranmer's *Prologue or Preface to the Bible* was put into the Bibles that were read in the churches in 1540, causing the Bibles to be called "Cranmer's Bibles." His principles emphasized the sole place of Scripture over all as well as the teaching of justification by faith alone. Furthermore, he spoke of the place of Jesus within the sacrament of the Lord's Supper and also the sufficiency of God's grace.

472. When Catherine of Aragon's daughter, Mary, became queen, she used her short, harsh reign to move England back to Catholicism. Burning 273 Protestants at the stake, she is remembered as "Bloody Mary." One of the last Protestants she put to death was Thomas Cranmer in 1556. Having been forced to recant in a signed statement, Cranmer later reaffirmed his Protestant beliefs and, at his execution, stuck his right hand into the flames so that the hand that signed the document might be the first part of his body to burn.

473. Lady Jane Grey was another one of Mary's victims. She was the daughter of Henry VIII's niece, and the Duke of Northumberland was hoping to put her on the throne instead of Mary I (or Mary Tudor). The plot failed when England instead stood by Mary. Mary had Lady Jane (the girl was only sixteen) imprisoned and later beheaded.

474. Regarding her faith in Christ, Lady Jane recorded her dialogue with Master Feckenham, a staunch Catholic sent to obtain her recantation. In one exchange, Lady Jane stated that the established (Catholic) Church of England "which denies us part of our salvation . . . is an evil church, and not the spouse of Christ but the spouse of the devil, that alters the Lord's Supper, and both taketh from it and addeth to it . . . shall I believe that church? God forbid." She was beheaded four days later.

475. Queen Elizabeth followed Mary Tudor to the throne in 1558. Under her direction England became the leading Protestant nation. She helped regain peace and unity among the divided and hostile factions of the Church of England, calling for the church to work toward unity and a middle ground rather than either end of the extremes of Catholicism or Protestantism.

476. The Act of Supremacy was passed by Queen Elizabeth in 1559. The order reestablished the acts of King Henry VIII and repealed the Heresy Act. It also gave Elizabeth (the crown) power over the church in England, which was to be an Anglican establishment with an established form of government.

477. Less Preaching! In 1576 Queen Elizabeth told preachers throughout England that they should preach less. She believed three to four sermons preached per year to the people was an adequate number. When Grindal, archbishop of Canterbury, protested, he was placed under house arrest.

478. King James I was the son of Mary, Queen of Scots, and was serving as King James VI of Scotland when Queen Elizabeth died in 1603. Ascending to the throne of England, James announced that he had a "divine right" to rule, took the title "Defender of the Faith," and pronounced himself leader of the Church of England. Though Puritans were hoping James would rid the church of Catholicism, he instead proved himself solidly Anglican and made life difficult for those who wanted to create independent churches.

479. Thomas Helwys led a congregation of English Separatists and Mennonites from Amsterdam back to London to start the first official "Baptist" church in England. The two core beliefs of the group were believer's baptism and independence from the state. Helwys, wanting to preach those two doctrines to the world, published a book entitled *A Short Declaration of the Mystery of Iniquity*. He then autographed a copy and sent it to King James with this inscription: "The king is a mortal man and not God, therefore hath not power over the immortal soul of his subjects to make laws and ordinances for them and to set spiritual Lords over them." Helwys was immediately arrested and thrown into Newgate prison. He died there.

480. English reformer and theologian John Rogers was the first Protestant martyr under "Bloody Mary" after she began her reign. He was burned at the stake for heresy in 1555.

481. John Knox was an obscure Scottish priest who had spent time as a galley slave off the coast of France. When he returned to Scotland in 1559 to pastor a church in Edinburgh, his nation was in the midst of a religious civil war. Though Mary, Queen of Scots, was an ardent Catholic, the Protestant forces defeated her Catholic army. The next year the Scottish Parliament adopted a Protestant statement of faith, forbade the Latin mass, and announced that the pope had no jurisdiction in Scotland. The statement of faith they chose was written by John Knox. When Mary finally abdicated her throne for her

Protestant son James, it was Knox who was chosen to preach at the coronation.

482. Mary, Queen of Scots, was beheaded in 1587, causing many Protestants to cheer. She had attempted to restore Catholicism to England and then began persecuting Protestants. Thanks to the work of John Knox, her attempts failed.

483. The Hampton Court Conference of 1604 took place just after the death of Queen Elizabeth, when King James I united England and Scotland. The leading Puritans, hopeful of seeing some changes made to the Prayer Book and the rule of bishops, presented their ideas to a man they thought would welcome them. Instead, James rejected their presentation and said that Scottish Presbyterianism "agrees with the monarchy as well as God and the devil."

484. The Separatists shared the desire to purify the Anglican Church, but they did so by separating themselves from the official state church and starting their own independent churches. Their leader, John Smyth, started a Separatist congregation in Lincolnshire in 1606, but when they, too, faced opposition from the state (particularly from the new sovereign, King James), they fled to Amsterdam and then to the colonies.

485. John Smyth, the leader of the English Separatists in the early 1600s, was a Cambridge graduate who had served as a pastor and lecturer in the Anglican Church. After spending time with Mennonite believers in Holland, he became convinced that infant baptism was both unbiblical and illogical. He proceeded to rebaptize himself and forty members of his congregation, thus starting the "Baptist" church.

486. John Winthrop, the Puritan leader in the New World, wrote that his colony must "be as a city upon a hill, the eyes of all people are upon us." Winthrop's followers believed that if they established a society based on the Bible, it would serve as an example for reform and renewal in England. Instead, the religious inclinations declined as monetary concerns increased.

487. Richard Baxter promoted religious tolerance during a difficult time in English history. He served as chaplain to Charles II, but his revised version of the *Book of Common Prayer* drew strong criticism when the Act of Uniformity restored the Anglican establishment to full authority of the church in 1662. He was denied the right of leadership and then forbidden to preach, but he preached anyway and suffered imprisonment twice as a result.

488. English poet and preacher John Donne, dean of St. Paul's Cathedral in London, was one of the most prominent preachers of the seventeenth century. Some of his most famous lines include, "No man is an island," "For whom does the bell toll? It tolls for thee," and "Death be not proud."

489. The Puritans were a group of believers within the Anglican Church at the time of Queen Elizabeth. The queen reformed the English church so that it was separate from the Roman Catholic Church, but she insisted that it should still share Catholic theology. A group of dissenters called for Christians to "purify" the church by disposing of many of the remaining Roman Catholic articles of faith. When the Puritans faced formal opposition, they moved to Holland, then they sailed to the New World.

490. Archbishop of Canterbury William Laud was beheaded in 1645 as a result of his persecution of the Puritans in earlier years. He found the tables quickly turned when the Puritan Revolution began in the 1640s.

491. Oliver Cromwell was the leader of the parliamentary army that led the Puritans to power in England in 1643. After defeating the armies of King Charles I, Cromwell was named "Lord Protector of England," a role in which he led with personal piety and brilliant administrative abilities. He had the king executed, held the nation together, and defeated uprisings by both the Irish and the Scots, but his attempts to reorganize the clergy and the Church of England into a Presbyterian form largely failed. Upon his death in 1658, his title was given to his son, Richard, who wisely stepped aside so that Charles's son, King Charles II, could be restored to the throne.

492. John Owen was considered by his friends to be the "Calvin of England" and one of the greatest of all the Puritan founding fathers. He served as Oliver Cromwell's chaplain from 1649 to 1651 on official expeditions to Ireland and Scotland. Owen wrote important books in later years and served as the chief architect of the Cromwellian State Church. He was forced out of his pulpit in 1660.

493. The National League of Covenant arose in 1625 when Archbishop William Laud, at the request of England's King Charles, insisted that all worship services in Scotland be based on the *Book of Common Prayer*. Rising in opposition, Scottish Presbyterians said they would dare to fight their king if necessary to defend their church. In response, King Charles convened Parliament, which proved a mistake. Disagreeing with Laud's decision to have the state take leadership over the church, Parliament brought Laud to trial, convicted him, and had him beheaded.

494. The Particular Baptists, a group that began in 1641, retained Calvin's theology of atonement but emphasized believer's baptism. They significantly shaped Baptist theology by announcing that, because the Greek word *baptizo* literally means "to dip in water," all baptisms were to be done by immersion. At that time, nearly all baptisms were done by pouring water on the head. From that announcement came an entirely new understanding of the theology of baptism—that baptism represents not only washing but a burial of the old life and resurrection into a new life.

495. John Bunyan could not read or write and was not a Christian prior to his marriage, but all of this changed after his wife insisted he read Puritan books and start shaping up his life. He was preaching within a couple years, but because he had no license, he was arrested by the local magistrate. He spent the next twelve years in and out of jail for his continued ministry.

While in prison he wrote books that had a huge impact outside the walls of his prison cell, including *Pilgrim's Progress.*

496. The Act of Toleration was passed by the British Parliament in 1689, recognizing the rights of Baptists, Quakers, Congregationalists, and Presbyterians to worship freely. The Church of England retained its favored position, but Christians in England had simply grown tired of fighting and losing their lives over theologies and doctrines.

497. The Wesley brothers, John and Charles, are generally thought of as popular revivalist preachers who brought bright singing and a message of grace to believers in America and England. But historians would argue that their greatest legacy is that, by accepting those who were different and encouraging a spirit of cooperation across denominational lines, their Methodist teaching changed the tone of the political debate in Great Britain during the late 1700s. While countries on the continent were fighting bloody civil wars, England transitioned from monarchy to democracy with relative peace.

498. "National Apostasy" was the title of a sermon preached by Pastor John Keble on July 14, 1833. Seeing the growth of Methodism and fearing that the Anglican Church was dying, Keble attacked the British Parliament for reducing the number of bishops in Ireland, claiming that the act constituted state interference in the church. As a result, pastors in Great Britain began seeing themselves as servants of God, rather than as civil servants working for the state. That led to a renewed spirit in the church, new and lively hymns, and a revitalized ministry to the poor and the hurting in British churches.

17

The Movements

499. The Apologist Movement began within one hundred years of the founding of the church, when learned Christians decided that they needed to respond to the wild accusations of critics. Celsus, a Roman historian, attacked the church for appealing only to "worthless and contemptible people, idiots, slaves, poor women, and children." Aristedes responded by noting that, while it was to the church's credit that it reached out to the poor and despised, many knowledgeable men were examining the claims of Christ. Relying on the writings of Paul, John, Ignatius, and Polycarp, apologists sought to define and explain the Christian faith.

500. The Ascetic Movement in the fourth century came as a backlash to the growing success, wealth, and popularity of the church. Renouncing sex, comfort, and possessions, the ascetics introduced the concept of penance to the church. This fostered the notion that there are two kinds of Christians: the "average" Christian and the "super-holy" Christian who finds a higher level of sanctity by denying himself or herself.

501. The Iconoclastic Movement of the eighth century took place because some believers wanted to replace religious icons such as shrines and statues with a limited number of images: the cross, the Bible, and the elements in communion. An "iconoclast" is an "image breaker," and those involved felt that icons were superstitious and unnecessary. The largely uneducated populace disagreed with them.

502. The Waldensians began in 1174 as a group advocating poverty and a strict adherence to the words of Jesus more than the words of the church. Followers of Peter Waldo, they were one of the first "back-to-the-Bible" movements, but their view of salvation was skewed by not enough emphasis on grace. Believing that true Christians will live in a perpetual state of poverty and penance, the Waldensian Movement died out when followers proved unable to fulfill the rigid rules.

503. The Albigenses Movement took place in the French town of Albi during the late 1100s when some renegade Catholics, who referred to themselves as "the pure ones," began preaching that there was a good Lord (the God of the New Testament) and a bad Lord (the God of the Old Testament) who battled for control of an empire. They preached total abstinence, vegetarianism, poverty, and saw Jesus as a sort of Buddha, offering nice life lessons but divine and not a man.

504. Menno Simons (1496–1561) knew the Bible would differ in theology from the teachings he had received as a parish priest, so he avoided reading the Scriptures for the first two years he was in the priesthood in Holland. When he finally read the Bible and also the writings of Martin Luther, there was no turning back. He renounced all ties with the Catholic Church and began leading the Anabaptists in Holland and those who lived along the German North Sea coastline, serving as a leading figure in that movement. His followers bear his name and continue today as the Mennonites.

505. The Mystical Movement in the 1500s was an attempt to move the church from the political realm back to the spiritual realm. Led by Teresa of Avila, the movement focused on finding a deeper walk with Christ and uniting with him through private prayer and meditation. In a tough, sometimes brutal world, the mystics called on people to remember the spiritual realities that are beyond natural perception.

506. The Bruderhof Movement of the early sixteenth century consisted of Anabaptists and others living in Christian communes. Though it's easy to suggest they did so because they wanted to follow the pattern of the early apostolic community, the real reason is that they created communes out of necessity. As condemned heretics of the Roman Church, they were outcasts and could not buy or sell necessities. Under the leadership of Jakob Hutter, they survived and became known as "Hutterites."

507. The Oratory of Divine Love was a distinguished group of believers in Rome who felt that the church was in need of change. Though it never claimed more than a few dozen members, it called for monastic and church reforms. It was ignored until Rome was sacked by a leaderless group of mercenaries in 1527. Sensing the attack was a sign from God, members issued a call for the pope and the cardinals to become less secular and more focused on spiritual renewal. Their recommendations were largely ignored.

508. The Catholic Reformation is the name given to the Roman response to Martin Luther. The Roman Church created a militant council in 1545 that reformed the machinery of the church, demanded priests go back to the business of spiritual concerns rather than political, and established the "Society of Jesus" (or "Jesuits") to serve as the "soldiers of Christ" and win back Protestant converts. It stemmed the tide of Protestantism in southern Europe.

509. The Pietistic Movement began when a young German university student, Philip Jacob Spener, found the Lutheran church services boring. In an attempt to apply spiritual truth to real life, he formed a small home group, the *collegia peitatis*. He and others in the group began praying and reading their Bibles together, and they re-introduced the notion of Christians singing together in worship. Though the church hierarchy hated the idea, it quickly became popular with laypeople. Centered at the University of Halle, those involved wrote hundreds of hymns, began sending missionaries around the world, and translated the Bible into Asian languages.

510. Puritanism maintained a severity toward indulgence that resembled the stringency of the Pharisees and their endless laws. As one historian noted, the Puritan who hanged a cat on Monday because the feline had killed a mouse on Sunday might be laughed at in contemporary circles, but in the age of Puritanism such righteous indignation was common.

511. The Philadelphian Society was founded in 1697. This American group was composed of Christians of all sorts to exchange "spiritual" experiences. It marked a trend in the church at that time to unify and bring together diverse Christian denominations.

512. The Society for Promoting Christian Knowledge (S.P.C.K.) was founded by British missionary Thomas Bray and four laypeople in 1698. The purpose of the S.P.C.K. was "to advance the honor of God and the good of mankind by promoting Christian knowledge both at home and in the other parts of the world by the best methods that should offer." The group became one of the major influences in starting the modern missionary movement.

513. The Moravian Brethren was a group of believers descended from Jan Hus, which meant they were neither Catholic, Lutheran, Calvinist, Baptist, nor Separatist. With no identity other than their Czech roots, and no country (due to their being forced from Bohemia), they spread out across Europe. In 1722 they heard that Count Zinzendorf of Dresden, a devout Lutheran, was interested in studying pietism. Appearing on his doorstep, the community asked if it could reside on his estate. He agreed, and within three years there were more than three hundred believers on his estate, speaking at least six languages and living in a Christian commune. When the government asked Zinzendorf and his group to leave the country, they moved to the New World and established a mission to the Indians, which became the city of Bethlehem, Pennsylvania.

514. The Oxford Movement (1833–1845) came about because of the growth of democracy. Some landowning Oxford scholars, worried that newly elected leaders would try to take authority over the Church of England, argued that "authority" comes from God, and that bishops were not empowered by the government but by apostolic commission. They published a number of documents, all of them in support of high church activities such as wearing clerical garments, lighting incense, and kneeling toward the front of the church while raising a cross. Eventually, the core group left to join the Roman Catholic Church.

515. Sunday school was the brainchild of Robert Raikes, a newspaper editor who in 1780 worried that working children were not being given the opportunity to learn to read and therefore better themselves. He hired Mrs. Meredith and paid her a shilling a week to teach a class of street children how to read, bringing them into her kitchen every Sunday afternoon. After the first three weeks, the abominable behavior of the kids caused Mrs. Meredith to quit, so the class moved into Mrs. Critchley's kitchen. Only now, there were three new rules: Children must wash their hands, comb their hair, and not peek into any kitchen drawers. Within three months, there were ninety children attending.

516. "Multitudes of wretches, who released on that day from employment, spend their day in noise and riot."—Such were the sentiments of one observer in the early 1800s of the Sunday school movement. Children who attended were uneducated, poor, and homeless. Lessons included reading and writing as well as stories of the Bible.

517. The Christian Socialist Movement of the mid–1800s preached that competition is evil and man is made to live in community. Largely the brainchild of novelist Charles Kingsley, it was an attempt to make the working class of England rise up against the wealthy and privileged. Though short-lived, this movement is responsible for keeping factories from hiring children under the age of ten and for limiting the working hours for women and teens to a ten-hour day.

518. The American Temperance Society, which was later renamed the American Temperance Union, was founded in Boston in 1826 to promote voluntary abstinence from liquor. Among the sixteen founders, seven were Protestant clergymen.

519. The Christian Union was formed in 1864. The members of this union were Protestant congregations who were opposed to "political preaching" during the Civil War. The group formed in Columbus, Ohio.

520. The Salvation Army was founded in 1865 by William Booth, who had a tent ministry aimed at helping the working class poor of London. Seeking to give his growing ministry organization, Booth created officers, ordered uniforms, established a brass band, and even created his own magazine: *The War Cry*. His greatest legacy was in helping middle and upper class Christians see that the urban poor constituted a "home mission" field, and that to minister to a person's physical needs made him or her more apt to listen to the gospel message.

521. The Christian Science Movement was begun by Mary Baker Eddy (1821–1910). She rejected Calvinism and gained a following through an ideology that emphasized divine goodness as a reality of existence and also the healing of the body through spiritual means. Her followers were largely of the middle class and brought wealth with them. She remained the spiritual leader of this movement until her death, but male leadership became the norm afterward. The Christian Scientists also use the name "Church of Christ, Scientist."

522. Seventh-Day Adventist doctrine leans heavily on the many writings and visions of Ellen G. White (1827–1915), this movement's prophetess. Through her writings she influenced this popular movement until her death. Evidence suggests her opinions were based more solidly on other writings rather than being from God, but her place has remained honored to this day in the history of Seventh-Day Adventism.

523. The Student Volunteer Movement was started at the Mount Hermon campground in Northfield, Massachusetts, in July, 1886. One hundred and fifty-one students gathered to pray and hear Rev. A. T. Pierson say, "All should go and go to all." A few days later, representatives from ten nations reported on the needs in their lands, and one hundred of the attending students volunteered to become missionaries. Under the leadership of John Mott, the SVM found, trained, and organized missionaries—five thousand in all by the outbreak of World War I.

524. The Christian and Missionary Alliance was formed by Albert Benjamin Simpson largely as an act of faith. He and his wife had moved to New York City after he accepted a call to a Presbyterian church in the early 1880s. Less than two years after he accepted that call, he resigned from Thirteenth Street Presbyterian and devoted himself to a ministry to the poor of New York City, though the alliance was not yet formed and he had no source of income. But he was blessed, and the work grew until it was a center for home and mission work and had a large and permanent structure of its own in 1889. Simpson became a strong proponent of the healing ministry as well as the social calling of Christian living.

525. The Niagara Bible Conference of 1895 featured many famous names in the American church, but it is most famous for affirming the five "essentials" of the Christian faith: the virgin birth, the inerrancy of Scripture, the substitutionary atonement of Jesus, his physical resurrection, and his bodily return. Endorsed by conservative churches worried about the rise of "modernism," it was the genesis of American fundamentalism.

526. Pastor Reinhold Niebuhr visited French-occupied portions of Germany in 1923 and was shaken by the hatred displayed by both sides in a time of "peace." Niebuhr became the national chairman of the Fellowship of Reconciliation (FOR) to further promote his position of pacifism. His thoughts on the subject became a book, *Leaves from the Notebook of a Tamed Cynic.*

However, as World War II approached and Hitler's machine of Nazism grew larger, Niebuhr began to critique the social thought of pacifism, and eventually he rejected it based on theological evidence. Christians, he maintained, live lives justified by grace through faith, and as a result they live in understanding of the serious and at times tenuous moments of life, but always they are grounded in the victory of God's sovereignty. With his reflections came thoughts and similar reactions from Christians worldwide.

527. The National Association of Evangelicals was formed in the 1940s, largely because of the fear that the ecumenical movement of various Christian denominations was ignoring the fundamentals of the gospel. Rather than focus on a "social gospel" of political activism and humanistic goals, the NAE held strongly to the veracity of the Bible and the need to evangelize the world.

528. The World Council of Churches was established in 1948 in Amsterdam. It describes itself as simply "a fellowship of churches which accept Jesus Christ as God and Savior," but has implemented an aggressive (some would say "revolutionary") campaign of social and liberal political activism. Some denominations—most notably the Southern Baptists and Missouri Synod Lutherans—have steadfastly refused to join.

529. The American Council of Christian Churches was a twentieth-century response to the World Council of Churches. Worried about the rise of ecumenism and the watering down of the gospel, conservative churches created their own council, which lasted until members began criticizing their own organization for being more focused on the social needs of humankind than on its spiritual needs.

530. The charismatic renewal began in early 1960 in Van Nuys, California, when Dennis Bennett, rector of St. Mark's Episcopal Church, was told by a local vicar that a couple in his church had "received the baptism of the Holy Spirit" and were speaking in tongues. Bennett, who didn't know what the term meant, met with the couple and he, too, experienced the baptism. Then other people in his church did, and because charismatic activity wasn't permitted in such a formal denomination, Bennett resigned and moved to Seattle where the same thing happened.

531. Christian Advance Seminars were formed in the early 1960s to acquaint traditional churches with charismatic gifts. Though many equate charismatics with Pentecostals, the former grew out of upper-class, formal denominations, while the latter developed from more working-class people who were raised with emotional revivalist meetings. However, the charismatic couple that were members at St. Mark's Episcopal Church in Van Nuys, California, were introduced to "the baptism of the Holy Spirit" by Pentecostal friends.

18

Christian Society and Culture

532. Kneeling for prayer may have become a requirement for those praying early in the twelfth century. The position of kneeling for prayer with the hands clasped together was the same position expected of people paying homage to an earthly figure of authority.

533. The prayer chain supposedly was born in 1727 in a Moravian community in Germany. It is believed there was at least one person in the community praying at any time of day or night, up to the minute, for more than a century!

534. Cannibalism (eating human flesh) was thought to be a common practice in the early church. During the persecution of Christians by the Romans prior to the time of Constantine, Christians were thought to practice cannibalism because of the language involved in the partaking of communion, which included the concept of "consuming" the body and blood of Jesus Christ.

535. Religious processions on church holidays held a very important place in the early church. For many people of the medieval period (1100–1400), being a Christian meant participating in festivals and ceremonies and listening to stories of legend, myth, and tradition. The church dictated what could be read and studied, few people could read, and fewer had their own copy of the Scriptures.

536. Christian occupations became an issue at the Council of Nicaea (325). At that time, certain activities were considered unsuitable for baptized believers: magic, idolatry, eroticism, and games in the amphitheater. In the second century some churches didn't allow believers to be magistrates or bear public authority. Church canons also specified which occupations were not acceptable for members of the clergy: banking, innkeeping, running a brothel, or being in the civil service.

537. The church acting as a bank was a concept that came about very early in the history of the Christian church. The clergy, as a wealthy segment of society, would make loans to Christian merchants. The Council of Nicaea (325), in an effort to forestall the practice of usury (charging excessive interest), forbade the lending of money at rates exceeding twelve percent each year. The ordinary lending rate was usually double to triple the Nicene limit.

538. "Christian" advertising had its debut very early in the history of the church. With persecution came public notice of Christian beliefs. In fact, more converts have been added to the church during periods of persecution than at any other time. Records kept by the leaders of the Roman Empire demonstrate their confusion over how those suffering might have influenced even more people to put themselves at risk.

539. Simony was a particularly ubiquitous problem in the church, especially during the Renaissance. Ever in search of funds to display and increase its power (for instance, the financing of impressive structures such as St. Peter's Basilica in Rome and the Sistine Chapel in Florence and papal wars against rival political powers), the church, being a nonpolitical system, had no tax revenue upon which to draw. Simony, the buying and selling of ecclesiastical appointments, was a common practice by the thirteenth century. Those who could afford to pay the most, regardless of their aptitude, character, or piety, were most likely to receive a seat within the clergy. Even the selection of popes was tainted by such practices, as cardinals' votes were increasingly bought off by wealthy families who sought to control the papacy.

540. Canute the Great, king of Denmark, was killed by his subjects in 1086. King Canute did much to make Denmark a Christian nation. He worked to restore churches and monasteries and also created laws to protect clergy members from the non-Christian factions. He may have gone too far, however, with an order that required mandatory tithes. The people revolted, and Canute was murdered. However, he was declared a saint in 1101.

541. Sunday recreation was not considered an appropriate activity by all factions of the church. *The Book of Sports* was written in 1618 by James I of England in response to Puritans, who believed no recreation was acceptable on Sunday afternoons following the church service. The book encouraged all manner of sports, from archery to dancing around maypoles, provided services had been attended.

542. Heinrich Jung-Stilling used his skills as a doctor in his evangelism work to help those who could not afford treatment. Making it a rule not to demand payment for his cataract operations, he helped many who were blind or who needed eye treatment. He and his wife never turned a single sufferer away. The couple remained poor throughout their lives, yet God provided for them faithfully.

543. The first American life insurance company was begun in Philadelphia, Pennsylvania, in 1759. It was called the "Corporation of Poor and Distressed Presbyterian Ministers and of the Poor and Distressed Widows and Children of Presbyterian Ministers."

544. William Wilberforce became a Christian after traveling with a local clergyman and reading the Scriptures with him. He was twenty-five years old at the time and went on to serve in the British Parliament. With strong convictions and a seemingly endless supply of patience, he battled for antislavery legislation. For eighteen years, he brought his bill to the House of Commons, acting as an ever-present reminder of the injustices being committed legally in England. In 1807, the antislavery bill was adopted by the House of Commons. The bill was fully implemented in 1833, just a few months before Wilberforce passed away.

545. Étienne de Grellet became convicted of the truth of the gospel while spending time with Pennsylvania Quakers after fleeing his native France during its revolution. In the late 1700s Grellet was a prosperous businessman; he spent the profits on numerous mission trips overseas and to Canada. He met with commoners, crown princes, and even military officials, seizing every opportunity to share the gospel and to preach a message of peace. Grellet was also deeply concerned about the conditions of those who were imprisoned in Europe and other places. His outspokenness led to much-needed reforms for prisoners as well as countless converts throughout the world.

546. The British Society for Promoting Reformation of Female Prisoners was begun by Elizabeth Fry, a Quaker and mother of eleven, who one day chanced upon a former inmate of Newgate Prison. Appalled at the conditions, particularly of the women prisoners who were largely there because of poverty, she began a regular visitation program, led Bible and literacy classes, and taught the inmates how to sew in order to help them find gainful employment. One of her supporters was Home Secretary Robert Peel, who pushed through the Prison Reform Act of 1823. The act severely restricted the incarceration of the poor and established the British police force. Police officers to this day are called "Bobbies," after Robert Peel's nickname.

547. F. B. Meyer's first convert may well have been the maid who overheard him preaching to his siblings while he was still a young boy. She was converted that very afternoon. He was a tireless Christian who longed to help his fellow human beings. Meyer pastored a church but went beyond serving those who entered the doors of the church and helped those who had nothing to give in return. He would meet convicts released from prison at the doors of the jail to help them start a new life. He led a movement to close brothels and saloons in order to remove temptations (nearly five hundred were successfully closed) and also established support groups for the poor, single mothers, and others in need.

548. Pastor Friedrich von Bodelschwingh of Germany believed preaching the gospel wasn't enough, saying, "It is a great injustice when one comforts the little man . . . merely with the promise of the next world." He believed in the social gospel, which meant "doing" for others. He felt a burden to help everyone who suffered. In the late 1860s he began a community dedicated to caring for epileptics. He worked tirelessly for the poor and unemployed, even going so far as to start a project for the unemployed in Germany that proved highly successful. He then ventured into mission work in Africa, establishing a refuge for African lepers, a colony for freed slaves, and an asylum for the insane.

549. Dr. William A. Passavant, Lutheran evangelist and minister, is considered a founding father of the evangelical social movement of nineteenth-century America. He started a hospital that provided care for those who couldn't afford it and also the first Lutheran orphanage in America. Many other orphanages and refuges followed, and not one person was turned away.

550. Abraham Kuyper led the Netherlands in a cultural revolution in the latter half of the nineteenth century in the name of Reformed Christianity. Disenchanted with the established church and the university, Kuyper converted to Christianity after a young girl from a poor family at his first parish witnessed to him.

Seeking to reverse the influence of modernism in Dutch society, Kuyper believed that the cultural role of Christianity was to be salt and light, to restore Christianity to a perfect state. Fundamental to his vision was the responsibility of Christians to vote, which led to the establishment of a Christian socialist majority. Kuyper directed an Amsterdam newspaper and became a prolific writer. He was considered the leading journalist of his nation. The Free University of Amsterdam was founded by Kuyper (the goal being to produce ministers for the many churches that had sprung up and away from the established rationalist-driven state churches). Similar Christian schools sprang up all over Holland because of Kuyper's influence.

551. Richard Niebuhr's book *Christ and Culture* (1951) is an in-depth study of culture and how Christians are to live within it, as they are inseparably joined to it. Niebuhr states, "When Christianity deals with the question of reason and revelation, what is ultimately in question is the relation of the revelation in Christ to the reason which prevails in culture. When it makes the effort to distinguish, contrast, or combine rational ethics with its knowledge of the will of God, it deals with the understanding of right and wrong developed in the culture and with good and evil as illuminated by Christ." He believed that there should be tension between Christians and the world around them.

552. Walter Rauschenbusch wrote *Christianity and the Social Crisis* after helping to establish the Brotherhood of the Kingdom group. His book gained a nationwide following when it was published in 1907. Rauschenbusch's premise was that American society was in the midst of crisis and that it was a result of the American church being in crisis. He urged Christians to condemn the wrong in the world and then work to fix it, not ignore the evil of it or conform to it. Thousands of Americans took a new interest in the social problems facing America. A social creed was adopted by the Federal Council of the Churches of Christ in America in 1908. Evangelism became a new focus for many, and new movements sprouted throughout North America.

19

Americana

553. A Christian missionary traveling up and down the Atlantic shores of the New World and visiting the various colonies in 1646 to gauge the spiritual lives of the colonists noted that there were church services being held in eighteen different languages along the Hudson River alone. The worshipers came from different races and cultures, but they all seemed to share one idea: Christians should be free to worship God in their own way.

554. Various religious groups settled in different places throughout America. Their individual locations were as follows: Roman Catholics settled around Maryland. Baptists, for the most part, stayed in Rhode Island. Dutch Reformed were in what is now New York. Puritans were in Massachusetts. Quakers settled in New Jersey and Pennsylvania. And Presbyterians settled in Virginia, the seaboard of Pennsylvania, and parts of North Carolina.

555. Rules for church attendance were quite strict in America in the seventeenth century, despite the fact that there was a multitude of different churches and belief systems in the colonies. In 1663 Virginia colonists faced fines of up to fifty pounds of tobacco for not attending church services.

556. Church attendance was required beyond Sunday, according to Dale's Laws in Virginia. "Everie man and woman duly twice a day upon the first towling of the Bell shall upon the working dais repaire unto the Church, to hear divine Service." The fines for missing service depended on how many times the offense had occurred: loss of a day's wages for the first instance; whipped for the second instance; and condemned to the galley for six months for the third instance.

557. Denying the Bible was considered a capital offense by the Massachusetts Bay Colony beginning in 1646. It's not surprising that few denied the authenticity of the Bible as the Word of God.

558. John Woolman was a Quaker and eventually became a minister within that denomination. He is noteworthy for his bold stand against slavery and how he roused the Quakers as a whole to fight that institution. He traveled throughout the colonies and was so distraught by the injustice of slavery that when he stayed with people who kept slaves, he would pay the owner a small amount and request that it be given to the slaves so that he would not be beholden to slaveowners for his lodging. In 1758 he led the motion of the yearly Friends' meeting which recommended Quakers free their slaves and also decreed that any Friend who participated in the act of buying or selling slaves was to be banned from participation in the business affairs of the Quaker Church.

559. The Age of Reason, or "the Enlightenment," refers to the mid–1600s to the late 1700s when philosophers (particularly Voltaire in France and John Locke in England) applied the laws of science to all of life. Arguing for social justice and education, they thought the universe could be understood by the human mind and that education could overcome sin. Their ideas about human dignity led to the French and American revolutions, but their rejection of passion and spontaneity eventually caused people to reject their rationality in favor of romance, emotion, and individuality. The church responded by either embracing their desire for truth or by rejecting their godless perspective.

560. Christ Church in Alexandria, Virginia, was completed in 1773 after six years of construction. The cost of the building was $4,070. George Washington purchased a pew for himself and his family for $100.

561. The Latin Seal is the phrase found on several pieces of United States currency. It reads, *E pluribus unum—coeptis—MDC-CLXXVI—Novus ordo seclorum,* and it means, "One out of many—God has smiled on our undertakings—1776—A new order for the ages."

562. Benjamin Franklin was originally not in favor of the Egyptian pyramid and the "all-seeing eye" that is still displayed on one-dollar bills. He suggested a depiction of Pharaoh's troops drowning in the Red Sea and the words, "Rebellion to tyrants is obedience to God." Thomas Jefferson, meanwhile, proposed a depiction of the children of Israel walking in the wilderness, being "led by a cloud by day and a pillar of fire by night."

563. "Congress shall make no law respecting an establishment of religion, or prohibiting the free exercise thereof . . ."—the words of the First Amendment to the United States Constitution, crafted by James Madison. Though taken for granted by most Americans, the idea that the national government would have no control over establishing a state church was profound. To this day, there is a small minority of countries that exist without an officially sanctioned church.

564. Harvard University, America's first college, was founded on October 28, 1636. Named after Puritan pastor John Harvard, the stated educational goal of the institution was to train pastors and missionaries to serve the spiritual needs of the people in the colonies. Six U.S. presidents have attended the school:

John Adams, John Quincy Adams, Theodore Roosevelt, Franklin Roosevelt, John Kennedy, and Rutherford Hayes, who attended Harvard Law School.

565. Yale University was founded in 1701 by Congregationalists. The institution was intent on turning out educated pastors and teachers because it was felt that Harvard no longer emphasized its Calvinistic roots and therefore couldn't turn out quality ministers.

566. The oldest Baptist church in America was founded by Roger Williams in 1639. This church in Providence, Rhode Island, has continued services for more than 360 years.

567. John Chapman's legendary work as Johnny Appleseed is an American tradition. While he is best known for carrying apple seeds all around America, Chapman also spread the gospel in his journey by handing out religious tracts.

568. Ninety-six Christian Native Americans were killed on March 9, 1782, in Ohio in retaliation for Indian raids that had been made elsewhere in the Ohio territory by other Indians. The converted Indians had lived peacefully in a Moravian Brethren town at the time.

569. *The Christian History* was America's first religious magazine. It was published in Boston in 1743 during the Great Awakening. The weekly publication told stories of what was happening in the revival and gave personal accounts of various Christians' experiences.

570. Francis Scott Key was born in 1779 and wrote the poem that eventually became the United States' national anthem: "The Star Spangled Banner." Key is also known as the cofounder of the American Sunday School Union.

571. Lemuel Hayes was the first certified African American minister of his race within the United States. Licensed in 1780 by the Congregational Church of Connecticut, this minister eventually went on to pastor an all-white church.

572. "'Twant me, 'twas the Lord," she said. "I always told him, 'I trust to you. I don't know where to go or what to do, but I expect you to lead me,' and he always did."—Harriet Tubman helped three hundred slaves to freedom with her nineteen rescues and gave the credit to God for showing her the way.

573. The best known man in America during the early 1800s was Francis Asbury, an English pastor and friend of John Wesley who was clearly ahead of his time. A circuit-riding Methodist preacher, he rode more than five thousand miles on horseback each year, stopping in so many small towns that his face was known throughout the country because most people had seen him preach. Asbury came out against alcohol and slavery decades before they were prohibited by law, and he called for the colonies to be free from British domination before the Revolutionary War began. He has a seminary named after him on the East Coast.

574. Trimountain, Massachusetts, took the name "Boston" in 1630 in honor of Pastor John Cotton (1584–1652), who was from Boston, England. Cotton was a prevalent figure as both a civil and religious leader in America after having to flee England because of his Puritan leanings.

575. Brimstone Corner, which was built in 1810, is the site of the Park Street Church of Boston. It is also where the sails for "Old Ironsides" were made. The place became known as Brimstone Corner because gunpowder was stored in the church for use in the War of 1812.

576. The first American anti-abortion rally occurred on December 3, 1846. The leading New York City abortionist of her time, Anna Lohman, or Madame Restell as she was otherwise known, found outside her home a rally led by a Presbyterian widow named Leslie Prentice, who was determined to pressure Lohman to discontinue her work.

577. President Abraham Lincoln faithfully attended Presbyterian churches both in his home state of Illinois and also in Washington, but he never became a member of a church. He once stated that "When any church will inscribe over its altar the Savior's condensed statement of law and gospel: 'Thou shalt love the Lord thy God with all thy heart, and with all thy soul and with all thy mind, and love thy neighbor as thyself,' that church I will join with all my heart." He read the Bible often and believed strongly in its authority over human morality.

578. The growth of American theological seminaries can be credited in part to the push made by evangelist Charles Finney for better training for ministers. The first seminary, Andover Theological Seminary, was founded in 1808 by the Congregationalists; it represented a reaction to the Unitarian theology at Harvard. Andover stood for the old Calvinism as well as new changes and styles implemented by Samuel Hopkins. The first year saw nearly one hundred male students enroll, far exceeding the founders' expectations.

579. Marrying "outside the fold" was considered an extremely dangerous undertaking. Unless one spouse or the other relinquished his or her religion, it was nearly impossible. One such marriage that appeared to work out was between Daniel Anthony, a Quaker, and Lucy Read, a Baptist. Though Lucy willingly married Daniel and attended Quaker meetings, she never joined the Quakers officially. According to stories, several nights before her wedding day she danced the entire night. It was something of a final hurrah because she would not be permitted to dance once she married a Quaker. Their union produced Susan Brownell Anthony in 1820.

580. Susan B. Anthony was raised as a Quaker. Though she is often hailed as being ahead of her time as a liberal-minded feminist, she grew up in a fairly typical and religious home. She was educated and became a gifted teacher and eventually the headmistress at a school for girls. Anthony first openly displayed her knowledge of inequality at a teachers' association yearly meeting. At that time, though women were allowed to attend, they were not to speak at the events. Anthony was the very first woman to speak at such an event. Her boldness inspired many to speak out against the inequality associated with less pay for the same work, the assumption that women are unable to keep up intellectually, and that women are of weak constitution and always frail.

581. Antoinette Brown, the first ordained female minister in the United States, trained at Oberlin College and completed the theological program there in 1850. She was unable to receive a degree, however. Her first pastorate, at a Congregationalist church, was in a small town. She asked to be dismissed after about a year because of the many trials she had faced at the church. The congregation in turn was upset with her, for, among other things, not preaching eternal damnation in her sermons. Antoinette went on to work in other ministry opportunities.

582. Wheaton College (formerly Illinois Institute) was chartered in Illinois on February 15, 1860. It has become one of evangelicalism's top institutions of higher education.

583. Swampscott, Massachusetts, was the setting for the introduction of premillennialism. Baptist pastor A. J. Gordon, speaking at a summer Bible conference in 1876, suggested that the world would continue to decline until the antichrist arrived, giving way to the return of Christ and the establishment of his reign for one thousand years. Up to that time, postmillennialism ruled the day. With the close of the American Civil War, the belief that the world was getting better and better gave way to a feeling that the world was declining into sin.

584. Evangelist Billy Sunday pitched for the Chicago White Stockings (the name later changed to the White Sox) baseball team at the turn of the century. Though he was a gifted player, he left his playing days behind him and became an evangelist. By the end of his ministry, he was said to have preached at least twenty thousand times and gained over a million converts for the church.

585. "Illegal kissing." In 1910 the Christian Endeavor Society of Missouri tried to ban all movies that showed kissing "between nonrelatives." Such bans and protests were common for that era, but the society was unsuccessful in this venture.

586. "Under God." These words weren't added to the pledge of allegiance of the United States until 1954. The amended language was put into law by Dwight Eisenhower, who was president at the time.

587. The ice-cream sundae was the result of Midwest soda-shop owners trying to get around a town law that prohibited the selling of ice-cream sodas on Sunday. The shop owners left out the carbonated water and used only ice cream and syrup, making a new and different dessert. The change was a big hit and eventually the sundae became a regular item on the menu.

588. The only American clergyman to have his own national holiday is Martin Luther King Jr. The pastor of Dexter Avenue Baptist Church in Montgomery, Alabama, King came to prominence when he led a boycott of the Montgomery bus system for treating African Americans unfairly. Influenced by the nonviolent methods of Mohandas Gandhi, he became the central figure in the Civil Rights movement of the 1960s.

589. "When a public official is inseparably bound by the dogma and the demands of the church, he cannot consistently separate himself from these."—Southern Baptist Convention decision, 1960. The Baptists did not want a Catholic to become president of the United States, but John F. Kennedy was elected six months later.

20

Revivals and Awakenings

590. The Awakening at Herrnhut sprang from nothing more than a confirmation service for two girls. The Moravian Brethren, living in a commune in Dresden, had brought together more than three hundred believers from all over Europe to study the Bible and pray together. On August 13, 1727, as the two girls were confirmed, "the Spirit of God" swept over the assembly. Some wept, others sang. People hugged each other. A twenty-four-hour prayer vigil sprang up. The people decided to send out missionaries, who wound up in Greenland, Lapland, Russian Georgia, Suriname, Ceylon, South Africa, Algeria, and the island of St. Thomas. Their work inspired John Wesley and William Carey and is generally viewed as the start of the independent missionary movement.

591. The Great Evangelical Awakening took place in Germany, Britain, and the American colonies in the 1730s. Coming as a response to the Age of Reason, it brought emotion and enthusiasm back into the church. Led by John Wesley, the movement gave life to the faith of thousands.

592. The Five Harvests was the name used to describe the growing spiritual renewal taking place in America during the early 1700s. Solomon Stoddard, a fiery preacher in Northampton, Massachusetts, began decrying the worldliness that marked the lives of people who had arrived in the New World to create a more godly society.

593. Jonathan Edwards was a devout Calvinist with a heart for God and a head for theology. He entered Yale when he was only thirteen. After going into the ministry and working first from the pulpit of his grandfather's church, Edwards resolved that Christ died for the elect, but he emphasized that he did not know whom the elect included. That being understood, Edwards began preaching a revival message based on the gravity of sin and the regenerating power of the Holy Spirit. He passionately called people to repent and put their faith in Christ. For five years, beginning in 1730, he prayed fervently that God would bring revival to his congregation in Northampton. Those prayers were answered in the Great Awakening.

594. The Great Awakening burst forth in Edwards's church in 1735. In the normally staid, unemotional lives of his congregation, there was weeping and wailing over sin, loud personal prayers, and reports of divine healing. Women fell over in a faint, overcome with emotion. Men driving their carriages by the church would suddenly stop, crying, struck by the convicting power of the Holy Spirit.

595. Theodore Freylinghuysen, a German immigrant pastoring a Dutch Reformed church in New Jersey, saw "God break loose" among his people. There were reports of miracles, of healings, and of incredible answers to prayer. Above all, there was a renewed spirit of devotion and evangelism among believers in the region.

596. The Pennsylvania Revival was led by Gilbert Tennant, a Presbyterian pastor. He, along with his brothers William, John, and Charles, began doing "revival" services featuring emotional prayers, vigorous singing, and dramatic preaching. Though mocked by more conservative clergymen, preachers like Edwards, Freylinghuysen, and Tennant spread the word that God was doing a great work in the colonies.

597. George Whitefield visited from England and tied together the various revivals in the nationwide explosion called "the Great Awakening." From Baptist churches in Virginia, to Presbyterian gatherings in Pennsylvania, to Reformed churches in New York and New Jersey, to Puritan congregations in Massachusetts, thousands committed their lives to Christ. When a revival meeting was announced, farmers and field hands would stream to the location. Whitefield preached to perhaps the largest crowds in American history to that date. The Awakening cut across denominational and racial lines and profoundly reinforced the American notion that churches were independent of the government.

598. The people of Philadelphia stormed the churches to hear George Whitefield, the magnetic preacher of the Great Awakening in the early 1700s. Benjamin Franklin said he was most impressed that people "admired and respected him [Whitefield]," given that Whitefield spent much of his time "assuring them they were naturally half beasts and half devils." Still, Franklin admitted the Awakening had had a positive impact on the morality of his city.

599. The circuit-riding preachers were men trained by John Wesley to take the gospel from town to town. Wesley himself traveled more than two hundred fifty thousand miles on horseback, appointing new preachers and assigning them circuits of their own. By organizing the people into classes and small groups, he set up a system that would take the Good News of Jesus Christ across the North American continent.

600. The Clapham sect was a group of wealthy evangelicals in eighteenth-century England that advocated for social causes.

The closely knit group, led by pastor John Venn but influenced by British statesman William Wilberforce, helped start the Church Missionary Society, the British Bible Society, the Society for Bettering the Condition of the Poor, and the Society for the Reformation of Prison Discipline. They were also the prime movers in the abolitionist movement in England and were the forerunners of modern evangelical groups, which attempt to influence politics for the sake of moral causes.

601. Swedish evangelists brought great revival in the first years of the nineteenth century by being followers of Henrik Schartau, a professor and theologian who inspired many to begin reading the Bible after a long period of rationalism had numbed the church. So angered were the established clergy that they actually pressed charges against traveling evangelists in Sweden for overfilling the churches. Despite such opposition, the evangelists continued to preach the Word and many came to a saving knowledge of Jesus Christ.

602. The Camp Meeting Movement started in 1800 when James McGready sent out announcements that there was going to be a revival at the Gasper River Church in Kentucky. Scores of families came from miles around in wagons or on foot, bringing tents and food with them, ready to watch the hand of God at work. Because the worshipers camped on the site of the revival, they began referring to it as a "camp meeting." The name stuck, and two hundred years later many cities, particularly in the American South, still have camp meetings.

603. The Western Revival came about one hundred years after the Great Awakening, but its roots lie in the same teaching of repentance and personal salvation. While the Awakening was spurred on largely by well-schooled Calvinists, the Revival came in the early 1800s as the result of rough Arminian circuit-riders preaching to frontiersmen while standing on the back of a buckboard. The Revival was also more individualistic, spawning a number of revivalist societies and "enlightened movements" like the Shakers, the New Light Movement, and similar groups.

604. "Mankind will not act until they are excited."—spoken by revivalist preacher Charles Finney in defense of his exciting camp-meeting preaching in 1834. A man who understood marketing, he was the first to post placards, distribute handbills, and take out advertisements in local papers to drum up a crowd for his revivals.

605. The first prophecy conference was held in Dublin in the 1830s at the behest of John Nelson Darby, a Plymouth Brethren who felt that the prevailing view of postmillennialism didn't square with his reading of the Book of Revelation. Darby, who had a long history of not getting along with people, went on to lead numerous prophecy conferences during the remainder of his lifetime. He noted in his talks that God, at various periods in history, has changed his relationship with humankind—an idea he called "dispensationalism," which is still an influential theme at prophecy conferences in the twenty-first century.

606. Dwight Moody was clerking in his uncle's shoe store as a young man when a Christian businessman, Mr. Kimball, met him. Kimball shared the gospel message with Moody and soon Moody's heart was opened. Fairly soon after he felt called into evangelism, at nineteen years of age, he moved to Chicago and tried to start a Sunday school class. However, he was told he couldn't teach because he had a problem with stuttering. Unfazed, Moody returned in one week's time with thirty young boys as pupils. He paid them to attend! The superintendent of the program then offered him a classroom, and within a year's time there were more than a thousand pupils in Moody's program. Moody went into full-time preaching shortly after this experience.

607. The Chicago Fire of 1871 burned down Pastor Dwight Moody's home, church, mission, and even the businesses of most of his financial supporters. Not knowing what to do, the self-taught former shoe salesman sailed for England and took that country by storm. Having never heard an American evangelist, the British were wowed by his emotional fervor and plain-spoken manner. Moody was the first modern evangelist, applying business techniques to the church and offering special music, counseling, and follow-ups to his revival meetings.

608. Jeremiah C. Lanphier was a godly man from New York City who held lunchtime prayer meetings for businessmen. His first meeting started on September 23, 1857, and within three weeks, there were forty people coming, with more wanting to attend. This incident contributed to the start of another spiritual awakening.

609. John Vassar began working for the American Tract Society in 1850. Vassar carried a suitcase of books and his Bible and went door to door "talking religion." He is said to have looked like a rough and hardy farmer yet he spoke like an apostle. Many testified that he did not want to sell books so much as he wanted to share the Good News of Christ. During one three-month period, he spoke with more than three thousand people about Jesus, and thousands of people came to Christ through his presentation of the gospel. He continued his work until he was unable to walk in 1877.

610. "There are lots of preachers in the beer-shops at this moment. What the church has to do is find them."—Rodney "Gipsy" Smith was born a gypsy and lived in England in the second half of the nineteenth century. After finding God at a revival in 1876, he gave his life wholly to God's work. For many years he worked for the Salvation Army, but he gained a greater following as a revival minister in Hanley, England. Thousands flocked to hear him as he conducted nine services each week. From England his work led him to America where he had five separate evangelical tours. It was in America that Gipsy was able to tell fellow evangelists Dwight Moody and Ira Sankey that it was during one of their revivals in England that he had felt God's calling.

611. "The Lord will make a preacher out of you, my boy," said one of the evangelizing duo with hands placed on the boy's head. That boy proved to be none other than Gipsy Smith. He was converted at a Methodist church during an altar call and later taught himself to read with a Bible and two dictionaries. He went on to write books of his own.

612. The "Second Blessing" was a phrase first popularized at the annual Keswick Conventions in Keswick, Great Britain, during the late 1890s. The teachers urged believers to "walk in the power of the resurrection" and to "let Christ reign in your soul"—words that led some to suggest that there must be a deeper, more powerful evocation of the Lord Jesus Christ than simple piety and propriety.

613. William Bryant's revival took place in Cherokee County, North Carolina, in the summer of 1896. During the revival people spoke in tongues and their bodies were "overtaken" by the Holy Spirit. Baptists, Methodists, Lutherans, and Presbyterians were a bit put out by such goings-on, and Bryant was shot at and his church building was burned down.

614. Evan Roberts was one of the men at William Bryant's revival. He was a Welsh miner who began proclaiming the miraculous power of the Spirit in revival meetings. Noting that speaking in tongues and other strange manifestations were taking place at scattered locations around the globe, Roberts became part of the Restorationist Movement.

615. The Restorationist Movement called for a return to tongues, miraculous healings, and other manifestations of apostolic times. One of the leaders, John Alexander Dowie, claimed he was Elijah the Restorer, and he set up a Christian community (later the town of Zion, Illinois). Meanwhile, in Maine, Frank Sandford was also claiming to be Elijah the Restorer, though he set up shop in the town of Shiloh.

616. Charles Fox Parham lived at Shiloh in 1900. He then moved to Kansas and set up a "healing home" in Topeka. Parham and his wife claimed to have "apostolic faith" and would invite people to live in their house so the people could wait for the Holy Spirit to miraculously heal them.

617. Agnes Ozman prayed to receive the Holy Spirit at Charles Fox Parham's home. She then, according to Parham, began speaking Chinese "and was unable to speak English for three days." Though Agnes was the first modern claimant to speak in tongues, most of the other people in the home claimed similar experiences. They said it was like the Spirit coming down at Pentecost, and by 1905 the Parhams were holding "Pentecostal" meetings across the lower central plains.

618. William J. Seymour, an African American Bible student, claimed to inherit the power of the Holy Spirit after spending time with Parham and set off to start a "Full Gospel" church (that is, a church service that didn't leave out the apostolic elements) in Los Angeles. Seymour's first service, which was covered by an *L.A. Times* reporter, made front page news and brought Pentecostalism to the attention of the nation.

619. The Hot Springs Gathering brought together leaders from Apostolic Faith churches, independent churches, and representatives of the Church of God in Christ in 1914, after years of bickering between the various Pentecostal groups. In an attempt to unify and stabilize this new form of Christianity and to establish a missions program and Bible school, the leaders formed "The Assemblies of God" denomination.

21

Churches

620. One of the earliest descriptions of a Christian worship service was written by Justin Martyr in the second century: "On the day called The Day of the Sun, all who live in cities or in the country gather together to one place and the memoirs of the apostles or the writings of the prophets are read, as long as time permits, then when the reader has ceased, the president verbally instructs and exhorts to the imitation of these good things. Then we all rise together and pray."

621. The Parthenon served as more than a Greek temple. After Emperor Theodosius I started crushing paganism, Athens's famed Parthenon became a Church of the Virgin Mary. Other pagan temples were also made into Christian places of worship. The change didn't last, however.

622. Early churches prior to Constantine's reign were structured around domes. The Syrians created this style for churches to represent the form of the universe. The domes were also mindful of the tent shape of the Syrians and recalled the Scripture that speaks of God establishing "heaven as a vaulted chamber and stretched out as a tent to dwell in." Other instances of the dome appear on early images of the biblical ark as well as respected tombs that were carved out to resemble domes.

623. The Church in Rome could have given "church growth" seminars to many modern congregations. By the year 255, it had approximately 30,000 members, 150 pastors, and wielded a huge influence. Like the empire it represented, the church came to adopt a hierarchical structure and claimed authority over small churches within its realm.

624. The Catholic Church split in 251 as a result of the arguments between Novatian and Cornelius. Novatian felt that people who had denied their faith during persecution could never again enter the church, while Cornelius, the bishop of Rome, believed God could forgive them. The two gathered followers, and Novatian was elected as the "antipope" of Rome. Creating an orthodox-but-graceless church, the Novatian congregations survived until well into the fifth century.

625. Another church split occurred after the Council of Chalcedon in the fourth century. There was no meeting in the middle on the official definition of Christ's two natures (human as well as God). The resulting split made three independent churches: the Armenian Church, the Coptic Church of Egypt, and the Jacobite Church of Syria.

626. The Church of the Holy Wisdom was rebuilt on the site of Constantine's Church in 538 in Constantinople (present-day Istanbul). The church and its famous "onion dome" were built by Justinian, emperor of Byzantium and creator of the famous *Corpus Juris Civilis*—the first modern compendium of legal principles and case law that remains the basis for the legal system in most western countries. Justinian saw himself as "Christian emperor," the executor of God's will, and used the term "body" to refer both to the church and the state. According to Justinian, the church dissolved into the Christian state.

627. The Great Division began on a summer's day in 1054, when Pope Leo IX and his representative, Cardinal Humbert, entered the Church of the Holy Wisdom in Constantinople and placed a document on the altar, excommunicating the church over its use of icons, its practice of Lent, its use of a creed, and (believe it or not) the type of bread they used for communion. They then left the church, shaking the dust off their feet as they went. A deacon grabbed the paper, ran after them, and asked them to remove it. Humbert refused and turned away, and the deacon threw the papal bull into the street. That event marked the separation of the Roman Catholic Church from the Eastern Orthodox Church.

628. Icons mark the theology of the Eastern Orthodox Church. An Orthodox believer, upon entering the sanctuary, goes first to the wall of paintings in the back (called the "iconostasis") and kisses the icons before taking his seat. An Orthodox Christian, upon visiting a home, will bow to an icon in the eastern corner of the room before greeting his host. The Orthodox Church believes images of Jesus and the saints are manifestations of the heavenly ideal—windows between the earthly and heavenly realms. Because people are created in God's image, they carry the icon of God within themselves. When they sin, they diminish the likeness to God. Salvation occurs when they restore the full image of God in themselves.

629. Incarnation, re-creation, and transfiguration are the three main doctrines of the Orthodox Church. The incarnation of God and the re-creation of man is the central theme of their theology. While Protestants and Catholics view man's relationship to God in legal terms, Orthodox believers see it in artistic terms— man should be transformed to best reflect God. The church, rather than being a formal structure, is a mystical body constantly seeking to renew man in the image of God.

630. In the Emperor Constantine, the Orthodox Church found its perfect leader. In allying the state and the church, he became the "holy initiator" of the Christian world and the connecting link between God and the world. While most western Christians see the alliance of church and state as the beginning of the problems for the church, most Orthodox Christians see the reign of Constantine as the apex of government on earth.

631. In opposition to icons, Pope Leo III sent an official representative to Constantinople in 718 to take down the image of Christ that rested over the Bronze Gate leading into the city and replace it with a simple cross. The legate was met by a mob who murdered him and sent his body back to the pope, the cross clutched in his dead fingers.

632. Window sponsors were an important part of how stained glass windows came to be put in the notable churches of Europe. In the twelfth century, guilds (the butchers, winemakers, merchants, tailors, etc.) took pride in sponsoring beautiful windows for the great churches of Europe. The scenes depicted showed their occupations. The prostitutes of Paris wanted to sponsor a window dedicated to Mary Magdalene, but their offer was quickly declined.

633. The Strassburg Cathedral, constructed during a frenzy of church building in the twelfth and thirteenth centuries, rises as high as a forty-story skyscraper. The Cathedral at Chartres is the equal of a thirty-story building. The architects who planned these structures wanted to create the illusion of soaring upward, but the majority of such buildings collapsed due to failures of design.

634. The Cologne Cathedral's construction was started in 1248. However, this beautiful building wasn't completed until August 14, 1880. It was completed the same day it had been started 632 years earlier. There was a 284-year break between 1558 and 1842.

635. Churches that were built from the heavy taxes demanded from congregations rather than the church's wealth received some negative publicity through Martin Luther's eighty-sixth thesis: "The pope's riches at this day far exceed the wealth of the richest millionaires, cannot he therefore build one single basilica of S.[aint] Peter out of his own money, rather than out of the money of the faithful poor?" Other buildings were funded by less respectable means.

636. St. Peter's Basilica was rebuilt by Pope Leo X in the early sixteenth century. Though the church needed to be rebuilt, the funds used to do so came from Leo's selling over two thousand high-level church jobs to those who could afford them.

637. The trial of John Wycliffe took place before the bishop of London in 1377. Wycliffe, a quiet man, was being tried by the Catholic Church for heresy because he had questioned papal authority, the selling of indulgences, and the worship of saints. But he had powerful friends in England who did not appreciate the high-handed manner Rome took in the matter. In the opening remarks, an argument broke out over whether Wycliffe should stand or sit during the trial. The argument turned into a fistfight, then a brawl, and eventually a riot. Wycliffe was whisked away by friends, the trial was suspended, and the only thing left for the bishop to do was to declare Wycliffe's writings banned, a decree certain to be ignored by both scholars and English believers.

638. The Church of "Our Lovely Lady" in Regensburg brought many people to her doors. In 1520 twelve thousand tokens were sold to pilgrims who wished to see and take part in the medical "healings" that were said to occur at a demolished synagogue which had been destroyed during a period of anti-Semitism. A statue and church were built on the site in order to continue the healings in a "Christian" manner.

639. The Anabaptists began as a group of believers in Zurich who believed that the Bible endorsed adult baptism but not the Roman Catholic practice of infant baptism. On January 21, 1525, they met and baptized one another, leading their detractors to call them "ana-baptists" or "re-baptizers." The Anabaptists took a strong stand for brotherhood, pacifism, and the separation of church and state, but adherents became known as "disrupters" for interrupting other churches' worship services. They were persecuted, but the movement proved popular, especially with the lower classes of the German Empire.

640. The Mennonites are the spiritual descendants of the Anabaptists; they were counter-culturalists whose goal was to reinstitute apostolic Christianity. They rejected infant baptism, holding political office, and bearing arms against anyone. Their leader, Menno Simons (1495–1561), traversed Europe, visiting small Anabaptist conclaves in secret nighttime meetings. Because of persecution, his followers fled to the Netherlands, then to the United States. The Amish and the Hutterites are branches of Mennonite followers.

641. The General Baptists got their name in the early 1600s for their belief that Christ died for all humanity, not merely for the elect. Their doctrine, which broke away from the Calvinist idea that Christ's atonement was limited because he died only for the elect, had been preached by Arminians and Mennonites for years. However, it wasn't widely believed in the church until it became part of Baptist theology.

642. Pietism grew out of the teaching of Philip Spener (1635–1705), pastor of a Lutheran church in Frankfurt. Gathering small groups in his house twice a week for reading and discussing the Bible, Spener and his excited band of believers were soon noticed and scornfully called "the gathering of the pious." Accepting the name gladly, they were one of the first modern groups to emphasize the need for being "born again."

643. The Evangelical Movement takes its name from the Greek word *evangelion,* which means "good news." In the 1730s, Christians across Great Britain began to believe the most important job they had was to spread the gospel of Jesus Christ. Allied with John Wesley and Jonathan Edwards, they traveled to America in hopes of spreading their message. The term changed a bit in the mid–1800s, when conservative Christians stressing the need for personal salvation delineated from Christians more concerned with the social needs of humankind.

644. The Plymouth Brethren was started in Dublin, Ireland, by a band of unhappy Anglicans who wanted to meet informally, pray with one another, and partake of communion regularly. One of the members, Anthony Groves, wanted to serve as a missionary in Persia, but the church hierarchy put so much red tape in his way, he eventually stopped trying. After talking with his friends, Groves decided he didn't need special training or an ordination but just the support of Christian friends. When they decided to send Groves to Persia, it caused a break with the church. Eventually, that group became a movement, which rejected "ordained" pastors and considered all members to be ministers.

645. "Methodist" is the term first used to describe renewal-minded Anglicans who relied on a stringent system of methods and behaviors in an attempt to develop a holy life. One of their number, John Wesley, abandoned those prescriptions in favor of a message of grace but relied on their sense of organization when setting up circuit-riding missionaries to spread out across North America. His reliance on one system brought back the title of "Methodist," but it also gave order to the movement so that it still lives today.

646. The "Free Church" Movement spawned a number of ideas that, though radical at the time, remain with us today. Believers of this movement gave us the modern concept of "discipleship," calling for a daily experience with God to transform a person's life. They were convinced of the priesthood of all believers and expected each individual to have a ministry of some kind. They called for the separation of church and state, so that government would have no control over their beliefs and practices. And they exercised congregational decision-making, relying on the body to be led by the Spirit of God.

647. African American evangelist William J. Seymour led a Holiness mission in 1906 in Los Angeles. The group grew larger as word spread of the amazing revival meetings and instances of speaking in tongues. Eventually, the mission moved to a run-down building on Azusa Street. This particular revival is often cited as one of the foremost beginnings of Pentecostalism.

648. The concept of denominations was popularized during the Evangelical Revival of 1740, but it was first conceived by the Puritans one hundred years earlier. Arguing that one particular Christian group is simply a member of the larger church, the Puritans felt that the cause of Christ could not be identified with any one group. Therefore, each group could be "denominated" by some similar characteristics or shared beliefs.

649. The Denominational Theory usurped the concept of apostolic succession by stating that true "succession" happens in the church, not with bishops or popes but with believers. Differences of opinion are inevitable, but the mere fact of separation does not constitute some sort of schism. At the Westminster Assembly in 1645, the Congregationalists pushed for Christian unity in belief and diversity in expression.

650. Church splits have been a staple of church history, but the curious case of the Plymouth Brethren offers one of the most unique stories in Christendom. During the 1800s, the group evolved into "the Exclusive Brethren" (they refused to fellowship with anyone who disagreed with their theology) and "the Open Brethren" (they, apparently, would). Begun by a group who disdained the formalism of the church, the denomination split over such issues as foot washing, prophecy, the role of elders, and the definitions of spiritual gifts.

651. The Disciples of Christ was started by Alexander Campbell and his father, Thomas Campbell, a pastor who had been a Presbyterian, then a Seceder (having pulled out of the Presbyterian Church), then a Baptist, and finally an independent church pastor. Alexander Campbell was continually trying to move the church away from formality and denominationalism, moving it toward a simple, personal faith based solely on the Scriptures. In 1832 he and his followers took the name "Disciples of Christ" because it sounded nondenominational, and that nontraditional approach blossomed in the expanding American West.

652. The first creedless church was organized by Richard Wolfe of Denver, Colorado, in 1912. Considered a fringe group, this sect believed in worshiping without any specific creed, theology, or dogma.

653. The Fundamentalist Fellowship began in 1920 when some conservative Christians, worried about the church's accommodation to modernism, believed that Christianity was acquiescing to the culture on the fundamental doctrines of the faith: the virgin birth, the lostness of man, the historical accuracy and authority of the Bible, and the need for salvation.

654. The first children's church was operated and attended solely by children. The built-to-scale Unitarian church was dedicated in 1937. The miniature church was located in Massachusetts and was only thirty-two feet long and eighteen feet wide, yet it had a steeple, belfry, and organ. The pews were just two feet by eight inches high.

655. More churches per square mile can be found in Jamaica than any other country.

22

Symbols

656. The word "symbol" comes from the two Greek words *syn,* meaning "together," and *ballein,* which means "to throw." Essentially "symbolism" is a "throwing together of an idea and a sign of it." Christian symbols were particularly important to the persecuted church as they allowed Christians to identify themselves and concepts of their faith while still keeping these beliefs somewhat hidden.

657. The cross is perhaps the most recognized symbol of Christianity. Over four hundred documented forms of crosses demonstrate the importance of this well-recognized symbol. Only about forty are used in Christian art, and of these, almost all can be found in both Catholic and Protestant churches. The cross is a sign of the atonement paid by Christ for our sins.

658. The all-seeing eye is a symbol that dates back to the sixteenth century. It is the sign of God the Father's omnipresence. In Great Britain the sign was often built into the wall behind the pulpit to demonstrate that God was watching the proceedings closely.

659. The hand of God is perhaps the most ancient symbol of God the Father. Like most symbols, it is referenced from Scripture. The symbol relates the creative power of God and that through his handiwork came forth the genius of creation.

660. A crown is a representation of the office Christ holds as king. The Scriptures teach that he is the "king of kings." The Bible also refers to Jesus as the "crown of life" which all who believe may take for themselves.

661. The unicorn is a symbol of the virgin birth of Jesus. It is interesting to note that this symbol is modeled after a fable of ancient pagans. Only with a virgin present could a unicorn be caught. Legend said the unicorn would run and place its head in the lap of the virgin, at which point it would be captured by those who had hidden in the woods.

662. The lantern is a symbol of betrayal that comes directly from Scripture. When Judas came with the soldiers to arrest Jesus, the group carried torches and lanterns to find Jesus. Alternatively, the lantern is a symbol of light.

663. Jesus is the Light of the world, the source that brings life to a dead world. Furthermore, Christ's two distinct natures, divine and earthly, are an important tenet of the Christian faith. The traditional symbol to display this doctrine is to light two candles during church services, with one on either side and a cross in the middle.

664. The Good Shepherd is a biblical reference to how Jesus described himself in the Gospel of John. As the redeemer of his people (the sheep), Jesus watches over them, protects them, and provides shelter for them.

665. The Holy Spirit is most often represented by a dove. This symbol recalls the story of Jesus' baptism. After Jesus was baptized by John the Baptist, a dove descended and God spoke from heaven. This is one of very few symbols for the Third Person of the Trinity.

666. Seven doves, or the seven lamps, or the seven-pointed star, all represent the seven gifts of the Holy Spirit stated in the Book of Revelation. The seven gifts are strength, honor, glory, blessing, power, riches, and wisdom.

667. Signs of the Trinity include the equilateral triangle or variations of it. The conception of the Trinity is the three distinct sides of the Godhead being three yet one. The equilateral triangle reminds us that all three sides (or figures) are equal. There are many variations on the triangle, including other such Christian symbols as three fish laid out to form a triangle.

668. The three-leaf clover is another sign of the Trinity, which goes back to a story about St. Patrick during his days as a missionary in Ireland. According to the story, Patrick was trying to explain the doctrine of the Trinity to the high king of Ireland around 464, but the king didn't understand and was getting frustrated. To illustrate his point, Patrick picked up a shamrock and gave it to the king, saying, "Here is a perfect leaf with three perfect parts." The king thought about it and came to accept the idea thanks to Patrick's object lesson.

669. The fleur-de-lys is a French symbol of the Trinity. The term means flower of the lily and demonstrates "threeness" throughout its structure. There are four sets of three within the symbol.

670. Color has long been used to symbolize particular emotions or sentiments of the church, particularly in connection with Christian holidays. *White* is a symbol of purity, light, and even the Godhead (the combination of the Father, Son, and Holy Spirit). *Black* has long symbolized death and mourning. *Purple* is the color most used to represent royalty; however, in the church it is also used as a symbol of fasting and penitence. *Red* is a symbol of blood, fire, and Christian zeal. *Green* is the most common color on earth; it is symbolic of hope, rebirth, and for Christians, a symbol of growth in their spiritual life.

671. The fish is used as a frequent title in inscriptions of the early church. The Greek letters for "fish" are formed acrostically by the Greek for "Jesus Christ, the Son of God, Savior." The symbol is also connected with baptism (converts, as small fish, follow the main fish).

672. A symbol of a fish was also a means of relaying a message. It could mean either a funeral was about to occur or that Christians were meeting for the sacrament of communion. According to historical records of the early church, the fish symbol displayed outside a pagan home meant someone had died. If the fish sign appeared outside a Christian home, it was a secret message that Christians were invited to come and share in the celebration of the Lord's Supper at night in secret.

673. Thistles are a symbol of a world that has fallen into sin. As Adam was forced to deal with thistles choking the good plants after his banishment from the Garden of Eden, so the thistle is a reminder of sin being all around us as a result of our fallen natures.

674. Passionflowers have become symbolic of the experience of Jesus before he was laid in the tomb. A central column in the center of the bloom is representative of the pillar Jesus was tied to during the beating he suffered from the soldiers. The ovary of the flower is symbolic of the hammer that drove nails into the cross, and the three styles of the flower represent the nails used. Five stamens within the center are representative of the five wounds Jesus suffered, and the ten petals found on the flower symbolize the ten apostles who fled the scene at Gethsemane, leaving only Judas Iscariot, who betrayed the Lord, and John, who witnessed Christ's death on the cross.

675. The phoenix is a symbol of Christian resurrection. According to legend the bird lived for five hundred to a thousand years, consumed itself by fire, and then rose again. Early Christians adopted the image as a symbol of both Christ's and their own future resurrection.

676. The butterfly is also used as a sign of resurrection. As the caterpillar goes through the stages to becoming a butterfly, it experiences a stage of "death" within the cocoon before breaking out with vibrancy, color, and wings. The death of Christ and his time spent in the tomb before he arose and eventually ascended into heaven (caterpillars are earth-bound, but butterflies can soar in the air) complete the image.

677. The peacock is another symbol of resurrection. A male peacock goes through a stage of molting when his beautiful blue and green feathers are lost. Eventually, new and even more beautiful plumage appears, but it is only through a time of molting that this is possible.

678. The fruit of the pomegranate bursts from the pressure of many seeds within. This fruit is a sign of Christ's resurrection, but it is also a symbol of the resurrection of his followers. All have a portion of the new life made possible by Christ's death on the cross; all that emerges in their saved lives is a symbol of the power of Christ to reproduce them.

679. Lilies are one of the most visible Easter symbols found in churches. The lily emerges each year from a bulb that is unseen in the winter, hidden in the darkness of a fertile grave. Yet with the coming of spring a stem emerges, then leaves, and finally flowers. Lilies are a symbol of Christ's emergence from the tomb.

680. The pelican became a Christian symbol due to a legend in which a mother pelican tears a hole into its own breast to feed her young with her own blood. (Pelicans in actuality feed their young by opening their beak so that the young may reach into the pouch beneath it.) This sign of giving oneself for others is a symbol of the atonement. That the sign receives its meaning from a legend seems likely; however, early references to the pelican can be found in writings of St. Augustine as well as Thomas Aquinas.

681. A favorite symbol of the sacrament of communion is the combination of heads of wheat and clusters of grapes displaying the two elements, the bread and the wine. Very often this particular symbol is found on communion tables and altars as well as communion serving elements.

682. Palm leaves are a symbol of the reward Christians have when earthly life comes to an end. The ancients often gave such leaves as a prize to the winners of athletic contests. A saying originated from this custom: "Let him bear the palm who merits it."

683. The rose is a sign of the promise of Christ's return. It is believed this symbol was first used by the church in the thirteenth century. The rose is mentioned in the Bible as a sign of new life that turns an arid desert into a beautiful plain.

684. Stars have long been a Christian symbol, with the number of points distinguishing the specific meaning of the representation. The *five-pointed star* is sometimes placed with images of Mary, the mother of Jesus. The Hebrew word for Mary, *Miriam*, means "star." The *six-pointed star* has long been the sign of the Jewish religion; it is the star of David. The *eight-pointed star* is the symbol of baptism or rebirth as the number eight symbolizes those ideas. The ten-pointed star is a symbol of the ten disciples of Jesus. There were twelve disciples appointed, but the star only references the ten who did *not* betray (Judas did) or deny him (Peter did).

685. The circle represents the doctrine of God's existence, which has no beginning and no end. The symbol demonstrates God's eternal presence from before the creation of the world until the end of the world.

686. Anchor symbols have been found in the catacombs, mixed in with other pictures and art. The anchor has long stood as a symbol of hope in Christ that "anchors" us to the faith. Often the anchor is placed with a cross and a heart to symbolize the three virtues of faith, hope, and love.

687. The Christian flag was a symbol given to America by Charles Overton in order to unite Christians behind a flag. A Sunday school superintendent, Overton gave an explanation of the colors and symbols of his suggested design at an 1897 rally when the original speaker didn't show up. The first red, white, and blue flag was sewn in 1907.

687. The twelve apostles are often represented by shields. This tradition is of an ancient origin and recalls the particular ways in which each apostle served or was martyred. The shields are fairly simple in form and color yet are most often meant to recall the gruesome ways they died. Many churches will pick one specific apostle to identify with and then use that apostle's shield for decoration within the church.

689. The design of churches is often a symbol in itself. Many churches are built in the shape of a cross to recall this most important Christian symbol. In general, churches following this layout have the main entrance on the west side and the sanctuary with the altar always within the east side. This might have originated with the ancient practice of looking to Jerusalem when one engaged in prayer.

690. Many Christian symbols correspond to specific doctrines and denominations. Research into symbols and their meanings is extremely important, particularly for churches redoing their architecture or adding stained glass windows with emblems. More than one Protestant church has unknowingly adopted Catholic symbols into new art for the sanctuary and suffered some embarrassment. The same can be said for Catholic churches adopting Protestant symbols by mistake.

23

Holidays

691. The Sunday Sabbath was instituted as a holiday by Constantine in 321 with the Constantine Edict. The edict proclaimed Sunday a national holiday and forbade merchants and craftsmen from working for hire on Sunday. Farmers were permitted to sow and reap on the Sabbath as a work of necessity.

692. The first Christian church calendar was organized from an earlier Hebrew calendar. Called the Julian calendar, it was accepted in 325 at the Council of Nicaea. Inaccuracies found in the Julian calendar after its acceptance at Nicaea were corrected by Pope Gregory XIII in 1582 with a new calendar, which was named for him: the Gregorian calendar. This calendar relies on the sun and has been in use throughout most of the world since its inception.

693. New Year's Day wasn't always January 1. Not until 1622 was the month of January made the beginning of the calendar year. Prior to the decision by the Roman Catholic Church, March was considered the first month of the year.

694. January 1 is also a religious feast day, in celebration of the circumcision of Jesus Christ. The day is a celebration of the Lord's submission to Jewish law and is a spiritual holiday observed by the Western church.

695. January 6 was originally the date celebrated as Christ's birth. In 548, the church proclaimed December 25 to be Christ's birth.

696. February 14, in the year 270, was the date that St. Valentine was beheaded. According to legend, his connection with the day of love and romance now celebrated is this: Claudius II had forbidden the rite of marriage so that he could recruit more soldiers. Valentine supposedly ignored this official order and performed secret marriages. As a result, he was arrested and then executed.

697. Shrovetide is the three days before Ash Wednesday. The dates are sometimes referred to as Shrove Sunday, Shrove Monday, and Shrove Tuesday. The main point of the holidays comes from the name "shrove," which means "to make confession and do penance for one's sins."

698. Ash Wednesday is the seventh Wednesday before Easter and also the first day of Lent. Many Christians attend special services and receive a mark of ash on their foreheads as a sign of their sorrow over sin and understanding of their mortality.

699. Palm Sunday is the Sunday before Easter. This holiday is often commemorated with displays of palm branches or parades with the carrying of palm branches in memory of Jesus' entry into Jerusalem the week before he was crucified. According to Scripture, the crowds laid palm branches in front of the donkey carrying him, and they praised Jesus, shouting "Hosannah!"

700. Maundy Thursday is the last Thursday before Easter Sunday. The day is considered very special to the church and is observed in memory of the Last Supper Jesus shared with his disciples. The term "Maundy" comes from the Middle English *maunde*. This refers to the ceremony of the washing of feet, which Jesus did and commanded of his disciples at the Last Supper.

701. In England the custom for Maundy Thursday used to include the reigning monarch performing the foot-washing ceremony on several persons and then distributing gifts to the needy. The custom of foot washing was dropped, but gifts are still handed out by English royalty.

702. Good Friday occurs on the Friday before Easter Sunday. Christians observe this day in memory of Christ's ultimate sacrifice, his earthly death on the cross. Church services are somber and reflect on Christ's love for his people in carrying their sins to the cross.

703. Easter Sunday rarely falls on the same Sunday as the year before, but its day determines many of the other Christian holidays. Easter celebrates the resurrection of Jesus from the tomb and can be determined as the first Sunday that follows the full moon occurring on or after March 21. The two branches of the early church (East and West) disagreed about what day Easter was to be celebrated on, and so the bishop of Rome threatened excommunication on those who did not adopt the Roman date.

704. Ascension Day is the fortieth day after Easter. Jesus' ascent into heaven is described in Scripture. The day of his ascension is considered the last time he was seen on earth in his physical, bodily form.

705. The Passover holiday falls on the fourteenth day in the Jewish month of Nisan, which corresponds to our calendar months of March and April. This eight-day celebration commemorates the exodus of the Israelites from Egypt.

706. Pentecost is the seventh Sunday after Easter and commemorates the descent of the Holy Spirit upon the disciples. The term comes from the Middle English *pentecoste*, which in turn is from the Latin *pentecoste* and the Greek *pentekoste*. They all mean "fiftieth" or "fiftieth day" and correspond to Pentecost's occurrence fifty days after Easter.

707. Another name for Pentecost emerged as a reference to the white robes that were worn for baptism on Pentecost Sunday: Whitsunday.

708. Trinity Sunday is the first Sunday after Pentecost. The purpose of this feast day is to honor and celebrate the three distinct figures of the Trinity: Father, Son, and Holy Spirit.

709. Reformation Day is celebrated October 31. Protestant Christians commemorate the day Martin Luther nailed his Ninety-five Theses on the door of a church in Wittenberg, Germany, in 1517. His declarations were the starting point of the Protestant Reformation. Many Reformed churches use this religious holiday as an alternative to Halloween, or All Hallows Eve, which is celebrated on the same day.

710. The Feast of Christ the King is celebrated by both Roman Catholics and Protestant Christians, but they celebrate Christ's position as the ruler of all nations on separate days. Roman Catholics observe this feast day on the last Sunday in November. Protestants celebrate this holiday on the last Sunday in August.

711. Advent Sunday is that Sunday nearest to November 30. Advent Sunday is a moveable holiday; the length of advent depends entirely on when Advent Sunday falls—this season of preparation for Christmas may be between twenty-two to twenty-eight days long.

712. December 25, Christmas Day, was not a permanent holiday until Pope Julius I made it so in the fourth century. Because the day coincided with the pagan rituals of winter solstice (return of the sun), the intent was to replace the pagan celebration with a Christian one.

713. The first living nativity scene was staged by Francis of Assisi on December 24, 1223. He used live animals with a cave as a backdrop near Greccio, Italy.

714. Saint Nicholas, who was bishop of Myra, was one of the most popular saints in Greek and Latin churches. He died in 345. Nicholas was Santa Claus's namesake, thanks to his penchant for giving gifts to needy children.

24

Heresies and Heretics

715. New Age religions didn't spring up in the late twentieth century. In the first century, the peace and prosperity brought by Roman armies led to a time of reflection. Masses of people seeking "new truth" began to embrace eastern religions. Along with the growth of Christianity came churches preaching the worship of Dionysus, Mithras, Cybele, Isis, and many other gods.

716. Gnosticism was a first-century heresy that taught that the physical world was evil, that God is distant and uninvolved, and that salvation is obtained by those who can understand special, secret teachings. The word *gnosis* means "to know," and the Gnostics believed they had special knowledge that was unavailable to most people. They denied the humanity and death of

Jesus Christ, took a stance against most Christians, and created false "gospels" purported to have been written by various apostles. Irenaeus, the bishop of Lyons, wrote *Against Heresies* as a response to gnosticism, contrasting the humility of true faith to the conceit of those who believe they share special knowledge, noting that the original apostles taught publicly and kept nothing secret. Irenaeus was the first to insist that all the "truth" believers require can be found in the Bible.

717. Docetism was a first-century heresy that claimed Christ was not a man but a phantom who only "seemed" like a man in order to share his moral teachings. The name comes from the Greek word "to seem"; Docetists rejected the notion of God in the flesh. It apparently was this heresy that led the apostle John to begin his first letter, "That . . . which we have heard, which we have seen with our eyes, which we have looked at and *our hands have touched*—this we proclaim. . . . The life appeared; we have seen it and testify to it" (1 John 1:1–2, emphasis added).

718. Belief in the virgin birth was not that difficult of a leap for first- and second-century spiritists. The problem they faced was in the concept that the Son of God could be "born" at all. Because they viewed God as purely good and spiritual and physical matter as base and evil, most people did not believe he could come in the flesh.

719. Marcion, a wealthy shipbuilder from Rome, was one of the most influential heretics of the early church. Preaching that the God of the Old Testament is different from that of the New Testament (in that the Old Testament God was wrathful and evil, while the New Testament God was loving and gracious), Marcion rejected the entire Old Testament, accepted the letters of Paul, and proceeded to go through Luke's Gospel and trim out the portions that didn't fit his theology. It was in response to Marcion's heresy that the church decided to clarify the canon of Scripture.

720. In rejecting Marcion, many in the early church rejected the apostle Paul. Tertullian once noted that most heretical groups referred more to Paul than to the Gospels and called him "the apostle of the heretics." However, taking Paul's writings in context, and seeing them as a link between the Gospels of Jesus and the growth of the church in Acts, the second- and third-century church decided to keep the letters of Paul in its worship services.

721. Montanus was the first Elmer Gantry. A charismatic speaker in the mid–second century, Montanus and his two assistants, Prisca and Maximilla, went about doing spiritual shows and prophesying, warning that the end times were at hand. He claimed to speak in a state of ecstasy, his personality suspended while the Spirit spoke through him. Churches split over his message, and eventually he was condemned for immoral behavior.

722. The Secret Book of James was a second-century forgery claiming to present "a secret book revealed . . . by the Lord." A mish-mash of Christ's sayings wrapped around a supposed dialogue between Peter and Jesus, the book calls Jesus the "Child of Humanity," decrees "woe to those who have found rest for their sickness," and offers enlightening lessons such as "To be filled is good and to lack is bad, yet it is also good for you to be lacking but bad for you to be filled."

723. The Secret Sayings of Jesus (also called *The Gospel of Thomas*) is a random collection of 113 quotes said to be from the Savior. They range from the silly ("Whoever interprets these sayings will not taste death") to the inane ("Cursed is the human that the lion eats, so that the lion becomes human") to the downright heretical ("Every woman who makes herself male will enter the kingdom of heaven"). A Gnostic book, it claimed to hold secret knowledge the average Christian had never heard. When Thomas, the purported author, was asked to reveal all the wise sayings of Jesus, he claimed he couldn't reveal them all for fear of "fire coming from the rocks" and consuming him.

724. The Secret Sayings of the Savior (also known as *The Book of Thomas*) was another Gnostic forgery, this time claiming to be a vision given to Thomas just before death. In it, the author promotes all the typical Gnostic heresies: The physical world is evil; sex is a curse; the human soul needs enlightenment; every person has an inner spark that offers wisdom and salvation; and we should all follow our inner desires. Recent New Age gurus have latched on to this and claimed it as a new teaching.

725. The Secret Book of John claims to be a second revelation, the first one apparently not having been explained adequately. It presents pantheism (the notion that everything is god) as the secret truth, wraps up the entire Christ story in a metaphor about a female angel, and then describes by name all the angels who are watching over the various parts of the body. ("Bilbo" watches over your kidneys.) A confusing mess, it covers all the typical heresies.

726. Pelagianism maintained that sin is not an inherited trait, but that people choose to obey or disobey. Proposed by the monk Pelagius, it asserted that a man, by way of ascetic self-control, could live a sinless life. Augustine, who knew what it was like to sin, argued successfully that both Scripture and experience reveal humankind to be hopelessly sinful, unable to save itself and therefore in need of the atonement found only in Jesus Christ.

727. Paul of Samosata was bishop of Antioch from 260 to 268. He encouraged applause during sermons and had choirs of women sing praises specifically to him. He wouldn't allow the congregation to sing hymns to Jesus. The bishop also served as chief finance minister to the crown, but he was removed in 272 after being charged with financial misconduct (embezzlement and bribes).

728. Arius denied the divinity of Christ in 315 and claimed Jesus was subordinate to the Father, a teaching called Arianism. His teachings caused great controversy in the churches in the East for many years. The Council of Nicaea in 325 refuted his beliefs.

729. Manicheanism, a third- and fourth-century heresy, taught that Jesus had no material body, did not suffer, and thus did not actually die. Instead, his purpose was to teach men how to be "light." Its founder, Mani, claimed the universe is in a giant battle between good and evil, and that every man must attempt to free the good in himself by abstaining from anything enjoyable. It is believed that Mani died by crucifixion in 276.

730. The Apollinarian Heresy, though it took place in the mid–fourth century, would fit right in with modern psychology. Apollinarius claimed that Christ, being divine, could not have been fully human.

731. The Nestorian Heresy came about in the early 400s, when Nestorius, bishop of Constantinople, tried to argue against the idea that Mary was "the mother of God." In doing so, Nestorius separated the human Jesus from the divine Jesus. While it isn't clear exactly what he meant, his political enemies used his words to have him excommunicated, claiming that he was teaching heresy. He received a letter in 431 from the church council addressed to "Nestorius, the New Judas." The Nestorian church that sprang up after him still exists in Iraq and Syria and has a long history of active missionary work.

732. Monophysitism ("one nature") was a heresy taught by Eutyches in c. 433. He claimed that Christ's humanity was lost in his divinity. Christian scholars immediately recognized that this teaching threatened the doctrine of redemption; if Jesus was not fully God and fully man, how could he redeem us? Those who agreed with Eutyches broke away and formed the Coptic Church, still the largest Christian group in Egypt, and the Jacobite Church, with followers in Syria and India.

733. The Cathari was a dissent movement in southern France during the early 1200s that wanted to reform the church by advocating extreme poverty. They set up communes in which "the Cathari" (which means "the pure ones") would avoid marriage, sex, meat, possessions, and money. They were also one of the first to try to expunge all differences between the sexes. However, they fell into heretical teaching by rejecting both the God and the text of the Old Testament, claiming that he was at war with the God of the New Testament. They came to believe that God could not come in the flesh, so they rejected Jesus as divine but revered him as a great teacher of truth. Though the Cathari had powerful German protectors, Pope Innocent III sent armies from northern France to wipe them out, then announced that he was "shocked" at the brutality.

734. The Brethren of the Free Spirit was a group of people in the 1370s who claimed to be in such a state of grace that God lived in them. Because they considered themselves perfect, they felt free to walk around naked, steal people's property, and practice adultery (those who left the group claimed there had even been orgies). They were called by commoners "the Beg-hards" because they wore tattered clothing and contrasted their poverty to the church's wealth while interrupting services and mocking priests. We get the term "free spirit" from this group.

735. The Beguines were a women's group, similar to the Beghards, but much more articulate. They were mystics, publicly read the Bible in French, and encouraged married women to go on retreats with them to get away from "the coercion of marital bonds." Their leader was Marguerite Porete, who wrote *The Mirror of Free Souls* and advocated a free lifestyle without moral boundaries as a means of finding salvation. Marguerite and her book were burned at the stake in 1310.

736. The Bloemardine was another group interested in free lifestyles. In 1372 they were condemned by the Inquisition, and their leader, Jeanne Dabenton, was burned at the stake along with the corpse of a male associate who had died in prison. The next year Pope Gregory XI began issuing orders that anyone taking the Bloemardine approach was in league with the devil, and he ordered both their members and their books to be sought out and destroyed.

737. Anabaptist heretics, particularly those who were women, garnered attention. Margareta Hattinger at one point claimed to be God. She spoke so that no one could understand her and claimed it was because she was speaking with God at a level known only to her. She was a target of reformers, but it is unknown what became of her.

738. Anne Hutchinson was banished in 1637 by the Massachusetts Bay Colony for her belief that moral law was unnecessary (due to the higher law of Scripture) as well as for her claim that she received messages from the Holy Spirit. She is perhaps the first heretic of the New World.

739. There were more than one hundred "Utopias" founded in the United States between 1580 and 1861. The country was large, land was cheap, and the sparse population allowed self-contained, experimental communities to practice their religion generally undisturbed by their neighbors.

740. Shaker Village was founded by Mother Ann Lee near Albany, New York, in the 1770s. Mother Ann, who had four stillborn children and who almost died in childbirth, became convinced because of her difficult pregnancies that "cohabitation of the sexes" was evil. She and her followers practiced celibacy as the means toward holiness. Mother Ann also believed the millennium was at hand and that Christ had returned to earth, residing in her person. After her death, the Shaker movement expanded, becoming a joyful and profoundly emotional religion whose practitioners lived together in harmony, gaining the name "Shaker" for their wild dancing and gyrating while "worshiping in the Spirit." They also produced remarkable furniture that was simple, beautiful, and still influential today.

741. Harmony, founded in western Pennsylvania in 1804 by George Rapp, a German immigrant, was another celibate, hard-working sect. They pooled their money and prospered greatly, but every aspect of life was ruled with an iron fist by "Father" Rapp (for example, anyone who had committed a sin during the day was required to confess it to Rapp before going to bed that night). He moved the entire community to Indiana purely on a whim, then back to Pennsylvania before dying in 1847. Harmony disbanded thereafter, but the land was sold to Robert Owen, an English industrialist.

742. New Harmony was a socialist community of nine hundred people founded by Robert Owen. Owen's son described it as "a heterogeneous collection of radicals, latitudinarians, and lazy theorists, with a sprinkling of unprincipled sharpers thrown in." The community quickly fell apart because of "the disease of laziness."

743. Nashoba in Tennessee was started by Frances Wright, a follower of Robert Owen. Nashoba was a plantation in which African American slaves and white laborers worked together in a friendly atmosphere, sharing skills with one another. The plan was for the slaves to be freed and set up with their own farms back in Africa, but the money quickly ran out, the slaves were sent to Haiti, and Miss Wright began a new crusade, advocating the abolition of marriage. In fact, she got into trouble when she criticized monogamy as unbiblical, and she was labeled by the press "the Priestess of Beelzebub."

744. Oneida was founded in 1848 by John Humphrey Noyes, who believed that once a person "converted," he or she should be free of sin and totally happy. Noyes designed his own marriage system, in which all the men were married to all the women and contact between the sexes was regulated by a leadership group. He also insisted all the children were to be raised in community nurseries devoid of sports and competition. Wrongdoers were subjected to "mutual criticism" by the leadership. While the socialism and complex marriage ideas proved disastrous, the high-quality silverware the commune produced to pay the bills ended up making them a fortune. Eventually, they dropped the religious aspects and became a corporation. Oneida is still in the business of making silverware to this day.

25

Missions

745. Saint Patrick is arguably the best and most neglected missionary in history. Captured in Britain as a boy and forced to work as a slave in Ireland, he eventually escaped to a Mediterranean monastery in France. But a dream of Irish children begging him to return caused Patrick to sail back to Ireland in 432. The church had never taken hold in Ireland, but Patrick knew how to reach the people. He established 300 churches, baptized roughly 120,000 converts, and ministered effectively in a land that had abused other monks who had made an attempt. He did this outside the established church hierarchy and without a single martyr or riot—an accomplishment almost unequaled in history. When missionaries came to Ireland more than 200 years later, they discovered thriving Irish churches.

746. Irish missionaries and churchmen made a huge impact on the world during the Dark Ages. While the Roman borders were falling to various nomadic tribes, libraries were being burned, and churches were being sacked, Ireland was a land of peace. Columba, an Irish missionary, took the gospel to Scotland and was the first to convert the Picts. Irish scribes also protected and copied many of the great ancient manuscripts, which kept them from being lost.

747. Cyril was a Greek missionary to the Slavic kingdom in the mid–ninth century. Though not knowing the Slavic language, Cyril and his brother Methodius created a written language (now known as the "Cyrillic" alphabet), translated the Bible into Slavonic, then began holding services in the Slavic language, because none of the commoners spoke Latin. He did all of this without the approval of Rome, which got him in trouble with the church hierarchy. However, his work renewed the biblical missionary strategy of visiting foreign lands, learning their language, and translating the Bible into the common tongue.

748. St. Boniface is considered by some to be the greatest missionary of the years between 700 and 1000. He strongly believed in preaching to heathens in every area that was reachable. His ministry led to the spread of the gospel in what would eventually become Germany, which was a hub for many other areas.

749. Cutting the "Thundering Tree" in Germany turned Boniface from just another missionary into a German hero. The church had struggled to take hold in Germany, where the people generally followed a mix of Arianism and pagan rituals. One of the symbols of their religion was the Thundering Tree of Hesse, which was supposedly the abode of the thunder god, Donar. Boniface, a missionary who had failed to gain the attention of the Germanic people, simply took an axe to the tree and chopped it down in 725. The crowd watching his action was stunned that Donar did not respond. As a result, they began listening to the message Boniface had for them.

750. Christianity came to Russia in 988 when a hard-partying ruler with five wives decided he wanted to use religion to unite his people. Vladimir, prince of Russia, sent out four representatives to investigate Judaism, Islam, the Roman Church, and the church in Constantinople. The representatives returned, saying the first three were too strict, but the latter, Orthodox Christianity, offered worship that had "beauty and splendor . . . We do not know whether we were in heaven or on earth." Appreciating a good show, Vladimir chose Orthodox Christianity. But to be fair, Vladimir, upon hearing the gospel, also changed his life. He put away his five wives, destroyed the ancient Russian idols, established schools and churches, and, upon his death, gave all his possessions to the poor.

751. Grand Prince Vladimir ordered that all people of Russia be baptized into the Orthodox Christian faith. He personally watched the proceedings take place in the capital city of Kiev and was himself baptized.

752. Anthony of Padua was called the "Hammer of Heretics" because he converted so many of the Cathari, a heretical sect in western Europe. He was the most effective preacher of the twelfth century, and according to legend, he was so passionate about spreading the gospel that he once preached to a school of fish!

753. Francis Xavier, a disciple of Loyola and founding member of the Jesuit order, traveled as a missionary to the seaport of Goa on the western shore of India. In preaching the gospel, Xavier led thousands to Jesus Christ. He went all over the region, teaching the people to recite the Lord's Prayer and the Apostles' Creed, and baptized so many believers (approximately 700,000) that at times he could no longer lift his arms. However, the caste system prevented the people of Goa from sharing their faith with the rest of India, so they became an island of Christianity, surrounded by a sea of Hinduism. Xavier died in 1552 while awaiting admission to China, where he wished to continue his work.

754. The Imperial Church was the title given to missionaries visiting remote people groups. Rather than living like the nationals, most missionaries saw themselves as conquerors, needing to destroy paganism and instruct the people in Christianity. Xavier tried to change that among the Jesuits by allowing people to adapt the Christian faith to their culture. When he traveled to Japan with that approach, he led more than two thousand to a saving faith in Christ. That group founded a city as a home for Christian believers in Japan—the city of Nagasaki.

755. The Jesuits of Nagasaki—Dozens of Jesuit missionaries were crucified at Nagasaki in 1597 in an attempt to wipe out Christian witness in Japan. Almost three hundred years later, when British missionaries returned to the region, they were shocked to discover some Japanese congregations still surviving that had been founded by the Jesuits.

756. The first mission to China was attempted by Francis Xavier in 1552. Unable to enter the country because of the policies of the Ming Dynasty, he smuggled himself into Canton aboard a ship. However, having to hide in the hold kept him in dank, filthy quarters. He fell ill on board, got as far as the coast of China, and died.

757. The door to China finally opened when, thirty years after Xavier's death, one of his disciples, Matthew Ricci, gained permission to visit. To prepare, Ricci spent three years learning the language and dressing in Chinese garb. He offered to come teach geography and astronomy to the Chinese emperor's councilors. By the time he died in 1610, his church numbered two thousand people.

758. The door to China closed when, after Ricci's death, some Dominican and Franciscan missionaries visited his church and were appalled to find the people living their Christianity through Chinese culture. They found it scandalous that the Chinese church didn't perform the ceremonies of Rome, and they appealed to the pope to change things. Pope Paul V agreed, and within twenty years the Christian church had all but died out in China.

759. "The only memorial I desire is prison reform."—spoken by John Howard, sheriff of Bedfordshire, when told that the members of his home church were raising money for a statue in his honor in 1787. Howard had seen the squalid conditions of English prisons and had watched poor people suffer merely for begging for bread. He traveled fifty thousand miles preaching prison reform in various Christian churches and spent thirty thousand pounds of his own money to move fellow believers to action, but his efforts were largely fruitless. Upon returning from a tour of French and Italian prisons, he discovered that his hometown friends (many of whom had refused to donate to prison reform) were planning to erect a statue of his likeness for the town square.

760. The small community of Herrnhut, Germany (six hundred people), sent seventy of its own as missionaries to slaves in the West Indies between 1732 and 1742, which shows how motivated they were to evangelize. Many lost their lives, and yet those sent received loving farewell celebrations that included the singing of one hundred hymns.

761. Junipero Serra is remembered as the "Apostle of California." He established nine of the first twenty-one Franciscan missions in the eighteenth century in what is now California. His work as a Franciscan missionary included baptizing six thousand Native Americans.

762. David Brainerd was best known for his evangelizing work with Native Americans in New Jersey beginning in 1744. His record as a student at Yale is less revered. Brainerd was kicked out after criticizing a tutor and attending a forbidden revival meeting. He died at twenty-nine of tuberculosis at the home of Jonathan Edwards. Edwards later wrote Brainerd's life story, which served as an inspiration to many to enter the mission field.

763. Alexander Smith was the only man to survive the mutiny on the famous *Bounty* in 1789. Smith ended up stranded on Pitcairn Island with other female survivors. He became a Christian after he accidentally found the ship's Bible and repented of his previous lifestyle. Smith went on to transform the community with the gospel message. The original Bible is still on display at a local church.

764. William Branwell played a key role in the English revival during the early years of the nineteenth century. He was famous for his five o'clock morning prayer meetings. He believed prayer was the key to revival and never began a circuit of preaching without preparing first with prayer. He would rise at four in the morning and then pray so loudly he could be heard for several blocks. If he didn't have a five o'clock meeting, he would continue to pray.

765. William Carey is often described as "the father of the modern mission movement," but he was a poor, self-taught cobbler, unable to adequately feed or clothe his children, and was married to a woman with serious psychological problems. After the family sailed to India in 1793, their youngest child died, the oldest ran away, and they didn't see a single conversion during their first ten years. On top of that, it turned out that Carey's physician partner had traveled to India to escape his creditors. But by the time Carey died in 1834, he had translated the Bible into forty-four languages, started the first Christian churches in India, and revolutionized the philosophy of missions by endorsing women in ministry, encouraging national pastors, and insisting "teams" of missionaries work together in a country.

766. The Free African Society was formed in 1787 and led by Richard Allen, an African American preacher who was born a slave in 1760 yet attained his freedom when his owner was converted. Allen loved to preach and desired to reach other Africans who were unchurched. The society was formed to act as a nondenominational society offering aid to those Africans in need.

767. The China Inland Mission was started by Hudson Taylor in 1865. The organization refused to accept any payment and their platform was to trust God for everything. That honorable position quickly became known across China, and many people who had refused to listen to the gospel decided to talk with the missionaries of CIM.

768. Hudson Taylor wasn't the first missionary to China; he was simply the first *modern* missionary. He dressed like the Chinese, wore his hair as they did, and eschewed all Western ways.

He also welcomed women missionaries (even *single* women, which was almost unheard of at the time), focused on medical assistance to minister effectively to a felt need, and ran his mission group as a collective. No one was guaranteed a salary, but each would share all income evenly. Taylor's work changed the face of missions, and his China Inland Mission grew into the largest mission effort in that nation's history.

769. **"Why need such a foreign aspect be given to Christianity?"** This was the question asked by Hudson Taylor when challenged to describe his unique approach to missionary work. Rather than asking the Chinese to conform to Western culture, he immersed himself in Chinese culture to win their trust, noting, "It is not their de-nationalization but their *Christianization* that we seek."

770. **The Taiping Rebellion,** which took place in China during the middle of the nineteenth century, was proclaimed as great news to Christian missionaries. Hearing that Christian rebels were attempting to oust the Manchu Dynasty, mission boards sent dozens of new missionaries in to support them. Unfortunately, the mission boards were mistaken. While the leader of the rebels had been influenced by Christians and wanted to rid China of idolatry, his theology was a mixed bag of animism, ancestor worship, and Christianity (he once proclaimed himself the "younger brother" of Jesus Christ). Millions of Chinese died in the civil war, and many missionaries lost their lives. Worse, the Christians had sided with the Taiping, who lost after much bloodshed, setting back the cause of the gospel for years.

771. **Three missionaries heard Henry Stanley's call** for missionaries to take David Livingstone's place on a mission into Uganda. The members of Alexander Mackay's Church Missionary Society team arrived in 1877. Though they did not see the work prosper, the Ugandan church grew quickly and strengthened after their deaths.

772. **The Boxer Rebellion** of 1900 was an attack on missionaries and westerners by Chinese "secret societies" (and backed by the Manchu government) in an attempt to rid China of Chris-

tian influences. The members of these societies were called "Boxers" because their martial arts ceremonial movements looked to westerners like shadow boxing. The Boxers killed hundreds of people, but a rescue force of eight nations, led by Great Britain, put down the rebellion and demanded reparations from the Chinese government.

773. Adoniram Judson, perhaps the first American foreign missionary, lived a life that would have been great movie material. A brilliant student, he left school to pursue an acting career in New York. When a friend who had encouraged him to reject Christianity died suddenly, Judson rededicated his life to Christ. After reading a book about Burma, he decided to go there as a missionary. But he needed the funds of the London Missionary Society, so he traveled to England by sailing ship, only to be captured by the French and held as a prisoner of war. Upon returning to America, he was greeted by a lovely girl serving as the church representative. They fell in love, got married, and immediately set sail for India as this country's first "missionary couple." Tossed out of India by the British in 1812, Judson was taken captive by Burmese guerrillas, jailed, learned the language while in prison, then was freed by the British, but chose to go back to Burma to plant churches. He served there for thirty years, planted sixty-four churches, and helped translate the Bible into Burmese.

774. The Gideons were founded in 1899 when four businessmen met in a YMCA and decided to organize a nonprofit business for distributing Bibles. The Christian Commercial Men's Association of America (later it was changed to the Gideons) started putting Bibles in hotel rooms nine years later. They have been immensely successful and now distribute 56 million Bibles to over 175 countries each year.

775. David Livingstone was one of the most well-known missionaries of his time. Livingstone only had one convert in his experience as a missionary, but he is popular today because his own experiences served as an inspiration for many more people who decided to enter the mission field.

776. The International Missionary Conference of 1910, meeting in Edinburgh, is generally regarded as the beginning of the ecumenical movement. John Mott, leader of the Student Volunteer Movement, led the thousand delegates to form a "Faith and Order Movement" to seek doctrinal agreement and a "Life and Work Movement" to coordinate missions work. The two movements immediately went in different directions, with the former led by conservatives and the latter led by liberals.

777. The Summer Institute of Linguistics started on a farm in Sulphur Springs, Arkansas, in 1934 by Cameron and Elvira Townsend. The goal was to train future missionaries to reduce a language to writing, then translate the Bible into that language. There were only two students the first year. Eight years later, they had so many translators they helped form Wycliffe Bible Translators to organize support in the United States for translation work around the world.

778. Missionary Dr. E. Stanley Jones felt most comfortable in India, witnessing in the name of Christ. He spent more than twenty years there before returning to America in 1928. The Methodist denomination elected him bishop, but within twenty-four hours he resigned after spending much time in prayer and hearing God's voice calling him back to the mission field. It is estimated that between 1921 and 1931 there were more than a million and a half Christians added to the national churches of India. This was in large part due to Jones's many books on the subject of Christianity.

779. The Sisters of the Common Life was founded by Amy Carmichael, an English missionary to India. Amy served as a missionary for more than fifty years in India, wrote thirty-five books sharing her experiences, and was an inspiration for many women to enter missions. She founded this organization in part to combat the loneliness so common among women missionaries who could not marry, or they would lose their funding from missionary agencies that only funded single women. The work proved a great success and provided single women with a family atmosphere. By the 1950s the members of this organization numbered nine hundred.

780. Wycliffe Bible Translators was formed in 1942 for the purpose of organizing and raising money to train translation experts. Taking a new approach, Wycliffe allied itself with governments, universities, and professors in foreign countries to reach groups of people without a written language. By the end of the century, Wycliffe had produced the Bible in more than 350 languages and were working on 900 more.

781. In 1956 five male missionaries, Jim Elliot, Nate Saint, Roger Youderian, Edward McCully, and Peter Fleming, were killed by Ecuadorean Indians near the Curaray River. Elliot's widow, Elisabeth, told the story of the missionaries the following year in her book *Through Gates of Splendor*.

26

People

782. Justin Martyr is generally recognized as the first Christian apologist. As a young philosophy student, he had explored the teachings of Plato, Aristotle, Pythagoras, and the Stoics, but was looking for Plato's promised "vision of God." When Justin met an elderly Christian man, he found the man to be wise, dignified, and humble, embodying the qualities the ancients had desired. Justin became a follower of Jesus Christ and wrote his *Apology* for Emperor Antoninus Pius, in which he used logic to show why the truth of Christianity exposes the falsehood of pagan religions. He was the first writer to explore the notion of Jesus as "the incarnation," and his exploration of Jesus as a part of God's essence, "as a flame lit from a flame," helped develop our understanding of the Trinity. Arrested in 165, he was tortured and beheaded, but he left the message, "You can kill us, but cannot do us any real harm."

783. Clement of Rome contributed much-needed writings of unity to the early Christians. As bishop of the church in Rome (sometime in the first one hundred years of the church), he was a strong leader for his congregation during the persecutions suffered under Emperor Domitian. He is considered to be one of the apostolic fathers of the early church.

784. Athanasius served as bishop of Alexandria between 328 and 373. He is considered one of the fathers of the church because of his unyielding stand against the beliefs of Arianism, a heretical system of thought. He endured five separate periods of exile for his beliefs.

785. Polycarp was the last living link to the New Testament age. The apostle John had discipled Ignatius, who in turn discipled Polycarp, who had spent some time with the old apostle during his last days. In 156, at the age of eighty-six, Polycarp was arrested in Smyrna for refusing to call Caesar "lord," burn incense to him, and acknowledge his "genius" as divine. Called unpatriotic and an atheist because he refused to participate in such public worship, he was tried before a large assembly. When urged by a judge to curse Christ, Polycarp responded, "Eighty-six years have I served him, and he never did me any wrong. How can I blaspheme my king who has saved me?" He was burned at the stake, but his faith in the face of danger encouraged the believers of his day to take a bold stand for Christ.

786. Irenaeus, the disciple of Polycarp, was born in Asia Minor but moved to Gaul (modern-day France) c. 160. As bishop of Lyons, he battled with Gnostic heretics, eventually writing *Against Heresies.* The book was largely responsible for destroying the Gnostic faith in the second century. A brilliant theologian, Irenaeus noted that the original apostles did nothing in secret, and he declared that "bishops" were the apostles' successors, the defenders of the faith. That argument enhanced the reputation of bishops, leading eventually to the notion of a hierarchical structure in the church.

787. Tertullian was an African writer who changed the face of Christian thinking. In 196 he began writing books in Latin, rather than the commonly used Greek, because Latin allowed more precision and less philosophizing. He elucidated the doctrine of the Trinity, posited the three-fold aspect of humankind (body, soul, and spirit), and was the first to create the theological constructs for baptism and the Lord's Supper. Tertullian eventually left the church to join a puritan movement because he was disturbed by the bishops' claim that they had the power to pardon sin and because he wanted to live in a community where there were no "professional" clergy. Once asked how he could believe the gospel account, his famous reply was "I believe because it is impossible."

788. Origen, the greatest scholar of the third century, was born to Christian parents in Alexandria c. 185. When his father was imprisoned and sentenced to death, the teenage Origen meant to go join him in martyrdom. Fortunately for the church, Origen's mother hid his clothes, keeping him from participating. When Rome confiscated all his property, Origen began teaching Greek literature to support his widowed mother. He would continue teaching the rest of his life and go on to write more than eight hundred books and hundreds of sermons, including the first attempt at a systematic theology, *On First Principles.* Unfortunately, Origen was deeply influenced by Gnostic thought, ignoring the clear words of Scripture in order to create allegorical interpretations that he claimed offered the hidden meanings of the faith.

789. Cyprian was a wealthy orator who became a Christian and tried to use his gifts to assist a divided church. When Emperor Decius had persecuted Christians, attempting to get them to say the words, "Caesar is Lord," some had given in to the pain while others had held out. Those who had said the words were known as "the lapsed," while those who had refused to say the words were called "the confessors." As you can imagine, the latter looked down on the former. Eventually, a priest, Novatus, started a church with a message of grace for the lapsed. In response, Cyprian created a system by which a lapsed believer could do penance and prove his or her faith. It involved wearing sackcloth, dumping ashes on your head, acting sorrowful, and appearing before the bishop to ask forgiveness. The idea caught on, and soon churches everywhere had designed elaborate methods of church discipline.

790. Ambrose was known as a just and capable governor of Milan when the bishop of the church died. Identifying a successor created such a ruckus that Ambrose had to move troops in to quell the strife. In doing so, the people called for him to become bishop. Ambrose may have been a believer but had never been baptized or held a church office. Nevertheless, he was elected, baptized, and moved through each ecclesiastical office in one day before being made bishop a week later. Though perhaps ill-prepared, Ambrose did great work. In one of the most important events in early church history, he refused to turn over the church of Milan to the Empress Justina, who wanted to use it for an Arian congregation. She sent troops, but Ambrose refused to yield, and in the end the troops left. Later, Ambrose would call on the Emperor Valentinian to repent, changing the relationship of the church and the government permanently.

791. Augustine is a towering figure, perhaps the greatest mind the church has ever known. After searching through many philosophies, he heard a child singing, "Take it and read; take it and read." Looking down, he saw a Bible, picked it up, and read Romans 13. "It was as though the light of faith flooded into my heart and all the darkness of doubt dispelled," he wrote later. He became bishop of the important African city of Hippo and began writing books that would dominate the church for a millennium. His *Confessions* tell of his conversion to Christ, but *City of God* is probably his most important work. When Christians were blamed for the fall of Rome to the Visigoths, Augustine explained that there are always two cities in this world: the City of Man and the City of God, representing pagan society and eternal truth. The City of God will endure.

792. John Chrysostom, whose name means "golden mouth," got his nickname for his oratorical skills. Once, when the people of Antioch were rioting over a new tax and the emperor was sending troops to put down the revolt, John stood before crowds of people and challenged them, rebuking them of their intemperance and encouraging them to change their lives for the better. The people relented and disaster was avoided. John, who became the bishop of Constantinople, broke with the tradition of the day and became known for his literal reading of Scripture and his exegetical style of preaching. He died in 407 when, after offending the empress by criticizing her suggestive clothing, he was sent into a remote exile in the rugged mountains around Armenia.

793. Eusebius Hieronymus Sophronius, better known as "Jerome," was hired by Damasus, the bishop of Rome, to create a Latin version of the Bible. Damasus had standardized worship and readings in his church, and he needed an accurate, single-language version that he could make the "standard" for the church. Beginning his work in 382, Jerome didn't finish his translation until 405 (long after the death of Damasus). The unique aspect Jerome brought to the table was that he moved to Bethlehem, consulted with rabbis, and translated the entire Old Testament from the original Hebrew rather than from copies of copies—a scholarly tradition that exists to this day. Jerome also tried to omit the Apocryphal books, because they did not appear in the Jewish Scriptures. His translation was so good it became the common Bible (or "Vulgate") in nearly every church. It was looked upon so highly that eventually church leaders prohibited the Bible from being translated into common languages.

794. Peter Waldo was a wealthy French merchant who, while sitting at a café, heard a wandering troubadour sing a song about the prodigal son. In the song, the son grows to appreciate the poor and says that he will be happy to meet a God who smiles on the unfortunate. Deeply moved, Waldo placed his daughters in a convent, gave away all his money, and began teaching the poor about Jesus Christ. He helped translate the Scriptures into French, encouraged Bible memorization, and encouraged people to follow the leading of the Holy Spirit. This got him into big trouble with the Roman Church, which did not believe the average person could understand the Bible and insisted that all preaching had to be approved by a bishop. Waldo and his followers, known as Waldensians, were excommunicated in 1184, not for teaching heresy, but for teaching the priesthood of all believers, for teaching the Bible to laypeople in their own language, and for rejecting holy water, vestments, saints days, pilgrimages, relics, and the doctrine of purgatory.

795. Arnold, the abbot of Brescia, is best remembered for insisting that clerical vice was a result of the church's attempt to control the world. Critical of papal authority and the lavish lifestyles of cardinals and bishops, he joined himself to Romans anxious to re-establish their empire. When the pope went to the Holy Land during the Second Crusade, Arnold seized power in Rome and set up a secular government. When the pope returned, Arnold was arrested and executed by fire.

796. Francis of Assisi, the son of a wealthy merchant, began to question the value of his wealth after he was captured and abused in war. One day in 1206, while riding his horse, he passed a poor beggar and was struck with the thought that the man had the face of Christ. Overcome with emotion, he gave the man his money and horse, then renounced all worldly possessions. He became a beggar, found eleven friends who joined him in poverty, and drew up a set of rules for living simply. The contrast between the poor followers of Christ and the powerful, wealthy churches of Europe was stark, and within ten years there were more than three thousand devoted Franciscans ministering to the needy in European cities.

797. Thomas Aquinas was the most influential theologian in Roman Catholic history. A Dominican with a brilliant mind, Aquinas (1225–1274) lived in France, studied at the University of Paris, and rediscovered the writings of the ancient Greek philosophers. His voluminous writings were an attempt to codify Roman Catholic theology and support the papacy, and he remains the patron saint of all Catholic colleges today. Aquinas's most impressive theory in the eyes of Roman Catholics is that the papacy and the church hierarchy are necessary in order to mediate the grace of God and pray dead sinners out of purgatory. In 1273 he had some sort of mystical experience, decided that his own arguments were "straw," and stopped writing.

798. Dante Alighieri, author of the *Divine Comedy*, recognized the outrageous actions of Boniface VIII. In his description of hell, Dante reserves a special place for Boniface. Within four years of Boniface's death, the College of Cardinals elected a Frenchman as pope—Clement V. The new pope never set foot in Rome, choosing to remain in France and setting up his base of operation in Avignon. It would remain the seat of power in the Catholic Church until 1377.

799. John Wycliffe was an Oxford professor who questioned the Roman Catholic Church for its sales of indulgences, its doctrine of transubstantiation, and its superstitious worship of saints and relics. However, what really got him into trouble was stating that, "As the Bible . . . is necessary for salvation, it is necessary for all men, not for priests alone." Wycliffe translated the Bible into English in 1382, then worked with the Lollards to distribute it. Thirty-one years after his death, the Council of Constance condemned Wycliffe for his actions. Excommunication apparently not being enough, they then exhumed his bones, burned them, and scattered the ashes on the river Swift.

800. Ignatius Loyola (1491–1556) was a Spanish nobleman who, after being badly wounded in a war with France, spent a year convalescing in a Benedictine abbey. Seeking spiritual peace, he eventually exchanged his wealthy life for the ascetic life of a monk, begging door to door, fasting for days on end, and even wearing a barbed wire girdle to keep himself uncomfortable. One night he experienced a spiritual breakthrough, felt he had become "a new man," and founded "the Society of Jesus," later called the Jesuits, who would become the frontline of the Roman Catholic Church in its battle for followers across Europe and around the globe.

801. Jan Hus was a Czech priest who, in his writings in the early 1400s, contrasted the pope and Jesus Christ: Jesus walked barefoot, while the pope rode a grand horse; Jesus washed his disciples' feet, while the pope had underlings kiss his feet. In *On the Church*, Hus asserted that Christ alone is the head of the church and no pope could establish doctrine contrary to Scripture. Summoned to the Council of Constance and promised safe passage, he was immediately arrested, imprisoned, and burned at the stake.

802. Desiderius Erasmus is said to have "laid the egg which Luther hatched" in reference to hastening along the Reformation. Martin Luther called him "an eel whom only Christ could catch." Erasmus's main contribution to Christian thought was his edition of the Greek New Testament, which was the very first to be printed. He was critical of the church and wasn't afraid to write about it in his other well-received satires on the church. The illegitimate son of a priest, he tried being a monk but found it wasn't for him. Instead he traveled, wrote, and studied. He is said to have been always poor not because his writings didn't sell but because he spent his money on books, good food, and fancy clothes.

803. John Calvin not only pastored a church in Geneva, he preached three sermons each day, wrote commentaries on nearly every book in the Bible, and produced his landmark *The Institutes of the Christian Religion* by the age of twenty-seven. His focus on God saving man, rather than man earning salvation, gave voice to the essential aspect of the Protestant Reformation. His emphasis on discipline leaves many students of history thinking that he was a somber, joyless man, but Calvin is revealed in his personal journals as a man who took great joy in knowing God. He once wrote, "There is not one blade of grass in this world that is not intended to make us rejoice."

804. Miles Coverdale, an English pastor and scholar, was a Roman Catholic friar who converted to Protestantism in 1528. After preaching a series of sermons on the theology of Martin Luther, he was run out of England and joined William Tyndale on the continent, where he helped with the translation of the Pentateuch from Latin into English. Inspired by that work, Coverdale became the first to translate the entire Bible into

English. Known as *The Coverdale Bible,* it was printed in 1535. He then helped revise *Matthew's Bible* into *The Great Bible* and was one of the committee members who produced *The Geneva Bible;* he did all this without a working knowledge of Hebrew.

805. George Wishart is considered to be one of the most gracious men in Christendom. Wishart was a Scottish Bible teacher who routinely came into conflict with the Catholic Church of the 1500s. Once, when a local cardinal hired a priest named John Wigton to kill Wishart after a church service, Wishart sensed that something was amiss. Seizing Wigton, he knocked a knife from the would-be assassin's hand. The congregation, realizing what had happened, raced to grab Wigton, but Wishart put his arms around the man and said, "If you are to hurt him, you must hurt me, too . . . I am not hurt, but this man has done us all a great favor, showing us what we are up against." Four years later, Wishart was arrested, strangled, and burned at the stake. But the leadership of the Scottish reform movement passed on to Wishart's bodyguard— a man named John Knox.

806. John Knox (1505–1572), a Scottish reformer, spent several years as a galley slave on a French man-o-war. When freed, he studied under John Calvin in Geneva, returning to Scotland in 1559 to launch the Scottish Reformation. He opposed the papacy and was challenged by Mary, Queen of Scots, but he helped develop an army that defeated Mary and ushered in a reformation. A strong preacher who wrote not only a Scottish liturgy (*The Book of Common Order,* 1564) but a *Book of Discipline* and a *Confession of Faith,* Knox was rigid and critical, eventually alienating most of his friends.

807. The Conscience of the New World was Bartholomew de las Casas, a Spanish conquistador who, after witnessing the suffering of the Native Americans, became a monk and began denouncing the cruelties of the Spanish armies. Making fourteen trips across the Atlantic, las Casas urged King Charles to protect the rights of the Native Americans, and argued that the way to win converts was to treat people with respect, not to try to force the Christian religion on them with the sword. Charles amended the laws in 1542, but Spanish atrocities would continue for years.

808. Nicolas Oresme thought that sorcery was a game and astrology was bunk, denied that anyone had magical powers, and preferred to look for natural causes behind alleged "miracles." Pointing out that magicians used illusions, mirrors, drugs, and sleight-of-hand, he was pointedly critical of priests who faked miraculous powers in order to increase donations. Oresme was probably the first to suggest that some visions were nothing more than hallucinations caused by mental illness.

809. Jacob Arminius was a Dutch professor in the late 1500s who tried to modify Calvinism, the dominant theology of his culture. Opposed to the doctrine of predestination (he claimed it made God "arbitrary" and "evil"), Arminius claimed that God willed the salvation of all people and that everyone had the free will to accept his grace. John Wesley took up the cause of "Arminianism" two hundred years later and founded the Methodist Church.

810. Matthew Henry was influenced most strongly by the Puritans. He was ordained in secret to get around Britain's Act of Uniformity. He is most remembered for his commentary on the Bible, and he rose before dawn each day to work on it. He was able to complete the commentary through the Book of Acts before his death in 1714. Friends composed the rest of the manuscript from his notes.

811. St. Vincent de Paul was born in 1581. He spent his life dedicated to working with the poor and providing for their well-being. The enterprise "St. Vincent de Paul" is now a well-known organization and continues to help those in need. De Paul was canonized in 1737 and became a patron saint in 1885.

812. Johannes Amos Comenius was a Protestant pastor in Bohemia caught up in the Thirty Years' War. Thrown out of Prague in 1628, he led a group of believers across the mountains and into Poland, stopping at the pass to look back on their country, kneel, and pray for peace. Spending the rest of his life as an itinerant pastor meeting the needs of small groups of Bohemian believers, he authored a series of articles on the education of children. Comenius advocated hands-on learning, the integration of activities rather than mere learning by rote, and studying science in nature rather than in a classroom. The first to write about learning as a matter of "growth" rather than simply the acquisition of information, Comenius recommended a three-part course of study: six years of elementary school, six years of secondary school, and six years of university study. Though largely ignored at the time, his ideas were put into practice throughout Europe and the Americas in the nineteenth century, and he is now referred to as "the father of modern education."

813. George Fox was a man uncomfortable with convention. Disliking the formalities of church, clergy, and worship, he said that all Christians were simply "the friends of Jesus," and he called on them to live simple lives, opposing organized churches, fancy dress, and all forms of war. When Fox was arrested in 1650 for his teachings, the judge mocked his group's beliefs, causing Fox to warn the man to "tremble at the Word of God." The judge quickly replied that Fox and his followers were the ones who were afraid. "You are the tremblers, the quakers," the judge stated. That name stuck, and today the Society of Friends are still referred to as "The Quakers."

814. William Penn, a nonconformist scholar influenced by the words of George Fox, founded the colony of Pennsylvania in 1682 as a refuge for Quakers. Named governor by King Charles II, he lost that title when he was presumed (wrongly) to have supported James II in his battle for the crown. In 1701 Penn made sure the province became a Crown Colony. His insistence on religious freedom had a profound impact on the creators of the American constitution, and his writings were quoted extensively by the founding fathers.

815. Sir Isaac Newton is best remembered for his law of gravity and his work on the physics of light. What is not as well known is that Newton believed his scientific discoveries were communicated to him via the Holy Spirit and that he regarded "the understanding of Scripture as more important" than his scientific work.

816. **John Wesley** was an Anglican pastor who, in an attempt to better himself, joined a "Holy Club" that relied on stringent methods to develop a holy life. Unsatisfied with the results, he sailed to America in hopes of finding meaning through missionary work. During that trip, a violent storm frightened Wesley, but he was struck by the calm faith of some Moravians sailing with him. When he returned to England, he was invited to a meeting, and there discovered that salvation is found in trusting Christ, not in one's actions. Turning his life over to Jesus, he began preaching a message of grace.

817. **John and Molly Wesley** didn't have the happiest of marriages. Molly nursed him back to health after he took a bad fall on some ice, and the couple, who had been engaged before John's fall, married and attempted to travel together. But the tough travel and sometimes difficult crowds made it a hard time. Molly abandoned John in 1758. When she died in 1781, John Wesley did not even attend her funeral.

818. **Hans Nielsen Hauge** is considered Norway's foremost evangelist but also a key figure of Norwegian history. Between 1798 and 1804 he traveled seven thousand miles on foot to share the gospel message with his countrymen. In good weather Hauge would knit as he walked, often talking at the same time with people traveling along the same roads. In the winter he would ski from place to place. His work brought many followers, and his followers' treks connected the people of Norway in a way that the isolated villagers could never have known prior to such evangelism tactics. The writings Hauge distributed helped many learn to read, and he encouraged his followers to increase their skills and make Norway a greater country politically.

819. **"Mountain Man" preachers** were the men taking the gospel into the unexplored wildernesses of the western North American continent in the early 1800s. Jedediah Smith was one of those preachers. Wearing buckskins and buffalo-hide moccasins, he worked with the likes of Jim Bridger and Mike Fink in ascending the Missouri River in search of beaver. A devout Christian who didn't smoke or drink or use the language that came with his territory, Smith discovered the South Pass through the Rocky Mountains, was the first white man to cross the Sierra Nevada, the first to walk to California, the first to taste the bitter waters of the Great Salt Lake, the first to enter Oregon, and the first to see the Great Basin. Having survived attacks by timber wolves and a grizzly bear, he died alone on the Sante Fe Trail, ambushed by Comanche Indians.

820. Charles Finney was a lawyer who began reading his Bible after noticing all the references to it in his law books. After becoming a Christian in 1824, he became an evangelist known for his exciting preaching style. There was shouting, groaning, sobbing, and falling on the floor at his services. Finney shaped the modern revival and insisted that local churches be involved with his services, pray with new believers, and arrange for follow-up meetings.

821. Charles Haddon Spurgeon was twenty years old when he was called to be pastor of New Park Street Chapel. A plain-spoken man who simply "told them what the Bible says," he built the church from eighty souls to more than ten thousand and brought about the Second Evangelical Revival, a movement that swept over England in 1861. The founder of a pastor's college, orphanage, and Bible press, he wrote more than 120 books, many of which still sell today.

822. "All his discourses are redolent of bad taste."—a review of Charles Spurgeon's preaching by the *London Daily Telegram*. Such criticism didn't stop people from attending his sermons. Unfortunately, when a crowd of more than twenty thousand arrived at the Surrey Music Hall to hear him preach in 1858, they found only twelve thousand seats. One angry rabble rouser yelled, "Fire!" and seven people died in the stampede that followed, causing the press to like him even less.

823. Søren Kierkegaard was a gloomy Dane who, in the late 1800s, tried to find answers to his search for God. His conclusions—that God is beyond a person's ability to understand, that

Christ's divinity is hidden by his humanity, and that the only thing we can do to know him is to take a subjective leap of faith—made him the father of existentialism.

824. Nobel Peace Prize winner Albert Schweitzer was a theologian, organist, musical historian, and medical missionary. His book *Quest of the Historical Jesus* (published in 1906) was considered a foundational work on that subject.

825. Eric Liddell's story became well known in the 1980s. The movie *Chariots of Fire* received much praise almost immediately. Liddell, an Olympic athlete, made headlines when he refused to run on Sundays for competition. The young athlete later headed to the mission field in China. He was captured in 1942 by the Japanese and died of a brain tumor in 1945 before his scheduled release.

826. A. W. Tozer (1897–1963) is said to have "spent more time on his knees than at his desk." The dedicated minister of the Southside Alliance Church in Chicago dedicated his life to spiritual study. He was converted as a teenager after listening to the words of a street preacher and became deeply involved with Christianity soon after.

Famous Christian Women

827. Marcella was born c. 322 and was greatly respected by Jerome. She came to him for theological teaching and ascribed her opinions and religious thoughts to him, even if they were indeed her own thoughts. She did this to be involved in teaching others while avoiding the office of teaching, which was not an acceptable practice for women. She is especially remembered for her efforts to bring heretics back into the church. She demanded they defend their views and argued strongly for the truth of Scripture.

828. Catherine of Sienna, a fourteenth-century mystic, is considered the most famous of all medieval churchwomen. The twenty-third of twenty-five children, she made a vow at the age of seven to remain chaste. She was an angel of mercy to those who were sick and suffering, and some said she could heal the sick that physicians could not. Catherine is most remembered, however, for her concern for the church's well-being in the midst of its most corrupt century. Many writings attest to her efforts at reform; she was prolific and made her cause known to anyone and everyone. She even marched to Avignon to see Pope Gregory XI in the hopes that he would return the papal seat to Rome, which he did.

829. Katherine von Bora became Martin Luther's wife after the man she was first in love with, Jerome Baumgaertner, broke their engagement off at the insistence of his family. Luther then tried to marry "Lord Kathe," or "Katie," as he affectionately called her in later years, off to an old and miserly man, Kasper Glatz. Katie objected and told a trusted friend of Luther, "If Luther or [you] Amsdorf are willing, I will readily arrange an honorable marriage with either, but with Glatz, never." Several months after Katie's proposal, Luther thought seriously on the matter. The two were married in 1525, and theirs was a long and happy marriage.

830. Katherine Zell led a similar life to Katie's. She married Matthew Zell, a Catholic priest who became a Lutheran minister. Their marriage was considered scandalous, and in 1524 the bishop attempted to annul it. They remained married, however. Katherine is remembered most for her zeal in practicing hospitality as well as her sharp tongue. She wasn't afraid to point out the errors of Catholics and Protestants alike. Katherine was trained in doctrine and theology and could converse easily with men, which unnerved many in the Reformation movement. She desired peace with other Christians most of all, which didn't fit the requirements of doctrinal unity that her contemporaries sought.

831. Marjory Bowes was only fourteen and John Knox, the Catholic priest-turned Protestant minister, was thirty-five when they first met. The prenuptial contract was signed three years later. Then Knox was forced to flee to escape being imprisoned for his Protestant beliefs. More than two years later, Knox sneaked back into England and the two were finally married when John was forty-two years old. They fled to Geneva, Switzerland, and Marjory became pregnant. John was then called back to Scotland to minister to persecuted Protestants there. Marjory and their son were able to join him several months later, but only for a short while. Marjory died when she was only twenty-five (they had one more son together), when they had at last been given permission to live in England and had established a home there.

832. Argula von Grumback (1492–1563) became a thorn in the flesh of Catholic leaders of Germany. She was an educated and intelligent woman of noble birth, and her letters in support of Luther and other reformers were honest, well-reasoned, and completely justified with Scripture. She felt compelled to speak out because men who felt as she did would not. She once wrote, after trying to garner the attention of the princes of Germany in 1523 to the situation of the Reformation, "I am distressed that our princes take the Word of God no more seriously than a cow does a game of chess."

833. Teresa of Avila (1515–1582) was a Carmelite nun and mystic. She became convicted of Christianity after reading Augustine's *Confessions*. After her conversion, she began to experience visions and even levitations, but as the clergy was skeptical of such things, she tried to keep her experiences secret. She is most remembered for her efforts to reform the Carmelite houses throughout Spain. She was against the Reformation itself but saw a true need for the Catholic Church to be transformed. Through her efforts she reorganized the Carmelites and also added fifteen new houses.

834. Idelette Calvin was a young widow with two children when she married the famous Geneva reformer, John Calvin. Though Calvin loved her, he married Idelette barely knowing her. She was, in fact, the fourth woman that was considered as a bride for him. Calvin had made arrangements when he was thirty years old to marry a wealthy woman from Germany, but it didn't work out. Then a friend suggested another woman, but

Calvin didn't like that she was fifteen years older than he was. Calvin then found another prospect of his own choice and even set a date, but the wedding fell through at the last minute. Finally Calvin chose Idelette, a woman who had converted from the Anabaptist faith and was in his own congregation.

835. Anne Askew was the most famous female martyr in the English Reformation. Anne was burned at the stake in 1546 after suffering torture on the rack. She refused to give up names of other Protestant women and showed bravery throughout her torture, which was chronicled in detail. Though she often defended her actions with Scripture, when she didn't want to answer a question, she would say resolutely, "I would not throw pearls among swine."

836. Jeanne d'Albert stood with the reformers. This French noblewoman and queen of Navarre made a profession of faith in 1560. Her husband was Catholic and their marriage was difficult and included a custody battle for their son. Jeanne refused to back down and did everything in her power to establish more firmly a place of refuge for Huguenots. She even cheered the Huguenot troops on in battle when religious wars broke out between the Catholics and Huguenots. She died prior to the St. Bartholomew's Day Massacre in 1572.

837. Women received little sympathy from their male clergy in regard to specifically female difficulties. Goody Taylor, a young pregnant woman of England, is an example. In the mid–1600s she complained to the archbishop that it was dangerous for pregnant women to climb up the steep stairs leading to the raised communion table. Nearly two dozen other women agreed with her and supported her claim, but the bishop stated unequivocally that if the women were to keep their standing with God and the church they would have to continue to make the climb.

838. Lady Eleanor Davis believed herself a messenger with instructions from the voice of heaven. Given to visions and prophesying, the seventeenth-century prophetess was also a writer. One of her writings, a commentary on Daniel, predicted a dark ending for the current king, Charles I, among others in positions of authority. She was fined and sentenced to prison, but it didn't change her behavior. She is also remembered for her unlawful entry into Lichfield Cathedral. Lady Davis sat on the episcopal throne and declared herself "the Primate of all England."

839. Anne Hutchinson is perhaps the most well-known female figure of colonial America. What is not so commonly known about the convicted heretic is that she was the mother of fifteen children. When brought to trial in 1637 and while under house arrest, she suffered a difficult miscarriage. Her accusers and detractors (all Puritan ministers) used this against her and claimed she gave birth to thirty monsters "not of human shape."

840. One follower of Anne Hutchinson was Mary Dyer. Though in good standing in her church, she walked out in protest on the day Hutchinson was excommunicated. Dyer became a Quaker in 1652 while visiting England, clearly unhappy with Puritan doctrine. When she returned to Massachusetts a few years later, she publicly professed her faith and was promptly banished. She was sentenced to hang in 1659 after returning yet again. But the magistrates couldn't bring themselves to hang a woman, so she received a reprieve. However, she returned to Boston less than a year later and was again sentenced to hang. Her sentence was carried out in 1660.

841. Margaret Fell did much to improve the situation of women within the Quaker religion. Margaret was active in both writing for the Quakers and speaking on their behalf. She even met with King Charles II. Margaret suffered imprisonment on several occasions, and because of those experiences she protested the poor conditions of the prisons. Margaret eventually married Quaker leader George Fox. The two weren't together often because traveling for the ministry took up much of their time, but both spent a lot of time in prison, though never together.

842. Sor Juana Inés de la Cruz of Mexico is thought to have had the largest library in the New World in the seventeenth century. A gifted scholar, she studied theology and literature for more than twenty years at the Convent of Saint Jerome. She read in Latin, Greek, Spanish, and Portuguese, and her greatest gift to other Christians was the translation of Jerome's works from the original Latin into Spanish. She was widely ridiculed by male members of the Catholic clergy but defended herself well and always according to a rational line of defense. At the age of forty she gave up her studies after being affected by a mystical experience.

843. Mrs. Attaway of Coleman Street Baptist Church in London was one of the more well-known "she-preachers." Though her pastor gave Mrs. Attaway permission, the gatherings this woman began holding in 1645 were not looked on favorably by English Puritans. Baptists, however, allowed women to have teaching ministries. She was criticized for her faithful group's tendency toward "lightness" and even worse, laughing. Her following grew, and at one point there were a thousand people attending her meetings.

844. Madame Jeanne Guyon (1648–1717) was a French Catholic mystic who, though she never came to the Protestant faith, was condemned by Catholic officials for her teachings. She had dedicated her life to Christian ministry after the death of her husband and proved to be a gifted teacher. She ministered to elite women of Paris, isolated monks who had not previously allowed women within their walls, and countless nuns as well. Her message was about the need for justification by faith alone. She also wrote more than forty books. She was eventually arrested and imprisoned for seven years, but she continued to share the gospel.

845. The marriage of Margaret Baxter to well-known Puritan minister Richard Baxter demonstrated an all-too-common scenario for pastors and their wives. Before marrying, Richard told his wife she shouldn't expect any of his time or attention because his ministry required it all. Baxter remained true to his word and later wrote that he often struggled over neglecting his family for the sake of his flock and felt "guilt about omitting 'secret prayer with my wife when she desired it, for want of time, not daring to omit far greater work.'" Later he said he felt marriage ought to be avoided by pastors.

846. Susanna Wesley, mother of John and Charles Wesley, was, by their own account, their "theological mentor." She bore nineteen children, of whom only ten lived. Susanna was an educated woman and passed her knowledge on to her children—both sexes—and took an active interest in their spiritual development. She also served as a teacher to her husband's parish during his absences. Susanna was often given a better reception than her husband, Samuel, because he was a difficult man prone to outbursts and intolerance. Susanna and Samuel often disagreed; their marriage was stormy, and they separated from one another at times.

847. It is both sad and interesting to note that five of Susanna's seven daughters experienced troubling marriages. Emilia, the oldest, married in her forties but was abandoned (along with her child) after only a few years of marriage. Susanna, the next daughter, married and produced four children with her husband before they separated. Hetty ran away with a man who promised to marry her. He didn't, her reputation was ruined, and she ran away with the first man who would take her. He was an alcoholic who abused her; she remained miserable throughout their life together. Martha, second to the youngest of the girls, married a minister. He ran off with a mistress after he and Martha had ten children together. Kezzy, the youngest daughter, had a love affair with the man who eventually married her sister Martha. She later fell in love with another man but died while they were engaged.

848. Mary Bosanquet Fletcher (1739–1815) gave her life to the movement of Methodism. At a young age she dedicated her life to a less worldly Christianity than her family was used to. At age eighteen she left home and became involved in Methodist volunteer work through her contact with John Wesley and other Methodists. Mary later inherited a large estate, which she turned into an orphanage and school. She devoted herself to establishing unity among the Methodists and Anglicans within her home parish, in part because her husband was Anglican.

849. Sarah Edwards began her life as the preacher's wife in Northampton, Massachusetts. When her husband, Jonathan, famed Puritan minister, preached his first sermon, Sarah sat on a high bench that faced the entire congregation. This was the customary seat for the "first wife," which allowed everyone a view so that she could not move or show any sign of boredom without being noticed. Sarah learned early on that she was expected to be a model Christian. If her dresses were too fancy (she had a knack for remaking clothes into the latest styles), board members complained. If her children misbehaved, it was taken as a sign of her inability to discipline properly. Though she and her husband had a happy marriage, she often felt confined by the "glass house" of being a minister's wife.

850. Eunice Beecher, described by a friend of her husband's as "one of the most jealous women that ever lived," had reason to question Pastor Henry Beecher's behavior. More than one rumor surfaced throughout the years of his ministry about his attention to women he was counseling. Eunice suffered greatly as a result, and when Beecher was brought up on charges of adultery with a woman from his congregation in 1871, she was deeply hurt. Newspaper articles about the affair were everywhere, and the trial made national news. Though he was not proved guilty, his congregation didn't believe his innocent pleas. Eunice quietly stood by her husband's side throughout the ordeal, to the very end a model figure of what was expected of pastors' wives in the nineteenth century.

851. Susannah (Susie) Spurgeon suffered from illness much of her life and was rarely able to attend the services her famous husband preached, but she supported him through his sermon preparations as well as through her own ministry. It was their habit that he would read the text he felt God had chosen, and then she would read back to him what the commentaries said on the given text. From there he would craft his sermon. On one occasion it was said that he fell asleep due to extreme exhaustion while trying to craft another sermon. As he slept he delivered a sermon! Susie took notes and had a full outline waiting when he woke up. She is also fondly remembered for her ministries in the church, despite being a lifelong semi-invalid. The first was the "Book Fund," which included sending the published works of her husband to those pastors (of all denominations) in England who couldn't afford copies. At one point there were six thousand names on the list and many volunteers doing the stacking and packing. The "Sermon Fund" was also established; it even paid for some of Spurgeon's work to be translated and taken overseas. She also was integral to the founding of the "Pastors' Aid Fund." This ministry collected suitable clothing for needy pastors and their families throughout England. She has been praised for how she wished to help all needy pastors, regardless of denomination. Her work helped to break down the societal pressures to separate Christians of a different rank or place in life.

852. Emma Moody met Dwight Moody when she was thirteen and they were both involved in Sunday school teaching. Four years later she was a full-fledged schoolteacher and engaged to Dwight. Dwight announced their engagement one night in this manner: "I have just become engaged to Miss Emma Revell, and therefore cannot be depended upon to see the other girls home from meeting." Emma was more cultured, civilized, and educated than her husband and worked hard to improve him so that his ministry would be well received. She continued to teach classes within his ministry, including classrooms full of men (a rarity at that time) with the full support of her husband.

853. Maria Taylor was the wife of Hudson Taylor, the famed missionary to China. She spoke fluent Chinese and was a gifted teacher. Maria's guardian, a prim schoolteacher/principal figure, made Maria refuse Taylor's proposal and even barred the two from communicating. Eventually, an uncle in England was consulted via letters from Maria, Hudson, and the schoolteacher. After several months of waiting, the uncle gave his permission, asking only that they wait to marry till Maria's twenty-first birthday.

854. Catherine Booth desired from a young age to serve those in need. She married William Booth, a minister, in 1855, and together they began a life dedicated to evangelism. Catherine was a strong preacher and joined her husband often in his work while also managing to have eight children. Later in life they founded the Christian Mission on the East side of London, which eventually became a worldwide organization called the Salvation Army.

855. Amanda Smith was born in 1837 to two African American slaves from Maryland, the first of nine children. Amanda's family was eventually freed and moved to Pennsylvania. As a young woman she heard a call and felt God's hand upon her. At the age of thirty-two she became a full-time evangelist and traveled from revival camp to camp, preaching and singing. Eventually, she felt called to work for revival in England, and for twelve years she witnessed there, holding meetings and speaking to anyone who would listen about her Savior. She later spent seventeen years laboring in Calcutta as a missionary and eight years more in Liberia, Africa.

856. Ann Judson deserves a more prominent place in Christian history. The wife of Adoniram Judson, she willingly joined him in a life of hardship in a primitive culture. Seeing herself as a true partner in the work, she learned the Burmese language, founded a school for girls, preached the gospel, stayed close when her husband was in prison, and translated much of the New Testament into Siamese by herself. The difficult lifestyle was hard on her physically, and she died at the age of thirty-six.

857. Mary Slessor was a typical missionary of the nineteenth century, though hardly typical in terms of the amazing ministry she began. Mary was a Scottish Presbyterian and moved to Africa in 1876 to become a missionary. She was twenty-seven years old at the time and had been strongly influenced by another missionary, David Livingstone. Both an evangelist and a preacher, Mary served thirty-eight years in present-day Nigeria, an amazing testimony to her faith in Christ. Though she fell in love, she never married. Instead she had a family of her own, taking in African children and remaining close to those she ministered to.

858. "Bible Women" were women who served missionaries in the capacity of teachers and interpreters, as well as Bible readers. The native women of the countries were paid only a small amount (either by the missionaries themselves or the churches) but served a vital role, working as laypeople and helping foreign missionaries gain acceptance with those being evangelized. In particular, "Bible Women" were helpful to those serving in Asian countries.

859. Charlotte Selina Bompass, the wife of an Anglican bishop, lived in rural Northwest Canada at the end of the nineteenth century. Her husband's traveling around his 750,000-square-mile diocese meant Charlotte was alone much of the time. She filled her time with teaching and volunteer work, including the first Yukon branch of the Woman's Auxiliary, a popular ministry organization at that time. She once spent a winter stranded from her husband and stuck with a minister's family due to the rivers freezing early that year. She was said to have endured hunger and loneliness and yet was constantly involved in teaching and ministering to the people of this rugged, lonely territory in the name of Christ.

860. Eva von Tiele-Winckler, the daughter of a Prussian aristocrat, began her ministry in the early 1900s in Poland. Better remembered as Sister Eva, she managed an outreach to more than two thousand children living in forty orphanages as well as a band of six hundred Christian deaconesses she had trained in the art of ministry. This faithful woman's work brought new meaning to the words "God will provide."

861. Daisy Smith completed her schooling and then headed to the mission field—the coal fields of West Virginia—around 1912. She eventually turned to another ministry opportunity: becoming a Presbyterian deaconess. Through the subsequent mission work that followed, Daisy discovered she had a knack for preaching. Shortly after, she married Oswald J. Smith, an up-and-coming minister who later founded the People's Church in Toronto after first suffering rejection at two other churches. Daisy's situation represented a common difficulty of marrying a minister: Often a partner's gifts are sacrificed in the name of supporting a husband's ministry, even if that ministry takes him far away. Daisy was a dedicated and supportive wife and did everything in her power to keep her husband's time free so that he could minister to his flock, but she often suffered alone and raised their three children on her own as he traveled widely on the mission field.

862. Aimee Semple McPherson is considered one of the most successful female Pentecostal evangelists of the twentieth century. She founded the International Church of the Foursquare Gospel in 1927. By 1993 that denomination included over twenty-five thousand churches in seventy-four countries. Her personal verse and theme came from Hebrews 13: "Jesus is the same yesterday, today, and forever." She is remembered most for her flamboyant style of preaching and her intensity, as well as for her miracles of healing. McPherson's ministry was plagued by scandal in 1925 as well as two divorces following the death of her first husband, Robert Semple, in 1910.

863. Henrietta Mears formed a ministry that was highly influential in the early 1900s. After achieving incredible results as a Sunday school teacher (her class grew from five to five hundred), she became the director of Christian education at a Presbyterian church and devoted her life to full-time ministry. People requested her Sunday school curriculum directly from her until the publishing firm Gospel Light Press was started. Henrietta also had great impact on a number of her students. Several of the men she taught went on to be great ministers, including Rich Halverson, who pastored an important Presbyterian church in Washington, D.C., and Bill Bright, who founded Campus Crusade.

864. Ruth Peale married a man considered America's most positive-thinking minister, Norman Vincent Peale, in 1930. His 1952 book *The Power of Positive Thinking* sold millions of copies. What is less known is how Vincent struggled with discouragement and experienced lapses of depression, as do most Christians. His wife, Ruth, was the constant, stabilizing, and supportive factor in his ministry. She also founded and directed the Foundation for Christian Living, a service organization, and wrote regularly for *Guideposts* magazine.

865. Catherine Marshall began her writing career as a way to make a living after Peter Marshall, her pastor-husband, passed away suddenly at the age of forty-six. She first published his sermons, which proved a great success. She wrote his biography in 1952 and was delighted when it became the national bestseller of that year. In 1959 she married Leonard LeSourd but kept her name as she was becoming a well-known writer by this time. Catherine's ministry to fellow Christians lives on through her many books, including the popular *Christy*. Her story of overcoming grief and launching her own ministry while furthering her husband's gifted teachings is truly inspirational.

866. Joy Davidman, the wife of C. S. Lewis, had been a card-carrying communist when she was younger. She was described as being sharp, witty, and the equal of Lewis's mind. She was also completely uninhibited and never shy. She and Lewis were married in secret long before their marriage became public. Joy would have been sent out of England (she was an American and her papers that allowed her to stay had expired), but Lewis married her so that she wouldn't have to leave England. Eventually, however, they fell deeply in love, and though the state Church of England wouldn't recognize the marriage (as Joy was divorced prior to her marriage to Lewis), they lived as a married couple. She was diagnosed with cancer very soon after their marriage and died after just two years of marriage to Lewis.

867. Mother Teresa was born in 1910 to Albanian parents in Yugoslavia. Her real name was Agnes Gonxha Bojaxhiu. She entered an Irish convent at age eighteen and began her lifework of serving those of greatest need. Her tireless ministry in India caused her to be named one of the ten most influential Christians in the twentieth century. She died in 1997.

27

The Twentieth Century

868. "Religion is the opiate of the people," wrote Karl Marx in his explanation of communist theory. Marx claimed that the wealthy classes had invented religion to keep the working classes in line by promising them a better life in paradise. Therefore the ideas expressed in church, according to Marx, exist only to pacify the masses and keep them in line. (It should be noted that Marx's mother once said that her son Karl would have been of more use if he'd gotten a job.)

869. Vladimir Lenin, supposedly the liberator of Russia, announced upon the eve of the Russian Revolution that the church would die a natural death once a classless society was created. Unwilling to allow any control of the church outside of the state, he confiscated church property, prohibited religious education for children, and decreed civil marriages. The Orthodox Church replied with defiance, which led to riots and the deaths of more than one thousand clerics.

870. The Scopes Monkey Trial was the ultimate battle between modernists and conservatives. The nation was transfixed as William Jennings Bryan (a conservative Christian politician who had four times failed in his bid for the presidency) battled Clarence Darrow (a famous New York trial lawyer) over the right of public school teacher John Scopes (a wannabe actor and publicity hound) to teach evolution. Bryan won, but Darrow made him look bad, leading to the mockery of fundamentalists in the press.

871. *Divine Redemptoris* was the official announcement of Pope Pius XI in 1937, condemning communism and expressing his sympathy for the Russian people. Coming from the Catholic Church, which had been separated from the Orthodox Church for centuries, and on the heels of Pius's criticism of Nazi policies, it was an amazing document. Though Protestants have criticized the Catholic Church for not doing enough to protect Jews and others from persecution, this encyclical put the Roman church squarely on the side of persecuted believers in totalitarian countries.

872. Anti-Semitism has been an ongoing accusation of Christians in general and the Roman Church in particular, but it reached its apex in Nazi Germany. Rejecting the theories of the Enlightenment, the Nazis magnified the racial ideas of ancient Germanic sagas, preached that German blood set them apart from all others, and viewed foreign ideas and persons as "corrupting." In an attempt to purge Germany of its impurities (including Christianity, which they labeled an "invention of the Jew"), the Nazis attempted to eradicate the Jewish race as an act of social purification.

873. The Confessing Church was a loose association of German churches arranged by Martin Niemoller to combat the Nazi takeover of Christian theology. Issuing a "Declaration of Truth" written by Karl Barth in 1934, it actually congratulated Hitler on his governmental success, but criticized the attempted coordination of all churches under one Nazi leader and rejected the racist elements of the "new theology." In 1935 Hitler cracked down, arresting more than seven hundred pastors and harassing church leaders and services.

874. "First they came for the socialists and I did not speak out because I was not a socialist. Then they came for the trade unionists and I did not speak out because I was not a trade unionist. Then they came for the Jews and I did not speak out because I was not a Jew. Then they came for me and there was no one left to speak for me."—Lutheran pastor Martin Niemoller

875. "The Cold War Church" was the name given to the Russian Orthodox leaders who, after the end of World War II, began using their influence to preach the benefits of communism and the necessity of freeing the masses "oppressed by imperialism." Particularly active in the Soviet-sponsored "peace movement," they were generally seen in the West as pawns of the anti-God, anti-Christian communist government.

876. The Cultural Revolution was the name given to a xenophobic movement begun by Mao Zedong in 1966. In an attempt to rid China of all western influences, all churches were closed and Bibles burned. But Mao's attempt to wipe out the church caused it to go underground, and persecution always strengthens the faith. By the time of Mao's death in 1976, the "secret" Christian church had grown approximately tenfold, making his attack on the church a waste of time.

877. The first pope to visit the United States was Pope Paul VI, who came in 1965.

878. Dietrich Bonhoeffer was a Lutheran pastor in Germany who became a leader of the "Confessing Church," a group of believers opposed to the new racist tendencies being espoused by many Lutheran and Catholic churches in Nazi Germany. After being forbidden to preach or write, he came to the conclusion that Hitler was the Antichrist and was involved in a plot to assassinate him. Arrested in 1943 for helping to smuggle fourteen Jews into Switzerland, Bonhoeffer was hanged for treason as the Allies approached Berlin in 1945.

879. Oswald Chambers served as a YMCA chaplain in Egypt during World War I after having founded the Bible Training College in London in 1911. His book, *My Utmost for His Highest,* remains a treasured devotional and has been a "top ten" bestseller in Christian circles since 1935.

880. Richard J. Foster's mission as a Quaker and a psychologist is to remind Christians of the importance of historic, unchanging, and utterly necessary practices of faithful Christian living such as prayer, Scripture reading, solitude, simplicity, and fasting. His Renovaré program is specifically geared to help Christian leaders restore these timeless disciplines to their rightful place in the Christian faith.

881. Billy Graham is, without question, one of America's greatest Christian figures of all time. He first garnered national attention at the Los Angeles Crusade of 1949, which lasted for eight weeks. Graham's ministry has continued for more than five decades and has touched millions. His many books, radio and television broadcasts, and even films and magazines *(Christianity Today)* are important avenues of evangelism throughout the world.

882. An interesting note on Graham: He preached his first sermon in 1937. He was so nervous that he went through four sermons in just eight minutes! Each sermon was supposed to be forty-five minutes long.

883. Vance Havner preached his first sermon in 1913 while standing on a chair behind the pulpit in North Carolina at twelve years of age. He was ordained at age fifteen and became a full-time evangelist in 1940. With no degrees or diplomas to his name, he joyfully followed God's calling. Many found him refreshing, simple, and direct, and were converted through his lifelong ministry.

884. Hannah Hurnard's missionary career spanned fifty years. Though she was a quiet child from a Quaker family of pacifists in England, she answered God's call to become a multilingual medical missionary to Jews in Jerusalem. Hannah was one of just twelve missionaries to stay in war-torn Jerusalem in the months of 1948 when Israel fought to win the right of statehood. Her book *Watchmen on the Walls* chronicles that amazing feat.

885. Clive Staples Lewis, better known as C. S. Lewis, touched millions with his books and radio broadcasts, reaching an expansive audience of adults and children alike across all denominational lines. Lewis was a professor and Anglican layman and rejected atheism to accept the saving grace of Jesus Christ. He wrote at the rate of one book a year, covering many topics and genres.

886. Watchman Nee, evangelist to his homeland, brought many Chinese to a saving faith in Jesus Christ. He suffered poor health due to contracting tuberculosis as a young adult and also had a heart condition that troubled him most of his life. Nee To Shen ministered to those living in extreme poverty but spent his last twelve years on a Chinese labor farm. After he died in 1972 a personal statement of the faith that carried him through and pushed him forward was discovered under his pillow: "Christ is the Son of God who died for the redemption of sinners. This is the greatest truth in the universe."

887. J. I. Packer is a professor, author, and Reformed theologian. His many books (more than thirty) and articles cover a variety of topics related to Christianity. He came to a saving faith in Christ during a chapel service at Oxford University and dedicated his lifework to Christ and the study of theology.

888. Dorothy Sayers graduated from Oxford and became an advertising copywriter in London just after the turn of the century. She began to write mystery novels, a passion for her, in her twenties. Born into an English clergyman's family, she returned to her Christian roots after a difficult home life brought her back to Christ. She wrote on Christian apologetics and religious dramas, in addition to her works of fiction, before passing away in 1957.

889. Francis Schaeffer (1912–1984) is considered a leading Christian commentator of the twentieth century. In 1955 he began a ministry called L'Abri. He and his family opened their Swiss chateau to those wishing to study the Bible. Schaeffer wrote books and reached thousands with his sincere message of the gospel. His twenty-four books direct the reader to the Bible as the single answer for every problem troubling humanity.

890. Schaeffer met his wife, Edith, at a church lecture on Unitarianism in 1932. Both of them responded with strong rebuttals to the Unitarian speaker, and both were impressed by the other's comments. Schaeffer walked Edith home that night, and they were together from that point on.

891. Corrie ten Boom is known for her ministry during World War II in a concentration camp, Ravensbruck, also called "the women's death camp." Corrie's family home in the Netherlands became a haven for Jews during the German occupation of Holland. When the family was caught, Corrie was sent to the camps. Her book *The Hiding Place* describes in detail the time spent there. Through both her and her sister's ministry, hope and faith in the promises of the gospel became possible for many victims suffering in the camps. Their barracks, #28, was the center of many secret Bible studies.

28

Quotes

892. "What do Athens and Jerusalem have in common?"—the question posed by church historian Tertullian in the 220s, when the leading Christian thinkers were influenced by Greek philosophy. Valentinus was a Platonist, Marcion a stoic, and Origen a mystic who had castrated himself. "Away with all attempts to produce a mottled Christianity of Stoic, Platonic, and dialectic composition," wrote Tertullian. "We have no need of curiosity reaching beyond Christ Jesus. When we believe, we need nothing further. Search that you may believe, then stop!"

893. "Worship what you once burned, and burn what you worshipped."—After being baptized, along with three thousand of his men, King Clovis I, the founder of France, was reportedly told by the attending priest to use this statement as a guideline in his future work.

894. "I believe in order to understand."—Those were the words of Anselm, archbishop of Canterbury, in 1095. Anselm believed that those who seek truth must first have faith, rather than vice versa. In his book *Faith Seeks Understanding,* he proposed that humankind, being sinful, demands the idea of a perfect being; therefore that being must exist. That argument, called "Anselm's Theory," has continued to fascinate philosophers and theologians.

895. "The successor of Peter," announced Pope Innocent III in 1204, "is the Vicar of Christ. He has been established as a mediator between God and man; below God but beyond man; less than God but more than man; who shall judge all and be judged by no one." Innocent, the first church lawyer to take the role of pope, was intent on increasing his power by decreeing himself greater than the government. He centralized the church hierarchy and insisted that all governors and rulers take an oath of investiture to him, becoming his vassals. Those who refused were excommunicated.

896. "My dearest child . . . you who are yet so young and whom I must leave in this wicked, evil, perverse world . . ."—the opening of a letter from an Anabaptist mother to her baby daughter. The woman had been condemned to death for choosing to be rebaptized as an adult but had been allowed to live long enough to give birth to her baby. Her husband had already been executed. "Oh, that it had pleased the Lord that I might have brought you up, but it seems that is not the Lord's will. . . . Be not ashamed of us; it is the way which the prophets and apostles went. . . . Though flesh and blood must remain on the posts and on the stake, well knowing that we shall meet in the hereafter." She was put to death the following day.

897. "We must imitate Christ's life and his ways if we are to be truly enlightened and set free from the darkness of our own hearts. Let it be the most important thing we do, then, to reflect on the life of Jesus Christ."—Thomas à Kempis, Dutch author of *The Imitation of Christ,* died in 1471. His words live on, however, in the second best-selling Christian book ever written. The book's popularity is second only to the Bible.

898. "It is altogether necessary," declared Pope Boniface VIII in 1301, "for every human being to be subject to the Roman pontiff." In the biggest grab for power in church history, Boniface succeeded in angering all the rulers of Europe. King Philip sent a squad of soldiers to arrest him, and the pope, clearly stunned by this action, died of a heart attack three weeks later. Europeans, who were beginning to think in terms of "nations," would no longer accept the pope as their political leader.

899. "Fear of God is thrown away, and in its place is a bottomless bag of money."—So said the mystic Brigitta of Rome during the fourteenth century, when the Catholic Church was at its all-time low. She also stated that all of the Ten Commandments had apparently been reduced to one: "Bring hither the money."

900. "The earth is round like a ball."—The opening words from a book by Nicolas Oresme in 1390, a man one hundred years ahead of his time. Oresme postulated that the earth rotated on an axis, insisted on scientific support for supposed miracles, and used mathematics to theorize some astonishing ideas about the world, nearly all of which were ignored.

901. "The Roman Church is . . . the essential interpreter of the Bible."—the words of a Catholic participant at the Council of Trent. While Protestants were emphasizing the authority of Scripture, Rome was insisting on a collaboration between God and people. Salvation according to Protestants was by grace alone, while the Catholic council proclaimed salvation came about through grace *plus* the cooperation of human effort with the Spirit of God. According to Loyola, that would avoid "the poison that destroys freedom." In his view, Christians were to "pray as though everything depended on God alone, but act as though it depended on you alone."

902. "Arise O Lord and judge Thy cause. A wild boar has invaded Thy vineyard."—the words of a papal bull condemning the words of Martin Luther in 1520. Specifically criticizing forty-one of his teachings as "heretical, scandalous, false, offensive to pious ears, seductive to simple minds, and repugnant to

Catholic truth," the bull called on Luther to repudiate his errors or face dreadful consequences. It gave him sixty days to think it over, and on the sixtieth day, Luther led a throng of supporters to the gates of Wittenberg, where he burned the bull and a copy of Canon Law.

903. "My God, my God, why hast Thou forsaken me?"—Upon reading those words of Scripture, Martin Luther began to wonder how a sinless Christ could identify with sinful humanity. That led to the young monk gaining a new perspective on God. When he read Romans 1:17 ("the just shall live by faith"), he would later write that he "saw the connection between the justice of God and the statement that 'the just shall live by faith.' Then I grasped that the justice of God is that righteousness by which through grace and sheer mercy God justifies us through faith. Thereupon I felt myself reborn." With his understanding that justification is by faith alone, the Christian church changed forever.

904. "Gunpowder against Indians is incense to the Lord."—This statement reflected the popular view of the Spanish conquistadors in South America in the sixteenth century. Such gross statements were ardently preached against by António des Montesinos in 1511. The brave missionary condemned Spain's actions and fought for Indians' rights until Spain eventually heard him and began to monitor its treatment of the Indians.

905. "As soon as the coin in the coffer rings, The soul from purgatory springs."—This rhyme was used by the German monk Johann Tetzel as well as other religious clergy who taught their listeners about pardons and indulgences and what the people had to do [give money] to receive forgiveness for their sins. Martin Luther attacked the notion in his Ninety-five Theses in 1517.

906. "This devil in the habit of a monk," declared Emperor Charles V of Germany in 1521, "has brought together ancient errors into one stinking puddle, and has invented new ones." The target of his abuse was Martin Luther, whom he declared "an outlaw."

907. "There is a lot to get used to in the first year of marriage," wrote Martin Luther after abandoning celibacy to marry a former nun. "One wakes up in the morning and finds a pair of pigtails on the pillow which were not there before."

908. "The world marches forward on the feet of little children."—Those were the words of Robert Raikes, creator of the first Sunday school class, which was designed to teach working class children how to read. Upon reading those words in 1785, England's Queen Charlotte formally endorsed the idea, summoning Raikes, a newspaper editor of modest means, to the Royal Palace and lending her name to a fund-raising letter. Raikes's genius was to teach children to read by using the Bible as the class textbook, thus introducing a generation of children to the wisdom of Scripture.

909. "If God did not exist, it would be necessary for man to invent one."—the words of Voltaire, a caustic critic of organized religion in general and Christianity in particular. Apparently believing in some sort of supreme being, he became the leader of the philosophes, who claimed that science was going to resolve all of people's problems.

910. "The funeral of bigotry."—These were the words of the London Missionary Society when, in 1795, it adopted as its "fundamental principle that our design is not to send Presbyterianism, Independency, Episcopacy, or any other form of church government" to foreign lands. Instead, its aim was to bring "the glorious gospel of the blessed God to the heathen."

911. "Unlearned fishermen did it for Christ, and if a farmer may not fish as well as they, he can at any rate sow the seed of the kingdom."—Hans Nielsen Hauge, late eighteenth century, on why evangelism is everyone's task

912. "If God wants to save the heathen, He will do so without your help or mine."—So said a pastor to William Carey, a self-taught Bible student who desired to take the gospel into unreached lands in the late 1790s. That attitude had prevailed for decades, until a group of Christian doctors agreed to send a trained physician to India, and he in turn asked Carey to come as his assistant.

913. **"God needs men like you in Parliament."**—the words of former slave trader John Newton, who authored the hymn *Amazing Grace,* to William Wilberforce, who had just been elected by his district. At Newton's urging, Wilberforce took his seat and submitted a bill to ban slavery in England.

914. **"They'll be no more plagued by us."**—the words of Richard Allen, an African American who was thrown out of a church service in Philadelphia for accidentally entering a whites-only worship section and kneeling to pray. Though Allen had donated money and helped lay the floor on which he knelt, two white ushers picked him up and tossed him outside the church doors. This event was the last straw after a period of segregation and poor treatment. The next Sunday, he and his friend Absolom Jones rented a storeroom and decided to hold worship services for African American Methodists. This was the start of the African Methodist Episcopal Church in 1816.

915. **"The loss is heavy, but as traveling a road the second time is usually done with greater ease and certainty than the first time, so I trust the work will lose nothing of real value. . . . We are cast down but not in despair."**—the words of William Carey, after a fire destroyed his missionary print shop in India in 1812. The disaster destroyed his polyglot dictionary, sets of type for fourteen eastern languages, and whole versions of the Bible. However, news of the fire brought Carey fame, much-needed funds, and volunteer labor.

916. **"Where the Scriptures speak, we speak; where the Scriptures are silent, we are silent."**—These words were spoken by Thomas Campbell, the extremely gifted founder, along with his son, Alexander, of the Disciples of Christ. In attempting to eschew the traditions and formalities that had developed in the American church, he changed his church's worship, moved from Calvinism to Arminianism, and challenged pastors to rethink everything from offering boxes to the need for church buildings. In an attempt to remake the first-century church, Camp-

bell once wrote a treatise entitled *A Restoration of the Ancient Order of Things.*

917. "**If someone proved to me that Christ is outside the truth, and that in reality the truth were outside of Christ, then I should prefer to remain with Christ rather than with the truth.**"—nineteenth-century Russian novelist Fyodor Dostoyevsky, author of *Crime and Punishment*

918. "Dr. Livingstone, I presume?"—the words uttered by *New York Herald* reporter Henry M. Stanley when he finally located David Livingstone at Ujiji, on Lake Tanganyika in 1871. Stanley could not convince Livingstone to come back to England and was so impressed with the man's character that he later became a missionary in Africa himself.

919. "Hold the fort. I am coming."—the words of Civil War General William Tecumseh Sherman to the soldiers under his command holding the Allatonna Pass fortification. Surrounded, the soldiers were about to give up when they received Sherman's message. They held, and Sherman's "march to the sea" began. One of the officers with Sherman passed the story along to hymnwriter Philip Bliss, who wrote a popular hymn: "'Hold the fort, for I am coming,' Jesus signals still. Wave the answer back to heaven, 'By thy grace, I will.'"

920. "It is not injustice to refuse a man permission to enrich himself by injuring his fellow man."—the words of William Jennings Bryan in support of prohibition. A three-time candidate for U.S. president and Woodrow Wilson's secretary of state, Bryan was criticized for prosecuting the John Scopes Monkey Trial. He won the Scopes trial but was made to look bad by his opponent and the press, who portrayed him as a closed-minded bigot. But he was a solid Christian citizen who did much to benefit his country.

921. "Evil-lution"—the phrase coined by William Jennings Bryan during his opening arguments of the Scopes Monkey Trial. Picked up by newspapers across the country, this phrase led to Bryan's being mocked as a backwoods zealot.

922. "Breathing strange utterances and mouthing a creed which it would seem no sane mortal could understand, the newest religious sect has started in Los Angeles."—the opening sentence of an article in the April 18, 1906, *L.A. Times,* reporting on African American Baptist pastor William J. Seymour, who was calling on followers to be "baptized in the Holy Spirit" and to "speak in tongues." The crowds that came to hear him speak established the Apostolic Faith Gospel Mission, from which modern Pentecostalism grew.

923. "Please send me; I am ready to go to India."—Dr. E. Stanley Jones heard God's voice throughout his life and made every effort to follow where God led. He penned these words in response to the missionary society letter that appointed him to travel to India in 1907.

924. "Women, children, and unsaved into the lifeboats!"—John Harper, a Scottish evangelist, uttered this call during the sinking of the *Titanic* in 1912. This heroic Scottish evangelist had been on his way to evangelize in America. He served God until his last breath, preaching the gospel in the icy waters of the Atlantic and converting several other passengers before he too drowned.

925. "A God without wrath brought men without sin into a kingdom without judgement through the ministrations of a Christ without a cross."—the definition of liberal theology, critically summarized by Richard Niebuhr in the 1950s

926. "I have a dream that one day my four little children will live in a nation where they will not be judged by the color of their skin but by the content of their character."—the words of Martin Luther King Jr. at the 1963 march on Washington. The next year the United States Senate passed the Civil Rights Act and the following year the Voting Rights Act—two pieces of legislation that had been considered impossible just five years earlier.

927. "Well, it didn't take, so you had better get really converted."—Ruth Peale lovingly supported her husband, Norman

Vincent Peale, but sometimes it takes tough love to open one's eyes. She brooked no excuses from him when he complained of what he felt was a "hopeless situation" in his pastorate. She demanded he be converted (again) and show some of the faith and trust he ardently preached to his congregation. He conceded and thanked her for loving him.

29

Books

928. *The Shepherd of Hermas* was a document written c. 140 that helped popularize the ascetic movement. It says that, while many of the New Testament documents do a good job of describing the life of Christ, they neglect to detail what one who aspires to the "deeper life" should do. The book, which was accepted as part of the canon in some churches, advocates self-denial and a difficult life in order to attain godliness.

929. *The Revelation of Peter*—The second-century church occasionally read from a book purported to be authored by the apostle Peter. It contained wild details of the world's doom, though in such florid, confusing prose it was difficult to discern the exact meaning. By the year 250, the book had come under heavy criticism, and by the councils of the third century, it was rejected as an outright forgery.

930. *The History of the Church* was written by Eusebius, who lived c. 260 and was bishop of Caesarea. He is considered the father of church history because of this book, which is a record of Christianity triumphing through pagan persecution. Eusebius spent time in prison and witnessed many instances of martyrdom. His purpose in writing was to commemorate some of the greatest Christians of the early church for future believers.

931. Justin Martyr's *Dialogues with Trypho* was one of the most influential books of the church's first three centuries. Developed as a conversation with a Jewish friend, the text of the book presented Jesus Christ as the fulfillment of biblical prophecy and the Jewish faith, and it encouraged believers to evangelize Jews, rather than view them as an enemy. Justin, a Gentile born in a Jewish city, helped bridge the division that had developed between Jewish Christians and Gentile Christians of the second century.

932. *From Bordeaux to Jerusalem*—In A.D. 333, a short pamphlet appeared throughout Europe, giving directions from France to Jerusalem. It was perhaps the first travel brochure and encouraged believers to make a pilgrimage to Bible lands, even offering tips on locating various biblical sites. The pamphlet also endorsed taking one year to make such a pilgrimage, thus setting up the first notion of a "Christian calendar" as a reenactment of Jesus' life. Eventually that pamphlet helped start the Crusades, making people think globally and giving them a renewed interest in taking back land in the name of Christianity.

933. *Pastoral Rule,* a handbook for priests written by Gregory the Great, was based on one premise: "He who, by the necessity of his position, is required to speak the highest things, is compelled by the same necessity to exemplify the highest." Always one to protest high titles, Gregory's passion was to get the church working to meet the needs of the common people.

934. *Ecclesiastical History of the English Nation,* written in 731 by a monk known as the Venerable Bede, was the finest church history book of its time. Dedicated to historical truth, Bede diligently sought out reliable witnesses and accounts in tracing the history of the church in England from the days of Julius Caesar to his own. His book is filled with stories of brave missionaries and pagan warriors whose lives changed when hearing the truth. He offered interesting snippets found nowhere else, such as the fact that Gregory the Great, in seeing fair-haired English slave boys for sale in Rome, was struck by the need to evangelize England, and the story of the evil King Edwin, who upon seeing a sparrow fly through his castle, turned to Christ when a priest compared his lifestyle to "a brief flit in a banqueting hall." Prior to this time, most history books were half truth, half fable. Bede presented inspiring stories of Christians as real men and women, sometimes flawed, but devoted to the spread of the gospel, and his book created a new way of reporting history.

935. St. Anselm's *Proslogion* was written by a man considered to be one of the most influential theologians of the eleventh century. This document attempts to prove God's existence by an ontological proof. It brought a level of scholasticism to his era that allowed scholars to analyze their beliefs through the trusted methods of classical philosophy.

936. *Yes and No*—the book by Peter Abelard (1079–1142) that posed 158 questions about the church, then answered each one two different ways, using conflicting passages of Scripture. Interested in getting his students to think about their faith, Abelard instead was arrested and condemned for creating "disputes." However, his students started dozens of schools, and his process of learning led to the creation of universities in France, Italy, and England.

937. *Summa Theologica* was the book Thomas Aquinas created in 1273 to reconcile reason with revelation. Aquinas, who was influenced by the non-Christian philosophers of his day, felt that reason can be based only on people's knowledge and that only revelation can fully reveal God and his workings. By combining revelation with logic, Aquinas attempted to create a comprehensive theology. At first, church leaders were not interested in a writer combining theology and philosophy, but eventually *Summa Theologica* became the basis of Roman Catholic doctrine. Interestingly, in 1274 Aquinas announced that an angel had revealed his writing was "so much straw," and he gave it up. *Summa Theologica* was never completed.

938. ***The Divine Comedy,*** written in 1321 by Dante Alighieri, is a three-part allegorical poem. *Inferno* explores the nine circles of hell (guided by the poet Virgil); *Purgatorio* describes the nine-tiered mountain that souls must traverse to work off their sins; and *Paradiso* details the nine circles of heaven, which happens to have hired Dante's love interest, Beatrice, as a tour guide. It's beautifully written and considered orthodox by the Roman Church, even though Dante placed the pope who was in power at that time in the bowels of hell.

939. ***Defender of the Peace*** was a treatise published in 1326 by two churchmen, Marsilius of Padua and John of Jandun, that questioned the legitimacy of the papacy. Asserting that the church is a community of believers and that priests are not superior to the laity, the authors called for an executive council to run the operations of the church and were particularly critical of Pope John XXII, who was trying all sorts of new schemes to raise money. Announcing that a bishop's first-year salary should be paid directly to the pope, John kept moving bishops around so that he was collecting continually. He also reintroduced the selling of indulgences for everything from divorce to waging war—a practice that created a storm of protests in Germany.

940. ***Spiritual Exercises*** was the name of the book authored by Ignatius Loyola in 1541. It prescribes four weeks of meditations on sin and judgment, then a study on love and prayer, followed by a meditation on Christ's life, death, and resurrection. Loyola also presented his thoughts on diet, lifestyle, and "desires" in an attempt to create a discipleship program for ascetics. Though a staunch Roman Catholic, he was so fervent in his beliefs that the Spanish Inquisition detained him three times to examine his theology and practices. Annoyed at their intrusion, Loyola abandoned Spain and moved to Paris, where he created a discipleship training program at the university.

941. *The Babylonian Captivity of the Church* was Martin Luther's attack on the practices of the Roman Catholic Church. The implications of Martin Luther's study would change the church forever. If salvation is through faith in Christ alone, then the intercession of priests is unnecessary, the sacrifice of the mass is superfluous, the prayers of the saints are unneeded, and the mediation of the Roman Church is meaningless. It is clear Luther didn't understand the enormous impact his ideas would have. In criticizing the sale of indulgences, he was simply trying to reform a corrupt system. Instead, he created a new church.

942. *The Freedom of a Christian Man* was Luther's follow-up book. The papacy had deprived individuals from approaching God directly without the mediation of priests. A reliance on "good works" for salvation enslaves a man in a system he can never uphold. The necessity of becoming a monk to be truly spiritual fosters the lie that serving God as a priest is better than serving God in some other capacity. "All callings are equally sacred in the eyes of God," Luther stated. With this book, he set out an entirely new understanding of what being a Christian is all about.

943. *The Institutes of the Christian Religion* was published in 1536 by John Calvin. Taking the first words of the Apostles' Creed ("I believe in God the Father . . . Jesus Christ . . . the Holy Spirit . . . the holy catholic church . . ."), Calvin took each phrase and defined a Protestant theology. The book is best known today for describing the doctrine of predestination, although that was not a concept Calvin invented. Luther, Hus, and others had believed in the notion that God, in his sovereignty, elects to save some people. But Calvin went on to note that believers will demonstrate their salvation through good works. That was significantly different from Roman Catholic theology, which argued that a person's works contribute to his or her salvation.

944. *The Book of Martyrs,* by John Foxe, is one of the best-selling books of all time. Published in 1571, it tells the gory stories of ancient Christians who died for the faith, many of whom were put to death by the Roman Church. The book horrified north-

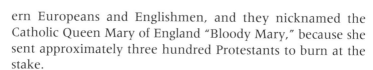

ern Europeans and Englishmen, and they nicknamed the Catholic Queen Mary of England "Bloody Mary," because she sent approximately three hundred Protestants to burn at the stake.

945. *The Discoverie of Witchcraft* was the first magic book ever written. Sir Reginald Scot was bothered by the tendency of people to attribute their troubles to evil powers and by their accusations of magicians he knew to be merely "performers." Because he enjoyed magic tricks as entertainment, Scot recognized the difference between the mighty power of God and the measly power of magicians. In 1581 he authored a book that unveiled some of the tricks and secrets of the people who worked at fairs and as street magicians.

946. *Paradise Lost* was written in 1667 by John Milton, the English poet and supporter of Oliver Cromwell. Milton was nearing the end of his life and was suffering from blindness when he wrote this epic poem discussing humankind's fall from grace.

947. *Pensées,* or "Thoughts," published in 1670, is a collection of writings by Blaise Pascal (for whom the computer language "Pascal" is named). The book describes the thoughts of a man facing doubts and hardships, and how his struggles with faith led him to trust God. Pascal argued that our experiences suggest the meaninglessness of life, but our hearts and consciences remind us that God is living and active. His thoughts lent vibrancy to the faith of many in France, and *Pensées* remains one of the best Christian texts ever produced.

948. *Pia Desideria* (or *Pious Desires*) was a small book written by Philip Jacob Spener in 1675 that argued for a personal experience with God over regular church attendance and acquiescence to a series of beliefs. He formed small groups in homes, called *collegia pietatis,* in which Christians would meet, pray together, study their Bibles, sing, and minister to one another outside the church walls. Church leaders of his day felt that this threatened the formal church, and Spener was hounded from one city to another. But his groups caught on with laypeople and started "the Pietistic movement."

949. *Pilgrim's Progress* is perhaps the greatest Christian novel of all time. Written by John Bunyan in 1678, it is an allegory that tells the story of a character, Christian, who faces temptations and trials in his walk toward maturity in Christ. Though Bunyan didn't have much formal schooling, his book gave the English language dozens of words and phrases still in use today: "muckraking," "house beautiful," "vanity fair," "Mr. Worldly," "the slough of despond," and that western favorite, "hanging is too good for him."

950. *The Analogy of Religion*, published by pastor Joseph Butler in 1750, sounded the death knell of deism. Butler didn't reject reason; he simply reminded readers that it fails to provide a "complete" system of knowledge; there are always problems and probabilities. Pointing out that nature is filled with unexplained mysteries, he asked if religion should be any different. And, citing the fact that much of science is discovered by experiences, he argued that religion has developed the same way. Deism could not explain why evils and disasters happen, but religion can—because God wills it. While the Age of Reason moved culture away from Christianity, the notions of deism failed to provide answers to the important questions of life.

951. *The Origin of Species*, published by Charles Darwin in 1859, was doubtless the most influential book of the century. After studying animals along the coast of South America, Darwin proposed that species make slight variations in order to survive. He called that process "natural selection" and noted that the process of "evolution" led to only the strongest surviving.

952. *The Descent of Man*, Darwin's follow-up book, applied natural selection to humans, concluding that humankind had probably evolved from monkeys. Christians argued that people are unique from animals, having a conscience and the powers of reason. Furthermore, if people are not specially created by God, nor fallen because of sin, there is hardly a need for a savior. The theory created more debate than any single topic in the twentieth century.

953. *Missionary Travels* was a hugely popular book by David Livingstone, an unhappily married physician who traversed back and forth across Africa in an attempt to spread the gospel, chart new territories, and help improve the African economy so as to eradicate slavery. Livingstone traveled the Zambezi River and a water route across the continent, but his passion was to share Christ with hostile tribes. When he died in 1873, the African people buried his heart in his adopted homeland, then returned his body to England.

954. The first Christian best-seller that wasn't purely theological or fiction was *In His Steps*, or *What Would Jesus Do?* by Rev. Charles Monroe Sheldon. Written in 1896, it pondered what the world might be like if people lived literally according to Jesus Christ's teachings. Over eight million copies in various editions were eventually published.

955. *The Fundamentals* was a series of twelve 125-page booklets, financed by Lyman and Milton Stewart between 1910 and 1915. Lyman, president of the Union Oil Company, invested a quarter of a million dollars and hired leading Bible teachers to write articles covering basic church doctrine. The booklets were immediately seized upon by conservative Christians, including a Baptist editor named Curtis Lee Law, who coined the movement "fundamentalism."

956. *Commentary on Romans* by Karl Barth was once described as "a bombshell on the liberal theologians' playground" by a reviewer in 1919. While liberal theologians had been hailing a God of mercy and the advancement of humankind, the pastor Barth noted that World War I had renewed a belief in the lostness of humankind and the judgment of God. His book was an attempt to turn people back to the Bible.

957. *The Cost of Discipleship* was an influential book by German pastor Dietrich Bonhoeffer. Accusing many Christians of relying on "cheap grace," he reminded his readers that being a Christian is more than believing the right things—it is following them, even during difficult times. Bonhoeffer was killed by the Nazis just before the war ended.

958. *The Faith of Modernism,* written by University of Chicago professor Shailer Mathews in 1924, set out to examine Scripture using "scientific investigations." In the text, Mathews describes the four hallmarks of modernism: religion, like humankind, has been evolutionary; people are basically good, but can become evil when shaped by an evil culture; the Bible is not historically accurate, but offers some spiritual insights; and God and morality are basically the same thing, and he (or maybe "she") can best be found by looking for an internal spark, rather than an external source of truth.

30

Trivia

959. The Book of Acts may have been written as a legal document to support the release of the apostle Paul from a Roman jail. The book, penned by a learned Christian named Luke, tells the story of Christianity's growth from the synagogues of Jerusalem to the cities of Palestine. It reveals that Paul, imprisoned for preaching the gospel of Jesus Christ, was an enlightened Jewish thinker. Because the Jewish faith was protected by Rome, this new faith, called "Christianity," deserved that same protection as Judaism.

960. The early church was protected by Rome because it was perceived as a branch of Judaism, a protected faith in the Roman Empire. That caused endless problems with the Jews, who viewed the Christian faith as a dangerous cult that wanted to do away with Jewish rites and ceremonies. In a document dated A.D. 58, the Roman historian Tacitus reported a violent disturbance in one of the poorer sections of the city. Tacitus wrote that the Jews were apparently fighting among themselves over the words of someone named "Chrestus"—a variation on the Greek name for Jesus Christ, *Christos.*

961. The practice of burying the dead, particularly the poor, was one of the appeals of first-century Christianity. The church in Rome bought a tract of land to use as a burial site. It featured some underground caves called *Catacumbas,* and ever since the Christian church in Rome has been associated with "the catacombs."

962. The Thomas Christians of India claim that "Doubting Thomas," one of the original twelve disciples of Jesus, traveled to their land in the first century to spread the gospel. That is very likely, because that sect of Christianity has existed since the earliest times, and a voyage from Palestine to southern India was certainly possible during the time of Christ.

963. Church titles have evolved with the church. Originally the leaders were called "elders," but the notion of a local "priest" was soon borrowed from the Jewish faith. Paul refers to "overseers and deacons" in his letter to the Philippians, and in trying to establish a hierarchy, church leaders soon developed the notion of "bishop" as the senior leader in a church. That was followed with the title of "archbishop" to recognize the leader of a city with several churches, which was followed in turn by the title "patriarch," given to the archbishop of a significant city. Later the Roman Catholic Church would create the title "cardinal" to refer to the pope's counselors. The word "cardinal" derives from the fact that some bishops were "incardinated," named to serve over an area other than the one where they had been ordained.

964. Agbar the Black was the ruler of the tiny kingdom of Osrhoene in the years 9 to 46. Eusebius, the respected Christian historian of the early church, records that Agbar once sent a letter to Jesus, inviting him to come visit his kingdom and asking the Lord to "heal the affliction that I have." According to Eusebius, Jesus replied by saying he could not come, but in the future he would send one of his disciples to heal the king and "give life to you and those with you."

965. Schools for Christianity became popular in the late 100s. A Sicilian named Pantainus established a school in Alexandria, letting pagans ask the great questions of theology, then answering them with Christian orthodoxy. He won many to Christ, including Clement of Alexandria, the greatest teacher of his time. Clement theorized that a man must understand his time and the questions of his time in order to reach people with the truth of the gospel. Many Christian teachers still hold to his philosophy.

966. The sacrament of penance came about in the middle of the third century, when Cyprian, bishop of Carthage, set up a system of absolving men and women of various "degrees" of sin. Only after a period of sorrow and the approval of the bishop could a "lapsed" Christian take communion. The scholar Novatian argued that the church had no power to grant forgiveness, nor did "time" have anything to do with "repentance." But the church, under the leadership of Cornelius, agreed with Cyprian and codified his theory into church doctrine.

967. The first Christian nation is believed to have been Armenia. According to legend, in 294 the entire population of Armenia was baptized into the faith.

968. Donatism takes its name from Donatus, bishop of Carthage in the early 300s, who was appalled that clergy who had renounced Christ and handed over the Scriptures for burning during persecutions were allowed to retain their positions in the church. Rejecting Roman rule, the Donatists proclaimed themselves the "true church." Augustine argued vehemently against their position, claiming the church is made up of various types, both sinners and saints. However, Augustine also relied on the use of force to suppress their teaching—an argument that later was used to justify the ruthlessness of the Spanish Inquisition.

969. A comet is said to have appeared on the day of Constantine's death, May 22, 337. The death of the great leader caused much sorrow, and many believed the comet was a sign that even the heavens were moved at the great man's passing.

970. "The Barbarians" was the name given to German tribes by the Roman armies because the Germanic people spoke neither Latin nor Greek. Rome, seeking to protect its borders from rampaging armies out of Asia, opened its borders to Vandals, Goths, Lombards, and the like. Within a century, the eastern edge of the Roman armies were made up entirely of Germans. Soon it became hard to tell the barbarians from the Romans. In 410 the Visigoths, under the capable leadership of Alaric, invaded Italy and sacked Rome, putting an end to the Roman legions that had been successful for so long, opening up Europe to hordes of rampaging barbarians and ushering in 150 years of chaos.

971. "At the voice of the saint, the monster was terrified, and fled more quickly than if it had been pulled back with ropes."—A biographer of Columba, a Celtic missionary, wrote these words to describe what Columba had seen in 565 during his travels. What monster was he writing about? None other than the famed Loch Ness Monster! The missionary was reportedly the first to ever lay eyes on the legendary monster.

972. The great missionary Cyril probably invented the "chalk talk." While watching his brother preach a sermon to the king of Bulgaria in 865, Cyril realized that the language barrier was keeping the audience from understanding the main points. As his brother continued preaching from Revelation, Cyril decided to illustrate the sermon by drawing a picture of the Last Judgment on the wall of the castle. That drawing helped the king grasp the point, and he gave his life to Christ that very night.

973. Rooster weather vanes were an important display item for church steeples in the ninth century. Pope Nicholas I decreed that every church should display a rooster as a strong warning against sin. The rooster served as a reminder of Peter's three denials of Christ before the cock crowed.

974. The East-West Schism reflected the Great Divide in churches. The Western church used Latin, the Eastern Church used Greek. Western priests were celibate and clean shaven, while Eastern priests married and wore beards. The West preached about things like purgatory and the holiness of Mary—things the Eastern Church found heretical. In 1049 Pope Leo IX demanded that the Eastern Church submit to Rome. When Michael Cerularius, the patriarch of Constantinople, refused, Leo excommunicated him. Michael's response was to excommunicate Leo. Though there have been countless attempts to reunite the Roman Catholic Church with the Eastern Orthodox Church, they remain separated on various points of doctrine. In 1453 when the Muslim Turks conquered Constantinople, the leaders of the church there proclaimed they would rather join the Muslims than the Catholics.

975. The "double excommunication" (church ban) that occurred in 1054 between Pope Leo IX (papacy side) and Michael Cerularius (Orthodox side) during the latter's visit to Constantinople had long-lasting effects. The two decisions were not revoked until 1965, more than nine hundred years later!

976. The Jihad, or "Holy War," was not invented by moderns. Saladin, sultan of Egypt and Syria, first used the term to battle the Christian forces of the Third Crusade in 1189. However, rather than fighting an offensive war, he set up defensive strongholds and warned his armies to "refrain from the shedding of blood," warning that blood that is shed "never slumbers."

977. The world's first "university" was created when a student argued against his theology professor . . . and won. Peter Abelard was immediately branded a heretic by his instructors and expelled from school. To earn a living, he began teaching students privately, charging a fee. When several friends were expelled from the monastery at Notre Dame, they set up a school and began teaching students in Paris. Because the workmen of the day all belonged to guilds or trade unions, the teachers quickly elected a leader (called a "chancellor") and created their own name: "The Universal Society of Teachers and Students." In 1200 King Philip II granted official status to the University of Paris.

978. The University of Paris was the hub of world scholarship in the twelfth and thirteenth centuries. As the world was emerging from the Dark Ages, teachers from several nations gathered in Paris to share their wisdom. Due to language differences, four separate groups, called "colleges," were formed: French, Norman, Picardian, and English and German. Students speaking the same language lived and studied together, giving rise to the idea of college dormitories.

979. The Papal Crown created by Pope Boniface VIII (1294–1303) contained seventy-two sapphires, sixty-six pearls, forty-eight rubies, and forty-five emeralds. He paid for it by declaring the year 1300 a "Year of Jubilee" and announced a pardon for all the sins of those who visited and brought an offering to the churches of St. Peter and St. Paul in Rome. A local historian noted that Boniface kept two priests busy day and night, "raking together his infinite money."

980. Saint Miles Partridge once played dice with Henry VIII for the bells at St. Paul's Church. The blessed gambler won and collected the bells.

981. The Spanish Inquisition was begun in 1478, but it took root much earlier. The Fourth Lateran Council had provided for punishing heretics, and in 1252 Pope Innocent IV authorized torture as a means of gaining heretical confessions. But in the late 1400s, Spain's Queen Isabella and King Ferdinand, determined to make their country "truly" Christian, asked the pope to establish an inquisition—inquiring about people's beliefs in order to aggressively pursue "heretics." Jews and Muslims were expelled, those who questioned papal decrees were tortured into recanting, and hundreds were burned at the stake.

982. Tomas de Torquemada was a cruel Dominican priest who was named Inquisitor General of Spain in 1483. He employed torture to extract confessions from "heretics" and even wrote a book about his methods—*A Compilation of Instructions for the Spanish Inquisition.* He personally oversaw the deaths of two thousand people who were burned at the stake for their religious convictions. Torquemada noted that because church doctrine prohibited the shedding of blood, the stake was preferred to beheading.

983. Christopher Columbus and other adventurers were certainly after fame and wealth, but any reading of the diaries of the New World explorers will reveal that they were also motivated by a desire to spread the gospel to unsaved peoples. King Charles V, before whom Martin Luther stood at the Diet of Worms, was the same man who sponsored numerous explorations to North and South America in hopes of spreading the Good News of Jesus Christ.

984. While Hernando Cortés was defeating the Aztec Empire in Mexico, his horse was badly wounded in battle. Leaving the horse with some local villagers, Cortés gave strict instructions to them to care for the horse and to worship the Christian God. They did so, but the horse died soon after of its injuries. When Cortés returned, he found that the Aztecs had equated "God" with "horse." They had erected an image of the horse over its grave and were worshiping it as the god of lightning.

985. Posting theses as Martin Luther did with his famous Ninety-five Theses on the door of the Castle Church in Wittenberg, Germany, on October 31, 1517, was not an unusual practice. It was a regular part of university life in that day to post notices of such disputes and thoughts on the door of the church.

986. The first adult baptism took place on January 21, 1525, in the home of Felix Manz of Zurich. Earlier that day, the city council had ordered Manz and his friend, Conrad Grebel, to stop holding Bible classes in their home. (They also warned all parents that they were to have their babies baptized within eight days or face banishment from the territory.) As the Anabaptist believers gathered to discuss their situation, one of their number, George Blaurock, a former priest, stood up and asked Grebel and Manz to baptize him "in the apostolic fashion." Upon Blaurock's confession of faith in Jesus Christ, Grebel baptized him. Blaurock then proceeded to baptize the others, in defiance of the city leadership.

987. Blaise Pascal invented the wristwatch, bus route, and first primitive counting machine before he became a Christian theologian following his conversion to Christianity.

988. The anxious bench was a church pew that revivalist preacher Charles Finney would place on stage with him at his camp meetings in the 1830s. It was reserved for "anxious sinners" who could come and request prayer. Interestingly, Finney allowed women to sit on the anxious bench and even to pray aloud, something local churches found scandalous.

989. The ricksha (also called "jinriksha") was invented by a Baptist minister in Yokohama, Japan, in 1869. The contraption carried people and belongings, with a person drawing it, and it was well-received and remains in use today throughout many parts of the world.

990. The reaper was invented by Cyrus McCormick in 1831. McCormick went on to found the International Harvester Company. He was an active Christian and shared his faith with many. His son, who shared his name, was an original trustee of the Moody Bible Institute in Chicago, Illinois.

991. The man who invented the telegraph and Morse code was the son of one of England's most prominent evangelical preachers, Jedediah Morse. Samuel's first message, sent to Baltimore from Washington, D.C., was "What hath God wrought," which comes from Numbers 23:23.

992. Orville and Wilbur Wright were brought up in the Evangelical Church, and their father was a bishop. The Wright brothers are the fathers of aviation. Their "flying machine" first flew in 1903, and their work brought about the modern field of aviation.

993. The two brothers once said no to the king of Spain's request that they take him for a ride in their primitive airplane. The reason? The brothers would not fly on Sunday and had to refuse him.

994. The Roman Question was on the minds of Italians throughout the late 1800s. The pope, angry with losing the papal states to the new nation of Italy, forbade Catholics from voting in political elections, thereby giving radical anti-Catholics easy victories. What to do with the pope remained a quandary until 1929, when Benito Mussolini offered sovereignty to "the Vatican State," which consisted of nothing more than the boundaries of St. Peter's Basilica and its surrounding buildings.

995. The pope was in exile from 1871 until 1929, withdrawing into the Vatican and refusing to come outside. The government of Italy had passed the "Law of Papal Guarantees," offering the pontiff all Vatican properties and 365,000 pounds per year, in addition to foreign rights for papal diplomats. Pope Pius IX rejected that law and went into exile inside St. Peter's Basilica, where all popes remained until 1929, when Mussolini agreed to the more favorable "Lateran Treaty."

996. Post Toasties was the second name given to the cereal C. W. Post invented in 1904. The first name for the product, a new breakfast cereal, was "Elijah's Manna," which Post had thought up by himself. The name was so unpopular with Christian ministers that he changed the name to "Post Toasties."

997. Wine for communion was an issue for many evangelical churches in the 1880s. Dr. Thomas Welch had an alternative: Dr. Welch's Unfermented Wine. In 1893 it received a new label, "Welch's Grape Juice," at its debut at the Chicago World Fair.

998. The first broadcast church service took place on the evening of January 6, 1921. A Westinghouse engineer who happened to sing in the choir at Calvary Episcopal Church in Pittsburgh thought his pastor's preaching would make a nice time filler for the new medium called "radio." But the pastor was skeptical, so his associate, Lewis B. Whittemore, preached the service. The response was so popular that Whittemore became a regular feature.

999. The Moody Radio Network began almost by accident in 1925. When studio musicians failed to show up for a live program for the Illinois Products Exposition, a quick-thinking engineer raced over to the Moody booth, grabbed the two students who had been playing trumpets to help gather a crowd, and asked them to play some music on the air. A few days later, the station asked the Moody Bible Institute to create a one-hour program each Sunday.

1000. **Donald Grey Barnhouse** became the first preacher to ever "buy time" on a radio network when he began airing the services of Philadelphia's Tenth Presbyterian Church on the local CBS affiliate in 1928.

1001. **Clare of Assisi** is the patron saint of television. She was made a saint by Pope Pius XII in 1958. According to legend, Clare, who died in 1253, once experienced a mass being celebrated miles away from her location at Assisi.

Bibliography

Cairnes, Earl. *Christianity Through the Centuries,* 3rd ed. Grand Rapids: Zondervan, 1996.

Cohn-Sherbok, Lavinia. *Who's Who in Christianity.* Nashville: Rutledge, 1998.

Flood, Robert. *The Book of Fascinating Christian Facts.* Denver: Accent Books, 1985.

Hodges, George. *Saints and Heroes, To the End of the Middle Ages.* New York: Books for Libraries Press, 1911, 1967.

Kane, Joseph Nathan. *Famous First Facts,* 5th ed. New York: H. W. Wilson, 2000.

Livingstone, E. A., and F. L. Cross, eds. *The Oxford Dictionary of the Christian Church.* New York: Oxford University Press, 1997.

Lo Bello, Nino. *The Incredible Book of Vatican Facts and Papal Curiosities.* New York: Liquori Press, 1998.

McManners, John, ed. *The Oxford Illustrated History of Christianity.* New York: Oxford University Press, 1990.

Miller, Basil. *God's Great Soul Winners.* Anderson, Ind.: The Warner Press, 1937.

Petersen, William J. *C. S. Lewis Had a Wife.* Wheaton, Ill.: Tyndale House, 1985.

Schaff, Philip. *The History of the Christian Church.* Peabody, Mass.: Hendrickson Publishers, 1996.

Shelley, Bruce. *Church History in Plain Language.* Dallas: Word, 1982.

Spitz, Lewis W., ed. *The Protestant Reformation.* Englewood Cliffs, N.J.: Prentice-Hall, 1966.

Stafford, Thomas Albert. *Christian Symbolism in the Evangelical Churches.* New York: Abingdon-Cokesbury Press, 1942.

Tucker, Ruth A., and Walter Liefeld. *Daughters of the Church.* Grand Rapids: Zondervan, 1987.

Walker, Williston. *A History of the Christian Church,* 4th ed. New York: Scribners, 1985.

White, Ronald C. Jr., Louis B. Weeks, Garth M. Rosell, eds. *American Christianity: A Case Approach.* Grand Rapids: Eerdmans, 1986.

Index

267